JOURNAL · OF

M · O · R · A · L

THEOLOGY

VOLUME 11, ISSUE 1
JANUARY 2022

APPLYING VIRTUES

EDITED BY
JASON KING
M. THERESE LYSAUGHT

J O U R N A L · O F

M · O · R · A · L

T H E O L O G Y

Journal of Moral Theology is published semiannually, with regular issues in January and June. Our mission is to publish scholarly articles in the field of Catholic moral theology, as well as theological treatments of related topics in philosophy, economics, political philosophy, and psychology.

Articles published in the *Journal of Moral Theology* undergo at least two double blind peer reviews. To submit an article for the journal, please visit the "For Authors" page on our website at jmt.scholasticahq.com/for-authors.

Journal of Moral Theology is available full text in the *ATLA Religion Database with ATLASerials®* (RDB®), a product of the American Theological Library Association.
Email: atla@atla.com, www: http://www.atla.com.
ISSN 2166-2851 (print)
ISSN 2166-2118 (online)

Journal of Moral Theology is published by The Journal of Moral Theology, Inc.

JOURNAL · OF
M ·O ·R ·A ·L
THEOLOGY

EDITOR EMERITUS
Jason King, *Saint Vincent College*

EDITOR
M. Therese Lysaught, *Loyola University Chicago
Stritch School of Medicine*

SENIOR EDITOR
William J. Collinge, *Mount St. Mary's University*

ASSOCIATE EDITORS
Jean-Pierre Fortin, *St. Michael's College, University of Toronto*
Alexandre A. Martins, *Marquette University*
Christopher McMahon, *Saint Vincent College*
Mary M. Doyle Roche, *College of the Holy Cross*

MANAGING EDITOR
Kathy Criasia, *Mount St. Mary's University*

BOOK REVIEW EDITORS
Mari Rapela Heidt, *Notre Dame of Maryland University*
Kate Ward, *Marquette University*

EDITORIAL BOARD
Christine Astorga, *University of Portland*
Jana M. Bennett, *University of Dayton*
Mara Brecht, *St. Norbert College*
Jim Caccamo, *St. Joseph's University*
Carolyn A. Chau, *King's University College at
Western University, Ontario, Canada*
Meghan Clark, *St. John's University*
David Cloutier, *The Catholic University of America*
Christopher Denny, *St. John's University*
Joseph Flipper, *Bellarmine College*
Nichole M. Flores, *University of Virginia*
Matthew J. Gaudet, *Santa Clara University*
Kelly Johnson, *University of Dayton*
Andrew Kim, *Marquette University*
Warren Kinghorn, *Duke University*
Ramon Luzarraga, *St. Martin's University, Lacey, Washington*
William C. Mattison III, *University of Notre Dame*
Cory D. Mitchell, *Mercy Health Muskegon*
Suzanne Mulligan, *Liaison with
Catholic Theological Ethics in the World Church
Pontifical University, Maynooth, Co. Kildare, Ireland*
Matthew Shadle, *Marymount University*
Joel Shuman, *Kings College*
Christopher P. Vogt, *St. John's University*
Paul Wadell, *St. Norbert College*

JOURNAL OF MORAL THEOLOGY
VOLUME 11, ISSUE 1
JANUARY 2022

CONTENTS

Editorial Essay

Jason King

ABOUT SIX YEARS AGO, DAVID MCCARTHY sent out an email to the editorial board of the *Journal of Moral Theology* asking who would be interested in being the next editor. The editorial board was primarily made up of people whom David had asked to review an essay, who had reviewed the essay by the deadline, had been asked to review a second essay, and had reviewed that essay by the deadline as well. In his wisdom, David had created a board of people who had the time and desire to prioritize the functioning of the journal. So, when David sent out the email asking for a new editor, I thought lots of people would volunteer. I said I would be interested in serving with the confidence that I would not be chosen. It was a miscalculation that resulted in David naming me the editor that January.

David had done so much to get the journal started. His energy and intuitions had conceived of it, developed its look, built a relationship with Wipf & Stock for paper copies, and got it indexed on EBSCO. When I took over, I saw my job as the routinization of this charisma (and, yes, this is a Max Weber joke). I needed to build out the journal to expand on what David started. I had no idea what I was doing though, so I sought help.

I talked with other journal editors, including Phil Rossi and Tony Godzieba. Tony said the journal would take over my life. It did. I began immediately with my first issue, editing it in the stands at t-ball games to meet the deadlines. Thankfully, Mari Rapela Heidt, the guest editor of the issue (and the current book review editor), was wonderful. I knew I needed more help though.

Kathy Criasia, the managing editor, knew the ins and outs of the production process and patiently taught them to me. I asked, begged really, Bill Collinge to come on board as the senior editor. Bill once caught transposed letters, in a footnote, in Latin, in a 200-page issue, just in case you want to know a little of what he brought to the journal.

I held a board meeting at The Society of Christian Ethics annual meeting to ask people for ideas on the journal. Stanley Hauerwas, who was not on the board, saw a bunch of people that he knew at the meeting and sat down. After figuring out it was a board meeting, he offered his advice. First, "keep doing themed issues." Got it.

Next, he said "administrative work is a real service." This helped me to understand what I was doing. I was working for others, and to really help others, I needed more people to help me. I needed to expand those contributing to the journal and those reading the journal. It wasn't a "growth strategy" but an attempt to create space where people in the field could share ideas. Such a place could bring us together in some small way, a way that might soften our divisions and make us all better through the sharing of our work.

Overwhelmed at how to do this, I spent hours brainstorming ideas with Christopher McMahon, whose office is next to mine. We tried lots of ideas, and he was always game, serving on the editorial board, as guest editor of issues, as book review editor, and, most recently, helping me incorporate the journal. At the prompting of David Cloutier, I worked with EBSCO to have entries include pdfs of the individual articles. Kent Lasnoski came on board to help start the book reviews.

At every conference I was at, I tried to reach out to people and encourage them to submit to the journal. So many people were doing such good work, and I preached my idea that JMT could be a place for them to share it.

A little more than a year into it, I was buried in work. I was sitting at a conference waiting for a session to start. The session was about the work of the Catholic Theological Ethics in the World Church network, and Jim Keenan was chairing it. He announced a book give away, *The Bible and Catholic Theological Ethics*, the latest issue in their book series. He gifted it to me for the work on the journal. It was a consolation, to use the Jesuit term, that I needed, reminding me that I was not alone.

To help with the work, I created a new position of Associate Editor. Like David, I sent out an email asking who would be interested. Like me, Therese Lysaught thought lots of people would volunteer. She said she would be interested in serving with the confidence that she would not be chosen. We know how that story ends. Once she was onboard as Associate Editor, we moved the journal to Scholastica, which helped streamline our production process and, more importantly, provided wider access to the journal. Articles could be found with simple Google searches and by anyone around the world with basic internet access.

This move had a financial cost, and it made us reflect on the nature of the journal. How would we raise money to cover the new platform? We could follow the typical route of making it a subscription-based journal or putting up a paywall or signup with a larger publishing company. None of these were appealing. If we wanted the journal to be a place for moral theologians, all moral theologians, we could not limit access to those few who had financial security and resources. We couldn't cut out graduate students, contingent faculty, moral theologians from around the world, and countless others. For our work, financial barriers would be in tension with, if not contradicting, Catholic social teaching. So, we committed to make the journal open-access, a decision that existed from the beginning but has become central to the journal.

Mount Saint Mary's University continued its financial support of the journal. Saint Vincent College added its support. Liturgical Press tested out a few advertisements with us. Others have been working to provide support, something difficult to do in the midst of a global pandemic and the precarious future of Catholic higher education.

Still, others kept supporting and contributing to the work of the journal. We started a book series with Catholic Theological Ethics in the World Church. With the help of guest editors, we did two special issues last year in addition to our regular issues in January and June. One of these issues was in Spanish, which required significant work from its editors, Alexandre Martins and MT Dávila. The Editorial Board gathered, and we made the decision to incorporate the journal. It should help secure the journal's future operations and enable us to better raise the necessary funds. The editorial board expanded to include a number of associate editors to help continue the work. We now have Mary M. Doyle Roche, Jean-Pierre Fortin, Alexandre Martins, Christopher McMahon, Mari Rapela Heidt, and Kate Ward.

With this issue, Therese Lysaught takes over as editor. It is an issue that I could not be happier to end on. It has an article by Cardinal Cupich and one by Charles Curran. The topics include environmentalism, racism, Lisa Sowle Cahill's contributions, faith, practical reasoning, biblical notions of justice, and Aquinas's view of grace and the unity of the virtues. Plus, book reviews. It has views from all corners of the field. It will be posted, open access, on our website. It will be announced on our newsletter that has over 400 subscribers. It comes from and reflects our scholarly community.

I now become Editor Emeritus, and Therese insists this position still requires work. I'm happy to do it. I'm happy to continue serving the community, even, as I remind Therese, in a more limited way. I have noted some of the contributions above, but these are just a fraction of the people who have helped along the way. I could list countless others. Megan Clark's advocacy and relentless work for the journal, Bill Mattison's and David Cloutier's ongoing advice, guest editing, and promoting the journal for others, Matthew Gaudet's work on several special issues, Ramon Luzarraga's willingness to review essays on short notice, the list could go on and on and I would still not be able to thank everyone who has done work on the journal.

And now, after five years, I'm able to see how much the journal has been a blessing for me because I was able to be part of this community. It is a community that, through its scholarship and its labors, shows its commitment to being disciples of the God who is love. **M**

Journal of Moral Theology, Vol. 11, No. 1 (2022): 5–11

From "Not Enough" to Bold Embrace: US Catholic Responses to *Laudato Si'*

His Eminence Blase Cardinal Cupich, Archbishop of Chicago

*Editor's Note: This essay was a keynote address offered by His Eminence Blase Cardinal Cupich at the second convening of "*Laudato Si' *and the US Catholic Church: A Conference Series on Our Common Home," co-sponsored by Catholic Climate Covenant and Creighton University. It was prepared for publication in the* Journal of Moral Theology *by Daniel R. DiLeo.*

"IN GOD WE TRUST," WE PROCLAIM ON our US currency; yet do we? To put it differently, in which god do we trust? Is it the god money, Mammon (Matthew 6:24), the idol who moves us *to have more,* and have more than others? Or do we trust in Jesus Christ, in whom and for whom everything was made (Colossians 1:16), who invites us to be more, and be with others? Mammon is a divisive idol, one that triggers the worst in us: individualism, indifference, and irrational competition, while distorting freedom and "bolstering a complacency and a cheerful recklessness" that give us permission to excuse ourselves from supporting social cohesion and environmental care (*Laudato Si'*, no. 59).

Here, I talk about how US Catholics could more boldly embrace *Laudato Si': On Care for Our Common Home,* in which Pope Francis offers a response through the best science available and the Christian faith to the most challenging sign of our time: the ecological crisis caused by human activity in the past two centuries (nos. 199-201). What does the pope's challenging message mean for a Christian community that professes a commitment to promoting a culture of life, yet acts with indifference to the call to make the sacrifices needed to protect this common home God has entrusted to us?

In the Christian tradition, the Holy Father reminds us, Christ is the destiny and the measure of maturity of all things and the perfect model of a human being (*Laudato Si'*, no. 83). By revealing the life of the Triune God, Jesus constantly invites and enables us to generate actual communion. Christ calls us to be open to ongoing conversion of our personal lifestyles and social systems, to be merciful and to freely love one another, especially the vulnerable. As such, *Laudato Si'* needs to be understood as a renewed call to conversion, to respond to Jesus's invitation to think differently about human beings, life, society, and our relationship with nature (no. 215). The first conversion involves a shift that affects our politics by moving from an economic model of development to one that emphasizes integral human development (no. 13). A second conversion leads us to become more aware of the interconnectedness of creation and the need for global solidarity through ecological education that is both informational and formational (nos. 209-215). A third conversion, which is fundamentally spiritual, provides us both passion and motivation in taking up the challenges we face (nos. 220–221).

FROM ECONOMIC DEVELOPMENT TO INTEGRAL HUMAN DEVELOPMENT

In *Laudato Si'*, Pope Francis recovers from our theological tradition the intrinsic interconnection that exists among ourselves, Creation, and the Creator (no. 66). In doing so, he urges us to remember our place in God's Creation as an integral component of the Earth's ecosystem. In the beginning, when God created the universe, He saw the goodness of Creation. All of this goodness was entrusted to humans, the only creatures created "in God's image and likeness...man and woman" (Genesis 1:27), who were put "in the garden of Eden to till it and keep it" (Genesis 2:15), meaning to live from it but also with it, and to take its fruits while caring for it (*Laudato Si'*, no. 67).

Somewhere along the way, we have forgotten the sacred relationship that binds us with nature. We falsely have come to believe that we have absolute dominion over the Earth and can exploit it at will. This "is not a correct interpretation of the Bible as understood by the Church," the pope observes (no. 67). We are called to love and care for the planet, not to treat it despotically. "We are not God," hence we are not at the center of Creation (no. 67). We are an important part of it, and in fact, are dust of the Earth (Genesis 2:7) for "our very bodies are made of her elements" (*Laudato Si'*, no. 2). The cry of the Earth now stirs our consciences to "acknowledge our sins against Creation" (no. 8).

This "Promethean vision of mastery over the world," as Pope Francis calls it, not only has had an impact on how we treat creation but is at the heart of the world's economic crisis, for we have come to adopt the false idol of economic growth as the sole purpose and overarching desire of society (no. 116). The desire for money has fomented division between winners and losers, where "the winners take it all." Having experienced the benefits of economic progress, so many of us turn a blind eye to the consequences this way of living has on people, our planet, and our own spirituality. By adopting this one-dimensional approach to the economy, we have fallen into the misconception that material growth is synonymous with human development. By neglecting the relational, spiritual, and emotional dimensions of development, we have inflated our desires and our greed for *more*: more income, more growth, more possessions; and more than others, expanding competition over cooperation. This paradigm has infiltrated all aspects of our lives and convinced us of the *"myth of progress,"* the illusion that we are free to exploit the Earth for personal and national economic growth, without considering the lasting consequences of our exploitation (no. 78, emphasis added).

The need of a new vision of the economy, the environment, and global solidarity comes into view as we look at the crises confronting the human family over recent decades. In 2008–2009, we suffered a severe financial crisis that spread throughout the globe.[1] This crisis was an opportunity to overhaul the global financial system and align it more closely with the real economy and the common good (cf. *Laudato Si'*, no. 109). Unfortunately, since the 2008 Recession, a widening of the wealth gap has worsened inequalities, which continue to tear at the fabric of humanity.

In 2015, world leaders, "painfully aware" of the effects of our economic choices on our common home, moved to act (no. 19). On behalf of more than 190 countries, they signed the historic Paris Agreement, which set a sustainable global agenda and goals. Fortunately, our country has re-joined this effort, although, despite this hopeful opportunity to change our development model, some polluting countries, including the United States, have been reluctant to live up to their commitments for the Sustainable Development Goals.

That, of course brings us to *Laudato Si'* when Pope Francis, in that same year, 2015, warned us about the lack of leadership and the weak political responses to the social, economic, and ecological crises (no. 54). He provided a thorough analysis, with the help of many conferences of bishops worldwide, including the US Conference of Catholic Bishops (USCCB), urging, as did St. John Paul II years ago, the need for a "global ecological conversion," both personal and structural (no. 52).[2] Sadly, however, we in this country have not, for the most part, taken this invitation to heart.

Pope Francis invites us to explore new ways of understanding progress, different from the "myth of progress" (no. 16). Particularly, this means an economy "which favors productive diversity and business creativity" while developing practices that preserve nature's gifts for

---

[1] For more details on the crises that marked the beginning of the 21st century, see Kate Raworth, *Doughnut Economics: Seven Ways to Think Like a 21st-Century Economist* (White River Junction, VT: Chelsea Green Publishing, 2017).

[2] See also, John of the Cross, *The Ascent of Mount Carmel* 2.6.6 and *The Dark Night of the Soul*, 2.21.11-12 in *The Collected Works of John of the Cross*, rev. ed., trans. Kieran Kavanaugh and Otilio Rodriguez (Washington, DC: ICS Publications, 2010).

generations to come (no. 129). Ultimately, in the words of Pope Emeritus Benedict XVI, the conversion of the economy requires "eliminating the structural causes of the dysfunctions of the world economy and correcting models of growth which have proved incapable of ensuring respect for the environment."[3] For that to occur, the economy should serve society and political life, not the other way around (no. 189).

What becomes clear in this analysis is that this misconception of development goes hand in hand with a distortion of freedom, which has impacted our approach to politics (nos. 6, 106). While the sense of absolute freedom without responsibility has led us to take from the Earth more than we need, it has also alienated us from our fundamental identities as brothers and sisters of the same human family. Let us be clear. Sharing, solidarity, and communion are neither anti-freedom values nor the basis of an anti-American "socialist" plan. They are first and foremost Christian values, deep human values that are vital for actual human development.

What is needed are new political systems "capable of reforming and coordinating institutions" and producing policies that are "far-sighted [...] and interdisciplinary" systems that intrinsically include the notion of justice (nos. 181, 197). We also need bold politics capable of challenging long-standing idols and free-market fundamentalisms, while also maintaining integrity and transparency (nos. 182, 189). Above all, we need open, participatory and inclusive political systems that involve all forms of wisdom (no. 63). Each of us must take responsibility for effecting change by becoming involved in the political process and by advocating for full participation of all citizens by protecting voting rights.

We have arrived at a turning point in history and must make some hard decisions, especially given how the COVID-19 pandemic has complicated these longstanding crises. The pre-existing socio-economic, ecological, and political crises are even more exacerbated as we see in underfunded public services, over-financialized economies that encourage perpetual risk-taking, continued environmental degradation and, worst of all, the absence of global solidarity.

That is why we must pause and reflect on our choices both communally and personally, for our current lifestyles and policies are inextricably linked with the current model of development. Our every action is relevant, since small gestures of love help change the world, Saint Thérèse of Lisieux reminded us (*Laudato Si'*, no. 230). As St. Francis of Assisi said, let us bring light where there is darkness, and hope where there is despair.

But to give space for God's light, each of us must at the least reject all attempts to divide us as a people. That would be a great place to

---

[3] Pope Benedict XVI, *Address to the Diplomatic Corps Accredited to the Holy See* (8 January 2007): AAS 99 (2007), 73; See also *Laudato Si'*, no. 6, cf. 2.

start. We have to understand, as the Holy Father reminds us, that "we are faced not with two separate crises, one environmental and the other social, but rather with one complex crisis which is both social and environmental" (no. 139).

CONVERSION THROUGH ECOLOGICAL EDUCATION

To sustain a process of global ecological conversion, we must prioritize education about ecology and the human place in Creation. For *Laudato Si'*, this education involves becoming familiar with scientific information and raising our consciousness about the complex issues involved: environmental justice, pollution, climate change, potable water access, biodiversity, and the breakdown of society amid global inequality. Could we not begin this education in our parishes, schools, and universities by arranging for small group gatherings to take up this dialogue?

But information about ecology is meaningless without the values needed to make important choices. Education is incomplete without formation, that is cultivating social virtues that help people make self-less ecological commitments (no. 211). To be complete, ecology education must provide a critical understanding of the "myth" of a modernity grounded in a utilitarian mind-set, e.g., individualism, unlimited progress, competition, consumerism, the unregulated market, etc. (no. 210).

Ecological education also involves promoting a new way of thinking about human beings, life, society, and our relationship with nature, which aims to promote a simpler and more "grateful" way of living, concerned with the needs of the poor and the environment (nos. 214–215). While this kind of education aims at forging a "culture of love" and care in each of us, a true ecological conversion will require the conversion of our national and international cultures that promotes a "new universal solidarity" and counters the laws of the market and "self-interested pragmatism" (no. 213). Pursuing the moral dimensions of culture has the promise of urgently moving society forward "in a bold cultural revolution" (no. 114).

A SPIRITUAL CONVERSION THAT PROVIDES PASSION AND MOTIVATION

Radical systemic change will not come—let alone be sustained—by mere political, economic, or scientific arguments (no. 202). What is needed is a conversion of the heart. In this regard, we as Catholics have much to contribute, since "authentic faith...always involves a deep desire to change the world, to transmit values, to leave this earth somehow better that we found it" (*Evangelii Gaudium*, no. 183).

Christian spirituality provides passion to care for and protect the world and all humans and impels us to reconcile our personal values with our everyday practices. Christian spirituality "proposes an alternative understanding of the quality of life and encourages a prophetic and contemplative lifestyle…marked by moderation and the capacity to be happy with little" (*Laudato Si'*, no. 222). As such, Christian spirituality ignites personal and social love because it favors "sobriety and humility" at a personal level while increasing "the capacity for living together in communion," moving from indifference to loving awareness and from individualism to solidarity (nos. 231, 224, 228, 220). And finally in our worship, Christian spirituality recovers our capacity to contemplate and celebrate the goodness of Creation; it is the antidote to "a more intensified pace of life and work which might be called 'rapidification'" (no. 18).

Ours is a radical spirituality, equal to the radical change necessary to save human society and our common home. Consequently, one vital element of Christian spirituality that must occupy a central role in the transition to a sustainable planet with a just economy is sacrifice. This is a topic that is usually avoided in discussions of how to meet the ecological crises that confront us for two reasons. The first is that speaking clearly about the level of personal sacrifice that will be required to move toward an equitable economy makes it more difficult to form a consensus supporting climate justice. The second is that any discussion of sacrifice will be distorted by climate deniers to make the pathway to sustainability seem impossible.

But the world's great religious and ethical traditions urge us to confront the reality that major individual and societal sacrifice are essential to saving our planet. And these same spiritual and moral traditions are equally united in demanding that the marginalized must not bear heavy burdens in moving to planetary sustainability.

It might seem that a society such as ours has lost its capacity for sustained sacrifice or at least lost sight of the ennobling role that sacrifice can play in our individual and communal lives. But if we look more deeply, we find in the enormous sacrifices that families make for their children a proclamation that sustained sacrifice is in fact all around us.

This is the linchpin for building a public ethic of sacrifice in pursuit of a just and sustainable world. Pope Francis devotes tremendous attention in *Laudato Si'* to the ethic of intergenerational responsibility, which is ultimately rooted in the spirituality of sacrifice for those who will inherit the planet. We must be willing to publicly advance such an ethic, not as a position we grudgingly acknowledge the need for, but as the great moral call of our age.

The transformative power of spirituality is contagious. Starting from promoting a personal rediscovery of the beauty of Creation through the grace of Christ, it can fuel a conversion towards new structures, instilled with universal love that can build up the common good (nos. 219, 235). In sum, Christian spirituality can provide a rich and balanced understanding of the meaning of our life on Earth, as well as the basis for a new understanding of growth, underpinned by an economic system that has people at its center, with long-term policies that care for future generations (nos. 125, 231).

CONCLUSION

The threefold conversion I have discussed will require ongoing dialogue, a commitment to education, and repeatedly tapping into the deep spiritual resources of our tradition, if our nation and our world are to move from "not enough" to a bold embrace of the vision of *Laudato Si'*. Likewise, I am convinced that it is useless to talk about advancing a culture of life absent a vigorous commitment—both by individuals and communities—to making the sacrifices required for improving the socio-economic, ecological, and political crises of our time.

Pope Francis has been clear about the interconnected nature and complexity of the challenges we face and the need to address them in unity, ever mindful that it is in God we trust. It is up to us to put aside any false idols and continually respond to the call to conversion that will lead to a more just, equitable, and loving future.

Let us be reminded of our mission to care for each other and for the Earth. Let us seek an interconnected response based on faith and science. Let us not be discouraged by the work ahead. Instead, let us trust and rejoice in God's promise to make all things new (Revelation 21:5), and take to heart the encouragement the Holy Father offers when he tells us that, in spite of the practical relativism and consumer culture we live in, "all is not lost." "Human beings," he notes, "while capable of the worst, are also capable of rising above themselves and their mental and social conditioning, choosing again what is good, and making a new start. No system can completely suppress our openness to what is good, true, and beautiful, or our God-given ability to respond to his grace at work deep in our hearts. I appeal to my sisters and brothers throughout the world not to forget this dignity which is ours" (no. 205). Thank you. M

Blase Cupich was named Archbishop of Chicago in 2014 and elevated to Cardinal by Pope Francis in 2016. He serves on the Vatican's Congregation for Bishops, Congregation for Catholic Education, and Task Force to Assist Episcopal Conferences, Congregations of Religious, and Societies of Apostolic Life. Cardinal Cupich also serves on the US Conference of Catholic Bishops' Ad Hoc Committee Against Racism. He was born in Omaha, NE and ordained to the priesthood in the Archdiocese of Omaha. Cardinal Cupich earned his STD in sacramental theology from The Catholic University of America.

Journal of Moral Theology, Vol. 11, No. 1 (2022): 12–22

Responding to the Invitation: Fostering a Bolder Response to *Laudato Si'*

Maureen K. Day

Editor's Note: This essay was a keynote address offered by Maureen K. Day at the second convening of "Laudato Si' and the U.S. Catholic Church: A Conference Series on Our Common Home," co-sponsored by Catholic Climate Covenant and Creighton University.

C LIMATE CHANGE IS A SERIOUS ISSUE FACING our global community and—thankfully—most Americans recognize this. According to a Yale study, 72 percent of Americans believe that global warming is happening, and 57 percent believe this warming is mostly caused by human activities.[1] Additionally, at least three-fourths of Americans support the funding of renewable energy sources, tax rebates for fuel-efficient vehicles and solar panels, and regulations on carbon dioxide emissions. Data from the Pew Research Center demonstrate that two-thirds of Americans think the federal government is not doing enough to reduce the effects of global climate change and three-fourths believe that it is more important to develop alternative energy than to expand our fossil fuel sources.[2] This is good news.

Here, I want to explore the impact of *Laudato Si'* on climate change attitudes and practices, to discover the lessons its release and the six years that follow bring us, so that we might learn from the ways its potential impact fell short and how we might embolden its impact going forward.

FOUR NEEDS….AND INVITATIONS

Laudato Si' made a difference. The Yale Program on Climate Change Communication and George Mason University administered two surveys seven months apart, the first in March 2015—two months

---

[1] Jennifer Marlon, Peter Howe, Matto Mildenberger, Anthony Leiserowitz, and Xinran Wang, "Yale Climate Opinion Maps 2020," *Yale Program on Climate Change Communication*, climatecommunication.yale.edu/visualizations-data/ycom-us.

[2] Cary Funk and Meg Hefferon, "U.S. Public Views on Climate and Energy," *Pew Research Center*, November 25, 2019, www.pewresearch.org/science/2019/11/25/u-s-public-views-on-climate-and-energy.

before the release of *Laudato Si'*—and the second in October 2015—five months after the release. These two waves of survey data allow us to see how people's views on climate change shifted with the publication of *Laudato Si'*. Generally, the findings show that *Laudato Si'* made a difference, with Catholics (35 percent) more likely to say that the encyclical shaped their thinking on the issue than Americans broadly (17 percent).[3]

One of the most obvious factors that allows Pope Francis to be such an influence is his popularity. Pope Francis's favorability among American Catholics was 82 percent according to the most recent Pew survey.[4] His popularity extends beyond Catholics, too. Although he is perceived somewhat less favorably among white evangelicals (45 percent), roughly seven in ten white mainline Protestants and six in ten of those not affiliated with any religious tradition have a favorable view of Pope Francis. For a religious leader, favorability easily translates into moral trust and influence, and Pope Francis clearly enjoys this in the impact of *Laudato Si'*.

But a more pressing question is why didn't *Laudato Si'* have more of an impact? I want to draw our attention to four needs that, if met, would effect a bolder appropriation of *Laudato Si'* by American Catholics: 1) healing our polarization, 2) increased discussion of *Laudato Si'* by Church leaders, 3) a deeper appreciation of the ways civic engagement intersects with our faith, and 4) a more accurate and life-giving understanding of humanity's relationship to the rest of creation. I believe that if we can begin to meet these needs, American Catholics—as well as Americans generally—will more effectively respond to climate change.

Need One: Healing Our Polarization

Beginning with the first need, American Catholics, like Americans generally, are characterized by polarization.[5] Data collected in 2017 by William D'Antonio's research team helps paint a quick picture of

---

[3] Edward Maibach, Anthony Leiserowitz, Connie Roser-Renouf, Teresa Myers, Seth Rosenthal, and Geoff Feinberg, "The Francis Effect: How Pope Francis Changed the Conversation about Global Warming," *George Mason University Center for Climate Change Communication and Yale Program on Climate Change Communication*, 15, www.climatechangecommunication.org/wp-content/uploads/2016/03/2015-Nov-The_Francis_Effect.pdf.

[4] Claire Gecewicz, "Americans, including Catholics, continue to have favorable views of Pope Francis," *Pew Research Center*, www.pewresearch.org/fact-tank/2021/06/25/americans-including-catholics-continue-to-have-favorable-views-of-pope-francis.

[5] Mary Ellen Konieczny, Charles C. Camosy, and Tricia C. Bruce, eds., *Polarization in the US Catholic Church: Naming the Wounds, Beginning to Heal* (Collegeville, MN: Liturgical Press, 2016).

Catholic polarization.[6] When we ask Catholics about their political ideology, 14 percent understand themselves as very conservative, 26 percent as moderately conservative, 31 percent as moderate, 19 percent as moderately liberal, and 9 percent as very liberal; so when it comes to ideology, Catholics lean conservative. But this lean goes the other way when asking about party, with 44 percent identifying as Democrat, 22 percent not identifying with a party, and 28 percent as Republican; Catholics lean conservative ideologically but lean Democrat when it comes to party affiliation. So, we are all over the political map, and I think this political diversity, when we're at our best, is a good thing.

The tricky thing about polarization when it comes to climate change is that political affiliation and ideology seem to be some of the strongest attitudinal predictors for the issue. The Pew Research Center found that there is a large gap between Democrats and Republicans in their belief that human activity contributes "a great deal" to climate change (Democrats 72 percent vs. Republicans 22 percent) and in their belief that the federal government is doing too little to reduce the effects of climate change (Democrats 89 percent vs. Republicans 35 percent).[7] We need to ensure that Catholic political diversity does not lead to factionalism with regards to climate change.

There are many political issues that red and blue and purple Catholics could all grow from with some robust and charitable dialogue.[8] I, for one, am thankful that Catholics are a politically diverse community and can have lively conversations on issues that affect the common good. We need politically different Catholics to pull us out of our political communities and back to our Catholic community where we can ask Catholic questions like: What does solidarity have to say to this issue? Does anything in this policy risk compromising the dignity of the human person? How are the poor and vulnerable going to be affected? Questions like these can mobilize more Republican Catholics to help curb climate change, and they are definitely open to it! Even with the political gap in attitudes about climate change, strong majorities of moderate Republicans support a variety of climate change efforts, including those that restrict industries and demand

---

[6] William D'Antonio, Michele Dillon, and Mary Gautier, dataset from "The Sixth Nationwide Survey of American Catholics in a Changing Church," 2017.

[7] Alec Tyson and Brian Kennedy, "Two-Thirds of Americans Think Government Should Do More on Climate," June 23, 2020, *Pew Research Center*, www.pewresearch.org/science/2020/06/23/two-thirds-of-americans-think-government-should-do-more-on-climate.

[8] Maureen K. Day, "Why are We at Each Other's Throats? Healing Polarization in Our Church," *National Catholic Reporter*, November 30, 2018, www.ncronline.org/news/opinion/why-are-we-each-others-throats-healing-polarization-our-church.

green innovation.[9] And progressive Catholics will be more successful if they use language that resonates with conservatives. Social psychologists have found that conservatives are more persuaded by climate change arguments when they are presented within a frame of purity, that is, a frame that keeps creation unpolluted, undefiled and prevents degradation.[10] Gather around what is held in common and appeal to the deeply held convictions of one another. Politically different Catholics share more in common with one another than they think. Let's have new conversations.

Need Two: Increased Discussion of Laudato Si' by Church Leaders

The second need is more frequent discussion of *Laudato Si'*, especially from Catholic leaders. Substantial percentages of Catholics (56 percent) and Americans generally (45 percent) had heard about the encyclical five months after its release.[11] These media numbers are much higher than those remembering the encyclical being discussed in their place of worship, with only 26 percent of Catholics, 16 percent of evangelicals and 9 percent of mainline Protestants reporting hearing *Laudato Si'* discussed in church. And additional research shows that less than one percent of diocesan publication columns written by nearly all US Catholic bishops around the time of *Laudato Si'* mention the phrases "climate change" or "global warming."[12] Public media is doing a better job at spreading the good news than we Catholics are.

We need to make sure we get the word out because reading or hearing about *Laudato Si'* is associated with greater belief in the reality of climate change. A 2016 CARA study found that reading or hearing about *Laudato Si'* was correlated with believing that the earth is warming and that this warming is largely a result of human activity.[13] The study also underscored the influence of Church leaders. Thirty-two percent of Catholics say that statements by Pope Francis led them to conclude or strengthened their belief that they have a moral responsibility to combat climate change. The percentages drop to the high teens when these respondents are asked about the influence of their bishop, pastor, or other Catholic minister. Given the other data, these

---

[9] Tyson and Kennedy, "Two-Thirds of Americans."

[10] Matthew Feinberg and Robb Willer, "Moral Reframing: A Technique for Effective and Persuasive Communication across Political Divides," *Social and Personality Psychology Compass* 13, no. 12 (2019): 5.

[11] Maibach, Leiserowitz, Roser-Renouf, Myers, Rosenthal, and Feinberg, "The Francis Effect," 5.

[12] Sabrina Danielsen, Daniel R. DiLeo, and Emily E. Burke, "U.S. Catholic Bishops' Silence and Denialism on Climate Change," *Environmental Research Letters* 16, no. 11 (2021): 114006.

[13] Center for Applied Research in the Apostolate, "CARA Catholic Poll (CCP) 2016: Attitudes about Climate Change," *Center for Applied Research in the Apostolate*, cara.georgetown.edu/climate%20summary.pdf.

lower numbers are likely not because these leaders are intrinsically without influence, but simply because many leaders have not raised the issue.

What prevents some of us from talking about *Laudato Si'*? It may be challenging for leaders to feel they have any influence at all when climate change has been made a partisan issue and few of us enjoy Pope Francis's popularity. The 2017 data collected by the D'Antonio team found that 84 percent of American Catholics were satisfied with Pope Francis's leadership.[14] But only 69 percent are satisfied with the national bishops, and it rises a bit with 74 percent satisfied with their local bishop and 78 percent with their parish priest. Bishops, especially as a body, need to build public trust so that they, too, may be seen as legitimate partners in dialogue and for their pronouncements to be more readily accepted.

So how do Church leaders initiate these discussions? Before we dive into dialogue, it would help to understand how the Church's influence and efficacy has changed, which is carefully outlined in Michele Dillon's *Postsecular Catholicism*.[15] A few decades ago, Catholic leaders only influenced Catholics. Our clergy were imagined to be moral authorities for Catholics but not beyond us. Further, their expertise was limited to the realm of theology, and other disciplines— like medicine, the economy, state governance—were left in the hands of their own experts. Now, we recognize that social concerns do not fit into a single discipline in a tidy way. Climate change, for instance, has biological, ecological, sociological, economic, ethical, religious, and other dimensions. We understand that a comprehensive solution will need experts from a variety of fields. This transition means that the Catholic hierarchy is no longer *the* voice of influence among Catholics, it is *one of many* influential voices. Despite this loss in exclusive authority, it is now a voice that is heard *beyond* Catholicism. This shift poses its challenges; no longer is office alone enough to claim moral authority. But this shift is also pregnant with opportunities. Catholic leaders, when they rely upon cogent and compelling arguments, become one among many authoritative voices in the public square, broadening the reach and influence of the Church.

Demonstrating this beyond-Catholicism influence, a CARA study found that among those of no religious affiliation, 95 percent who recall hearing about *Laudato Si'* believe society should be taking steps to combat climate change; only 77 percent of those unaffiliated who have not heard about *Laudato Si'* feel this way.[16] We don't want to

---

[14] D'Antonio, Dillon, and Gautier, "The Sixth Nationwide Survey."

[15] Michele Dillon, *Postsecular Catholicism: Relevance and Renewal* (New York: Oxford University Press, 2018).

[16] Center for Applied Research in the Apostolate, "CARA Catholic Poll."

make causal leaps from correlations, yet these findings tell us something very important. They show that the Church is being heard by audiences beyond Catholics themselves; let's continue, and even increase, the dialogue.

We must also consider ways Church leaders might rebuild their trust. Yes, one of the reasons that *Laudato Si'* was able to have an impact was Pope Francis's favorability, a level that few Church leaders can match. But we should recognize that speaking courageously and acts of valor do not need to come *after* we have become popular; being virtuous is attractive and can actually increase popularity and influence. The Yale study reveals that American (from 53 percent to 60 percent) and American Catholic (75 percent to 88 percent) favorability toward the Pope increased after *Laudato Si'* and his visit to the United States.[17] Likewise, a greater share of Americans (from 51 percent to 62 percent) and American Catholics (from 65 percent to 71 percent) trust the Pope as a source of climate change information after the publication, as well.[18] In short, Pope Francis's popularity and trust as an authority on this issue grew after *Laudato Si'*. Bishops can do the same thing. They can talk to leaders and experts in their dioceses and beyond to have a better sense of the issue and how it will affect our country. Bishops need to talk to one other, especially the bishops who are more ambivalent or are unsure how to effectively speak on climate change. In becoming savvier on the issue, they can share the most inspiring aspects of *Laudato Si'* with the faithful, demonstrating the relevance of Catholicism in our public life and proclaiming the goodness of God's creation with confidence. In initiating a dialogue that many lay Catholics recognize is a pressing issue, the bishops are displaying shared concern and solidarity with their flock, truly smelling of their sheep. The bishops can then take what they've learned and more boldly proclaim—as a national body as well as individually—the urgency of climate change for American public life, supported by the hope of their people.

We should also note that women religious are seen as a legitimate moral voice for Catholics and their potential influence is virtually untapped. A 2012 Pew survey found that 83 percent of American Catholics are satisfied with the leadership of US sisters.[19] Through their tenacity, efficiency, and devotion, they are a vivid reminder that virtuous living increases authority and moral status. Catholic sisters carry a tremendous amount of moral capital in American society. However,

---

[17] Maibach, Leiserowitz, Roser-Renouf, Myers, Rosenthal, and Feinberg, "The Francis Effect," 7.

[18] Maibach, Leiserowitz, Roser-Renouf, Myers, Rosenthal, and Feinberg, "The Francis Effect," 8.

[19] Pew Research Center, "Catholics Share Bishops' Concerns about Religious Liberty," *Pew Research Center*, August 1, 2012, www.pewforum.org/2012/08/01/2012-catholic-voters-religious-liberty-issue/#leaders.

much of their work is away from the public eye. I want to invite sisters to consider the ways they might more publicly utilize the trust and moral capital they so obviously enjoy shaping the American imagination more robustly. Our society needs the wealth of your communities' experiences to have renewed conversations about climate change. Please help lead us in this. Finally, those who are ordained or professed, elevate the voices of lay experts and empower everyday lay people who have much to share on this. Too often Catholics turn to clergy and religious for moral guidance; know when to shift our attention to the laity. In short, leaders—whether ordained, professed, or lay—even while being sensitive and humble, consider the ways you might more boldly speak, dialogue and act in ways that will make manifest the vision articulated in *Laudato Si'*.

Need Three: Understanding the Relationship Between Civic Engagement and Faith

The third need for a bolder appropriation of *Laudato Si'* is a greater appreciation among Catholics for social reform. Several studies have found this aversion to political action when examining Americans and the way they view social problems and choose to engage (or not) in American public life; often citizens, including Catholics, opt for personal changes over social changes.[20] Sometimes even activists themselves employ personal language, such as protecting their families, to explain their activism.[21] This political aversion is not unique to Americans.[22] Although the publication of *Laudato Si'* saw a seven point increase in the number of Americans who believe that the United States should reduce greenhouse gas emissions regardless of what other countries plan to do, rising from 54 percent to 61 percent, far fewer changed in their perception of which political actors these responsibilities should fall to.[23] While many Americans identified corporations and industry (roughly two-thirds), citizens themselves (roughly two-thirds), Congress (just under six in ten) and President Obama (just under half) as political agents who should do "more" or "much more" to address global warming, these numbers were very stable before and after the publication of *Laudato Si'*. Similarly, although the majority

[20] Nina Eliasoph, *Avoiding Politics: How Americans Produce Apathy in Everyday Life* (New York: Cambridge University Press, 1998). Maureen K. Day, *Catholic Activism Today: Individual Transformation and the Struggle for Social Justice* (New York: New York University Press, 2020).

[21] Paul Lichterman, *The Search for Political Community: American Activists Reinventing Commitment* (New York: Cambridge University Press, 1996), 87–88.

[22] Bin Xu, *The Politics of Compassion: The Sichuan Earthquake and Civic Engagement in China* (Redwood City, CA: Stanford University Press, 2017), 137–142, 198–199.

[23] Maibach, Leiserowitz, Roser-Renouf, Myers, Rosenthal, and Feinberg, "The Francis Effect," 36.

support the United States undertaking large or moderate efforts to curb global warming, *Laudato Si'* did not seem to affect people's responses; the encyclical changed our personal attitudes but not our political buy-in. We need to remember that public engagement and social reform is part of being Catholic.

An important aspect of my research, and troubling to my American Catholic sensibilities, is that Catholics have lost sight of the importance of participatory democracy. The bishops' document, *Forming Consciences for Faithful Citizenship*, is clear that Catholics should be active citizens writing, "[R]esponsible citizenship is a virtue, and participation in political life is a moral obligation."[24] While we might more readily feel compassion, encounter, and kinship when we provide aid at the individual level, these feelings should propel us into long-term and larger-scale change.[25] St. Thomas recognized that a human person is a "civic and social animal" (ST I-II, q. 72, a. 4), but we are turning increasingly inward.[26] Let us remind one another of the ways our personal holiness is connected to visions of the common good and see ourselves as citizen-disciples.

Again, we need interdisciplinary conversations if we are going to solve this complicated and urgent issue in a timely and effective way. For most of us, to be active in climate justice does not require understanding all things political; rather it means bringing a Catholic voice to the table. *Laudato Si'* provides tremendous wisdom for the spiritual, moral and human dimensions of the climate change issue. We can bring good news of hope, liberation, compassion, fidelity, and justice as we call for a restraint of greed and a right relationship with our common home. We can help illuminate the issue, offering our piece and learning from others, expanding everyone's imaginations. Let's stoke an old fire and remember that social reform is a part of the American Catholic tradition.[27]

We see some promising evidence that *Laudato Si'* did shift people's imaginations. Before *Laudato Si'*, 32 percent of Americans considered climate change to be a moral issue.[28] After *Laudato Si'*, just seven months after the first survey, that percentage jumped to 38 percent. Likewise, we saw an eight-point gain among those who viewed

[24] United States Conference of Catholic Bishops, *Forming Consciences for Faithful Citizenship: A Call to Political Responsibility from the Catholic Bishops of the United States* (Washington DC: United States Conference of Catholic Bishops, 2020), no. 13.
[25] Day, *Catholic Activism Today*, 197–198.
[26] Robert Putnam, *Bowling Alone: The Collapse and Revival of American Community* (New York: Simon & Schuster, 2000).
[27] Sharon Erickson Nepstad, *Catholic Social Activism: Progressive Movements in the United States* (New York: New York University Press, 2019). David J. O'Brien, *Public Catholicism*, 2nd ed. (New York: Orbis Books, 1996).
[28] Maibach, Leiserowitz, Roser-Renouf, Myers, Rosenthal, and Feinberg, "The Francis Effect," 6.

climate change as a social justice issue, and a four-point gain among those understanding it to be a spiritual and a religious issue.[29] *Laudato Si'* is slowly expanding people's imaginations, giving people more tools to think about and effectively respond to climate change. And, as experiences are one of the most powerful tools for seeing our reality in a new way, inviting Catholics into political engagement through parish and diocesan opportunities could be transformative. If you are not sure where to start, programs like those offered by JustFaith Ministries are excellent.[30] Talk to one another, see what is out there; we are in this together! Let us work to foster a greater understanding of the citizen-disciple for American Catholics.

Need Four: A More Robust Understanding of Humanity's Relationship to Creation

The final need is to totally dismantle false notions of humanity's relationship to creation in favor of what is articulated in *Laudato Si'*. Until very recently, environmental concerns were often framed as the environment versus people. Do you remember when it was the spotted owl versus loggers who needed to feed their families? Then it was reducing beef in our diet to curb methane versus ensuring that growing children got enough protein and iron. It was developing genetically modified corn to feed more people versus the survival of the monarch butterfly. This discursive frame was present not only in popular thinking but in Catholic discussion of the issue as well. Until recently, American Catholic media outlets framed these issues as a choice between the environment and human beings.[31] The dominant way of thinking was that environment supplied jobs and resources to further human life, and streams might have to be polluted and animals might have to go extinct in the process. The bad effects were seen as unfortunate, but morally necessary given the alternative. While this view was certainly waning before *Laudato Si'*, the encyclical powerfully admonishes this false binary, condemning both a "tyrannical anthropocentrism" and the technocratic paradigm that allows modernization, technological developments, and the unbridled appropriation of resources to run its course with little ethical scrutiny (no. 68). The old paradigm is obviously destructive and *Laudato Si'* clearly spells out that humans are not to exploit creation, rather we exist as a part of creation. We need to help shift imaginations, to help us see that it is a gift to depend upon other creatures and to live humbly as human persons.

---

[29] Maibach, Leiserowitz, Roser-Renouf, Myers, Rosenthal, and Feinberg, "The Francis Effect," 6, 32.

[30] JustFaith Ministries, "Our Programs," *JustFaith Ministries*, 2021, www.justfaith.org/programs.

[31] Nepstad, *Catholic Social Activism*, 151–154.

This is an invitation to plumb the resources of our tradition and amplify aspects that have always shown our connection to creation. I would argue that the Franciscan tradition has much to offer here. Pope Leo XIII's 1879 *Aeterni Patris* established St. Thomas Aquinas's thought as the dominant philosophical viewpoint in Roman Catholicism. However, we can still look beyond Thomas when other traditions offer us relevant insights. For instance, Thomas—a Dominican—and his contemporary St. Bonaventure—a Franciscan—emphasized different aspects of God. When Thomas discussed God, the vast majority of the time he emphasized the oneness of God; Bonaventure, on the other hand, leaned into the triune nature of God.[32] That is, Bonaventure lifts up the qualities of distinction, particularity and relationship within the Trinity, and this triune understanding of God has been the core of Franciscan thought ever since.[33]

How we view God must matter for everything and emphasizing God's oneness will illuminate some things while it obscures others. Consider solidarity. If we start with an image of God that amplifies God's oneness, our solidarity will rest on a universalism. We'll easily see the characteristics creation shares. But in only emphasizing what we universally hold in common, we risk missing what distinguishes us. The Franciscan approach highlights what sets each species apart, the special role each plays in its particular ecosystem and the relationships each shares with other creatures. It calls our attention to our shared interdependence. Of course, hang on to the universal commonalities we share that Thomas highlights, but hold these beside the realization that I need you, you need me, and we all need earthworms, streams, sharks, honeybees, fireflies, mushrooms, elephants, amoebas, glaciers, old growth forests and the whole rest of our earth. We all matter, and we each matter. Nothing is insignificant. The whole and the parts and the web of relationships connecting all of us are precious. Let's plumb the riches of the Catholic tradition and discover the depths of the invitation we are being offered.

In closing, I want to fully admit that some of the needs I have highlighted are great. Healing our polarization and revivifying the social reform tradition of Catholicism will take long-term, coordinated, cooperative efforts. Other needs, like hearing more on *Laudato Si'*, especially from our leaders, and plumbing our tradition to rediscover the resources it provides for understanding our relationship to creation, can start tonight. But large or small, a common thread to all these

---

[32] Joseph Chinnici, Mary Beth Ingham, and Thomas Nairn, "Franciscan Moral Vision: Responding to God's Love," Presented at Franciscan Forum X, Colorado Springs, Colorado, March 27–29, 2014.

[33] Kenan B. Osborne, *The History of Franciscan Theology* (St. Bonaventure, NY: Franciscan Institute Publications, 2007); Thomas A. Nairn, *The Franciscan Moral Vision: Responding to God's Love* (St. Bonaventure, NY: Franciscan Institute Publications, 2013).

needs is an invitation to be more deeply, more intentionally, more authentically Catholic. Both as individuals and as Church, let us bring our faith to public life and work toward a more just, compassionate, and wondrous relationship with our common home. M

Maureen K. Day teaches and researches on faith and public life. With training in theology and the social sciences, she focuses on Catholicism, family, young adults, social ethics, and religion in American civic life. Dr. Day has published *Catholic Activism Today: Individual Transformation and the Struggle for Social Justice* (NYU Press 2020) and *Young Adult American Catholics: Explaining Vocation in Their Own Words* (Paulist Press 2018), and authored scholarly articles, book chapters, and popular essays. She holds a PhD in ethics and social theory from the Graduate Theological Union.

Lisa Sowle Cahill: Five Significant Contributions to Reimagining Christian Ethics[1]

Charles E. Curran

L
ISA SOWLE CAHILL IS A LEADING AND very important contemporary Catholic moral theologian. She started teaching at Boston College in 1976 and has held the J. Donald Monan professorship since 1996. She began her academic career in what can be described as the second wave of contemporary moral theology. The first wave dealt directly with the realities of the Second Vatican Council (1962–1965), the papal encyclical *Humanae Vitae* (1968), and the reactions to them. Cahill dealt with the aftermath of these two events and directly contributed much to the ongoing development of moral theology until the present.

Her writings, her awards and accomplishments, and her many doctoral students objectively prove the tremendous impact she has had on Catholic moral theology.[2] Cahill has published eight books dealing with the method of moral theology and particular issues, such as sexuality, gender, family, bioethics, global justice, pacifism, just war, and peace building. In addition, she has edited or co-edited six other volumes. Cahill has also co-edited nine volumes in the well-respected international journal *Concilium*. Her CV at the Boston College website includes ten pages of book chapters and articles. It is customary in festschrifts to include all the publications of the honoree, but the recent festschrift in her honor simply gives the books and the volumes of *Concilium* that she co-edited.[3] The logical conclusion is that these book chapters and articles are so numerous that listing them in the book would take up too much space!

Lisa Cahill has served on numerous boards and committees dealing with a wide variety of subjects. She was president of the Catholic Theological Society of America in 1992–1993 and president of the Soci-

---

[1] This essay was originally the plenary address at the celebration at Boston College of the contributions of Lisa Sowle Cahill to Christian ethics, September 10–12, 2021.

[2] For Cahill's curriculum vitae, see www.bc.edu/content/dam/files/schools/cas_sites/theology/pdf/lcahill_cv.pdf.

[3] Ki Joo Choi, Sarah M. Moses, and Andrea Vicini, ed., *Reimagining the Moral Life: On Lisa Sowle Cahill's Contributions to Christian Ethics* (Maryknoll, NY: Orbis Books, 2020).

ety of Christian Ethics in 1997-1998. In 1996, she was elected to membership in the American Academy of Arts and Sciences, the oldest and most prestigious academic society in the United States.

Cahill's influence on moral theology has been extended through the work of her graduate students. Seventeen of her doctoral students contributed to the 2020 festschrift published in her honor—*Reimagining the Moral Life: On Lisa Sowle Cahill's Contributions to Christian Ethics*. At meetings of the CTSA and the SCE in the evenings after the academic sessions have ended, I have many times seen her leading her former and present graduate students into the bar for further discussion and celebration. She has devoted much time and effort to mentoring many who will make significant contributions to moral theology in the future. Thus, no one can doubt that she has been a very important major figure in Catholic moral theology.

Inspired by the title of the festschrift in her honor, this essay develops five methodological contributions Cahill has made to reimagining the discipline of Christian ethics. These five significant methodological contributions have ramifications for many content issues she has discussed over the years. In my judgment, what is characteristic of her methodological approaches is the emphasis on "and." The emphasis on the "and" is a hallmark of the Catholic theological ethical tradition with its emphasis on Scripture and tradition, faith and reason, grace and works, Jesus and the Church. Her methodological "and," however, has its own particular characteristics, which will be developed in the subsequent sections of this essay. Cahill insists on both theological and philosophical sources of moral theology, but the theological is primary. Her philosophical notion of human flourishing is based on Thomism and feminism. Cahill's approach is both Catholic and ecumenical. Whereas many distinguish between the individual and social aspects of ethics, her "and" in this case insists on the social aspect of what previously had often been considered as merely individual ethics. Catholic moral theology in the past insisted on proposing the moral truth. Her "and" in this case adds the need for action to achieve what is the moral good.

THEOLOGICAL AND PHILOSOPHICAL SOURCES

In her first major work, she mentions four complementary sources of Christian ethics: the scriptural witness and the philosophical accounts of human flourishing received the most attention here and in her later writings. The other two sources are the community's tradition of faith, theology, and practice and the role of the empirical sciences.[4] This essay will develop in greater detail only the theological source involving the scriptural basis and the in-breaking of the reign of God

---

[4] Lisa Sowle Cahill, *Between the Sexes: Foundations for a Christian Ethics of Sexuality* (Philadelphia, PA: Fortress, 1985), 1–6.

with its particular values and the philosophical source of human flourishing.

Primacy of the Theological Source

Throughout her many writings, following the example of her mentor and friend James Gustafson, she has emphasized the primacy of the theological aspect of Christian ethics.[5] The theological source of Scripture and the values of the in-breaking reign of God are not primarily interested in developing norms that exclude but rather a vision that inspires the Christian community and its public life today. New Testament values of the vision of the in-breaking reign of God challenge existing human relationships by reordering relationships of domination and violence toward greater compassion, mercy, and peace, especially by acting in solidarity for justice with the poor.[6]

Cahill applies this theological vision with its scriptural values to three important content issues—the social-political order, human sexuality and the family, and the call to peace-making. The discipleship nourished in the Christian community challenges the realities of human inequality, poverty, violence, injustice, and ecological destruction in the social and political orders. Such realities are evil and wrong, unjust, and unacceptable to the Christian. The Christian community is called to a preferential option for the poor that strives to overcome the injustice, poverty, and powerlessness of so many people in our world. New Testament values are not the liberal values of freedom and self-determination but the integration of all human persons, especially those who are powerless and on the margins, into a new communal unity and inclusiveness in Christ.[7]

With regard to sexual morality, the first function of Christian morality is to encourage disciples to do good, not to set boundaries and condemn and exclude those who fall outside of the boundaries. The positive theological and ethical vision of Christian sexuality focuses on faithful heterosexual marriage. She insists on equality and no subordination in marriage. Unfortunately, early Christian practice existed in a very patriarchal society and environment. Even here, however, Christians made some transformation in the existing realities. The emphasis on virginity, for example, was a rejection of the hierarchically controlled functions of the patriarchal family. Cahill notes that, in the

---

[5] Cahill, *Between the Sexes*, ix; Lisa Cahill, *Global Justice, Christology and Christian Ethics: New Studies in Christian Ethics* (Cambridge: Cambridge University Press, 2011), 111.

[6] Lisa Sowle Cahill, *Sex, Gender, and Christian Ethics: New Studies in Christian Ethics* (Cambridge: Cambridge University Press, 1996), 123.

[7] Cahill, *Global Justice*, 1 and throughout.

New Testament itself, there are some small changes and transformations regarding women and slaves toward greater compassion and solidarity.[8]

Cahill recognizes in her earlier discussion of sexuality some departures from the biblical and theological vision of sexuality if they represent the most morally commendable course of action concretely available to individuals caught in difficult situations.[9] Committed homosexual relations, as well as remarriage after divorce, are examples. In a later book, Cahill discusses "adverse virtue." When choices represent attempts to act with integrity in the midst of unavoidable conflict and adversity, one has what might be called "adverse virtue." These choices are not virtues in the sense of fulfilling totally all that humans are meant to be, but they also are not essentially sinful.[10] Other theologians are more willing to see actions such as a permanent homosexual relationship and divorce and remarriage as fundamentally good in the proper circumstances.[11] The core of the problem is the relationship between the ideal and the present reality.

With regard to sexuality, Cahill is quite critical of the existing hierarchical Church teaching. This teaching is captive to some patriarchal assumptions, defines woman's nature in terms of reproductive functioning, ties sexual meaning to the biological structure of sex acts, and focuses on the morality of individual acts instead of emphasizing the personal, familial, and social relationships in which they occur. The greatest liability of Catholic hierarchical teaching on sexuality is its lack of demonstrated commitment to equality and the wellbeing of women worldwide.[12]

With regard to the family, Christian commitment calls for marital and kin bonds as the foundation for affectionate, mutual, and just internal family relationships and for compassionate and sacrificial outreach to those beyond one's family, especially the powerless and those in need. Notice once again the emphasis on the social aspects. The Christian family and its values are not the same as many contemporary understandings of family with exaggerated values of family security and advancement, and definitely not the same as the family of modern liberal individualism where commitments are based on individual choice alone.[13]

---

[8] Cahill, *Sex, Gender, and Christian Ethics*, 154–165.

[9] Cahill, *Between the Sexes*, 143–152.

[10] Lisa Sowle Cahill, *Theological Bioethics: Participation, Justice, and Change* (Washington, DC: Georgetown University Press, 2005), 117–120.

[11] See, for example, Margaret A. Farley, *Just Love: A Framework for Christian Sexual Ethics* (New York: Continuum, 2006).

[12] Cahill, *Sex, Gender, and Christian Ethics*, 236.

[13] Lisa Sowle Cahill, *Family: A Christian Social Perspective* (Minneapolis: Fortress, 2000), 130–135.

Her 1994 book *Love Your Enemies: Discipleship, Pacifism, and Just War Theories* basically follows the same method of starting with the biblical and theological vision as she discusses how Christians down through the centuries have dealt with the issue of violence. The book does not develop in any detail her own moral evaluation of the issues. Cahill, however, insists here again on the broader methodological issue giving primacy to the biblical and theological vision. The book takes seriously Jesus's call to peace-making and the rejection of violence. The question for the Church and the individual Christian believer today continues to be how the mandate of Jesus to live in love, peace, and forgiveness is to function in our contemporary public life. Cahill again emphasizes the biblical notions of discipleship, the reign of God, and the Sermon on the Mount, while recognizing the eschatological reality that the fullness of God's kingdom will only come at the end of time. Just as the New Testament community itself borrowed some forms of moral knowledge and understanding from its own culture, so the Christian communities today must be in conversation with their cultures and their understandings. But the final criterion of appropriate Christian action today must be the experience of discipleship. The danger of the philosophical just war approach is the use of violence that begins as an exception too often becomes expanded and even normative.[14]

Lisa Cahill's emphasis on the theological aspect of moral theology goes further than the approach of any other Christian ethicist or moral theologian in this country. She has brought together the two separate disciplines of systematic or dogmatic theology and moral theology to deal with the realities of human inequality, poverty, violence, and ecological destruction in our contemporary world. Her characteristic "and" thus brings together what previously had been considered two very different types of theology. However, she points out that religious experience of God involves a moral way of life as its equally original counterpart. In fact, this is the thesis of her 2013 book, *Global Justice, Christology, and Christian Ethics.*[15] In this volume, she shows that the topics usually considered in dogmatic or systematic theology can contribute to dealing with our contemporary global moral problems—salvation, creation and evil, the kingdom of God, Christology, the Spirit, the cross, and hope. This is a most significant and original contribution to the discipline of moral theology or Christian ethics.

---

[14] Lisa Sowle Cahill, *Love Your Enemies: Discipleship, Pacifism, and Just War Theory* (Minneapolis, MN: Fortress, 1994), 236–246.

[15] Cahill, *Global Justice*, 1–4.

Philosophical Source

The last section discussed the theological source for Cahill's approach while this section discusses her philosophical basis. The philosophical deals with the fundamental question—what contributes to human flourishing? Here again Cahill appeals to her characteristic "and." Feminist ethics and Aristotelian-Thomistic realism form the basis for her philosophical approach to human flourishing.

Feminist Ethics

Cahill develops her understanding of feminism in a number of places but especially in her 1993 presidential address to the forty-eighth convention of the Catholic Theological Society of America.[16] In fact, this was the first presidential address of the society dealing with the issue of feminism. At the very beginning of this address, she succinctly summarizes her approach to feminism. Feminist theological ethics is thoroughly historical and cultural beginning with the experience of women. The emphasis on the historical and particular explains the many types of such ethics based on different historical situations and circumstances. In the United States, Black women have developed a womanist theology; Latina women, a *mujerista* theology. In addition, throughout the world, women are theologizing from their own particular historical and cultural circumstances.

Feminist ethics, however, issues a universal moral imperative: justice for women! While feminist ethics is particular in its origin, it is universal in its agenda. Out of the particular, feminists recognize what furthers or damages full humanity for women and men. Feminist ethics is not just description, dialogue, and understanding. Feminist ethics, like all ethics, is critical, judgmental, interventionist, and even in a certain sense coercive. It is a form of liberation ethics. We can and should judge certain practices, institutions, and acts as wrong. Feminists work for justice and equality for women and men in all aspects of their lives.

In this address, Cahill recognizes some positive contributions of postmodernist and anti-fundamentalist approaches in pointing out the many false universals which have been held down through the years. But postmodernism by definition cannot take the second step of building up what justice and equality call for in human relationships, communities, and social and political life.

Thomistic Realism

For Cahill, the meaning of Christian love must be further specified in terms of what dispositions, practices, relationships, and actions do

---

[16] Lisa Sowle Cahill, "Feminist Ethics and the Challenge of Cultures," *Proceedings of the Catholic Theological Society of America* 48 (1993): 65–83.

or do not serve human welfare. In other words, the practice of Christian love must be structured by justice. Justice and ethics identify the basic human goods which all require and the reinforcement of human equality. In addition, such a theory must also account for how practical moral decision making occurs, especially why there is both greater variety and some basic similarities in how goods are perceived and decisions made. Many Christians recognize a role of common morality, respect for persons, and human rights.[17] Cahill herself proposes a revised contemporary version of Thomistic natural law to develop further what justice requires today. The language of human nature expresses what constitutes human beings as distinctively human, what connects us to other human beings and how humans are related to the natural world, what justice calls for in these relationships, and how and why conversations about justice can be carried on across the many differences that exist in our contemporary world, such as in culture and religion. What appeals to Cahill in Thomistic natural law is its basic insistence on realism. All humans cringe at the horrors often seen and experienced in our world today—murder, pillage, rape, discrimination against immigrants, women, minorities, and the poor, as well as the poverty and hunger that affect so many people in our world. Here Cahill appeals not only to human reason but also to human emotions reacting against the violence and suffering imposed on others. These reactions reveal the existence and importance of our common human nature and the claims it makes. The evils and injustices in our world against the poor and the innocent are appalling and call all of us to hold the perpetrators to account for their atrocities.[18]

An important characteristic of Cahill's realism is the recognition of certain basic human goods that are common to all human beings, exist in quite different cultures, and constitute human flourishing. Some Thomists, such as John Finnis and Germain Grisez, have proposed seven goods that all societies in some way observe—life, knowledge, play, aesthetic experience, sociability or friendship, practical reasonableness, and transcendence. Many Thomistic authors agree that moral debate and some consensus are possible among different cultural goods because all people and all cultures have at their core a common human way of being in the world, including our bodily make-up; our abilities to reflect, choose, and love; and our dependence upon a community of all other human beings for survival and especially for meaning. Cahill opposes the contention that these basic goods are equally basic and incommensurable, meaning that one cannot prioritize any basic human good and cannot directly sacrifice any basic good.[19]

---

[17] Cahill, *Global Justice*, 248–249.

[18] Cahill, *Global Justice*, 251; *Sex, Gender, and Christian Ethics*, 52–53.

[19] Cahill, *Global Justice*, 259–260.

A second characteristic of her natural law approach is that morality is teleological. Aquinas recognized that the ultimate end of human beings is happiness. Every agent acts for a purpose or end. A primary way of expressing the teleological aspect is the claim that human flourishing is the end and purpose of morality. A third characteristic of her natural law approach is its inductive nature. Inductive consensus building identifies patterns of continuity within great change, incorporates new insights such as the need for human equality and participation, and recognizes that bias and invested interests must be overcome. Knowledge of human goods, needs, and all obligations approaches universality only if the inductive reasoning process is expansive, inclusive, and critical.[20] In summary, what is worth recovery in Thomistic natural law theory is a view of human existence and morality as purposeful; a conviction that basic moral goods are objective and shared among culturally different human beings; and a moral epistemology of inductive, experience based practical reasoning in which contingent contexts are highly influential in discerning priorities among goods and concrete choices about them.[21]

Cahill also sees an important role for virtue in her natural law method. Virtues modify the basic human inclinations to do the good. In Aquinas, the four cardinal virtues modify the inclinations of reason (prudence), will (justice), the irascible appetites (fortitude), and the concupiscible appetites (temperance). The two most important virtues for Cahill and for Aquinas are justice and prudence. Aquinas gives more space to justice than to any of the other virtues. Justice governs right relationships. General justice disposes the agent to act for the common good. Particular justice is a disposition to act for particular goods in the relationships among parts in a whole (commutative justice) and in the relations of a part to the whole (distributive justice). Prudence involves practical reasoning that deals with contingent matters and is very much in keeping with the inductive approach to our moral knowledge. Justice and prudence for Cahill thus support the recognition of great diversity in our world, but also assert basic goods that all human beings need and have a right to.[22]

Cahill's understanding of Aquinas differs greatly from the Neo-Scholastic approach that was commonly accepted in Catholic hierarchical teaching and in most of the pre-Vatican II understandings of Thomism. This Neo-Scholastic approach insisted on human values as unchanging and universal. Human nature was the same everywhere in this world. There was basically no recognition of historicity and historical consciousness. Neo-Scholasticism used a deductive methodol-

---

[20] Cahill, *Sex, Gender, and Christian Ethics*, 46–55.
[21] Cahill, *Global Justice*, 250–251; *Sex, Gender, and Christian Ethics*, 57.
[22] Cahill, *Global Justice*, 269–270.

ogy as illustrated in the syllogism. The syllogism was a form of deductive methodology with the conclusion derived from the major and the minor; and if the logic was correct, the conclusion was just as certain as the premises. In addition, Neo-Scholasticism too often identified the moral human reality with the biological aspect as based on Ulpian's understanding of the natural law as that which is common to human beings and all the animals. While not developing Ulpian's understanding, Cahill sees this Neo-Scholastic approach as failing to recognize that the person is more than the biological. Thus, she strongly criticizes the Neo-Scholasticism that had been generally accepted in Catholic theological circles up until recently.[23]

Cahill is also strongly critical of US culture with its emphasis on individualism and the absolutization of freedom and autonomy. She opposes injustices and inequalities that exist precisely because of the failure to recognize that every human being has an equal right to the basic needs of food, clothing, shelter, education, and healthcare. In the economic sphere, she insists on the preferential option for the poor. The kingdom values from her theological perspective are consonant with her understanding of true human flourishing developed in her Thomism and form the basis for her criticism of American culture today.[24]

On the basis of this long section, two important contributions of Cahill to reimagining Christian ethics stand out. The first is the primacy of the theological aspect, which brings together both dogmatic or systematic theology and moral theology. In the past, especially in light of the need to prepare ministers for the sacrament of penance, the emphasis in Catholic moral theology was on what actions were right and what were wrong. This same emphasis on the morality of particular acts and a casuistic approach also are found in contemporary bioethics with its emphasis on law and public policy. The theological vision proposed by Cahill is not primarily concerned with the margins of the Christian life or the minimal requirements but with the fullness of the Christian life with its emphasis on the call to discipleship.

Cahill's second contribution occurs on the philosophical level where she brings together feminism and Thomism. In the eyes of many, there is only opposition between these two approaches. But Cahill's Thomism is not that of the Neo-Scholastic approach that was *the* Catholic method from the end of the nineteenth century until the post-Vatican II era. She emphasizes the realism of Aquinas as well as the importance of the virtues. Again, her primary concern is not casuistry. Thomism and feminism are involved in promoting true human flourishing. This goal of human flourishing is an important aspect of her

---

[23] Cahill, *Sex, Gender, and Christian Ethics*, 49, 67; *Global Justice*, 250–265.
[24] E.g., Cahill, *Global Justice*.

methodology but is subordinate to the theological aspects of discipleship. She does not neglect casuistry, but it is truly secondary in her approach.

OTHER ILLUSTRATIONS OF CAHILL'S "AND"

This section considers three other illustrations of Cahill's "and"— Catholic and ecumenical, individual and social, knowing moral truth and doing it.

Catholic and Ecumenical

Ecumenism became a living reality in Catholic theology only with the Second Vatican Council. My own pre-Vatican II training in theology and especially moral theology gave little or no attention (except perhaps under the category "adversaries") to Protestant theology. As a result of Vatican II, in this country there began a strong and significant dialogue of Catholic moral theologians with their Protestant counterparts. One important illustration of this ecumenical approach from the Protestant perspective was James M. Gustafson's very significant 1978 book *Protestant and Roman Catholic Ethics: Prospects for Rapprochement.*[25]

Catholic moral theology has had explicit ecumenical dimensions since Vatican II. At the very beginning, only a few Roman Catholic theologians did their graduate studies at non-Catholic institutions. In the aforementioned book, Gustafson mentions the first five Catholics whose thesis he directed. The last of these is Lisa S. Cahill.[26] Gustafson directed the dissertations of more than twenty Catholic doctoral students, most of whom became quite productive scholars. Cahill, unlike Gustafson's earlier Catholic students, came to the University of Chicago Divinity School immediately after graduating from Santa Clara University with a double major in theology and English and no further work in theology. Her 1976 dissertation written under Gustafson's direction was "Euthanasia: A Protestant and a Catholic Perspective."[27]

Cahill's first book, *Between the Sexes: Foundations for an Ethics of Sexuality*, was published in 1985 by Fortress Press, which is associated with the Lutheran Church. The book originated from the E.T. Earl Lectures at the Pacific School of Religion in Berkeley, California, and is written from the Christian perspective, not the Catholic. The

---

[25] James M. Gustafson, *Protestant and Roman Catholic Ethics: Prospects for Rapprochement* (Chicago: University of Chicago Press, 1978).

[26] Gustafson, *Protestant and Roman Catholic Ethics*, xii.

[27] Lisa Sowle Cahill, "James M. Gustafson and Catholic Theological Ethics," *Journal of Moral Theology* 1 (2012): 92–115.

book includes two chapters recognizing the strengths and weaknesses of Thomas Aquinas and Martin Luther with regard to sexuality.[28]

Cahill's earlier books and articles were written from a broader Christian and ecumenical perspective and published often by Protestant publishers. To this day, she generally refers to the discipline as Christian ethics (not moral theology), the name usually used in Protestant circles. As time went on and she became a more prominent figure in Catholic circles, she wrote primarily from a Catholic perspective. Her 2005 monograph *Theological Bioethics: Participation, Justice, and Change* was her first book published by a Catholic publisher—Georgetown University Press. Even when writing from a primarily Catholic perspective, she often brings in the ecumenical dimensions. Thus, her third major contribution has been her emphasis on both the ecumenical and Catholic aspects of Christian ethics.

Individual and Social

Most varieties of ethics—both philosophical and religious—have tended to discuss both individual and social ethics. In this case, however, the "and" is disjunctive, referring to two different types of ethics. Cahill, however, has strongly emphasized the social aspect of what is often called individual ethics. This emphasis on the social aspect of all ethics constitutes a very significant contribution she has made to moral theology.

According to Cahill, the legacies of negativity and oppression connected with sexuality were very present in an earlier day in the Christian tradition. Christian sexual ethics today with its recognition of the sexual body as pleasurable, the interpersonal meaning of sex, and the priority of equality and freedom in defining sexual morality has been effective in overcoming these problems that existed in the past. However, this individualistic approach will not be adequate to the task of shaping a positive ethics of sex and gender for the future. This emphasis on the person-centered understanding of sex with a focus on sex as a pleasurable and intimate activity of couples neglects the social meanings of the body involving parenthood and kinship. [29] Historically, we are reminded again how economic and social conditions have affected sexuality in the past with regard to patriarchy. Christian ethics today needs an analysis of the social ramifications of sex, which is both critical and constructive. Cahill herself with her feminist ethics of liberation opposes the individualism of the Western liberal culture by giving attention to the social and political dimensions of supposedly private and personal sexual relations in marriage. Our United States culture has seen sex primarily as individualistic and even narcissistic and has

---

[28] Cahill, *Between the Sexes*, ix.
[29] Cahill, *Sex, Gender, and Christian Ethics*, 9–10.

disassociated sex from parental fulfillment and social responsibility.[30]
There is an important social dimension to sex that is too often over-
looked in our culture and in our ethics.

Lisa Cahill's primary interest coming out of graduate school was
bioethics. Married Catholic women theological ethicists were very
rare birds when she started teaching in the mid-1970s. Cahill was overwhelmed by invitations to speak, teach, and write about issues dealing
with sex, marriage, the family, and women's issues. The social dimension of the family that first concerned her as a feminist was patriarchy
as experienced here in the United States and even more prevalent in
the Third World. In the 1990s, she became involved with the Religion,
Culture, and Family Project directed by Don Browning at the University of Chicago Divinity School. This involvement gave rise to her
book as an attempt to understand the Christian family as critically informed by the Christian tradition and as responding to today's social
realities. Here she explains what might be called the internal life of the
Christian family and its relationships, but also the social relationship
of the family working to transform the broader society with its concerns of the common good and the preferential option for the poor.[31]
The next section also emphasizes the social dimension of her bioethics. The emphasis on the social aspect of what has often been thought
of as individual ethics (e.g., bioethics) constitutes Cahill's fourth important and distinctive contribution to the reimagining of moral theology or Christian ethics.

Moral Truth and Action

In her book, *Theological Bioethics*, Cahill makes the claim that
theological ethics should make justice in access to healthcare resources its first priority.[32] For most bioethicists, this is a strange and
even wrong and harmful claim. Their position has tended to reduce
theological bioethics to the private sphere. Much of the work of bioethics as it grew in this country involved service on boards and commissions dealing with public policy, law, and institutional procedures.
Participants in these public policy discussions approached the issues
and problems based solely on human reason, which is common to all.
Religious perspectives were considered highly particular since all people did not share this approach and knowledge. In fact, many early
theological bioethicists wrote for the general public and served on
these boards or commissions dealing with law and public policy and
gave up their theological perspectives because they could not be
shared with all people.

---

[30] Cahill, *Sex, Gender, and Christian Ethics*, 64.
[31] *Family: A Christian Social Perspective*, xi–xiv.
[32] Cahill, *Theological Bioethics*, 1.

Cahill insists that theological bioethics has an important and primary role to play in trying to overcome healthcare inequities. The predominant approach to bioethics today based on philosophical liberalism and market forces reduces all moral values to autonomy and informed consent and conceals the harm done to a more just healthcare system providing care for all in our country and especially throughout the globe.[33] Her approach, as in other areas, insists on the common good and justice for all with a special recognition of the preferential option for the poor.

Cahill's approach once again is based on the "and"—this time, thought and action, theory and practice, truth and action. Her book argues that theological bioethics must go beyond just talk and knowledge and even the vision of a more just distribution of healthcare in a more egalitarian and solidaristic fashion. Theological bioethics must participate in a global social network of mobilization for change. Edward Schillebeeckx, the Dutch Catholic theologian, calls theology "the self-consciousness of Christian praxis" and links theology to Christian practices by calling for a critical examination of the existing practices and working for newer, more just approaches. Cahill herself, then, insists on giving priority to distributive justice, the common good, and the preferential option for the poor in theory and in practice. Cahill calls such an approach participatory theological bioethics. The key contribution of participatory theological ethics is to instantiate, as well as advocate for, practices of healthcare justice and thereby nourish the hope that change is possible.[34]

The primary focus of participatory theological ethics in action is not the narrow political area but the broader social or civic area. Cahill appeals here to the Catholic theory of subsidiarity, which recognizes the myriad social institutions, structures, and practices that exist in the space between the individual person and the government. She gives special attention here to the role of community organizing as seen especially in the work of the Industrial Areas Foundation.[35] After establishing the need for such a participatory theological ethics in chapter 2, in the subsequent chapters she offers further examples of successful local and international religious-theological action for health equity and justice. These include Catholic healthcare ministry and its mission to the poor and underserved; the hospice movement; religiously sponsored pressures for healthcare reform, both nationally and internationally; religious networks supporting the availability of AIDS drugs and working for overcoming the AIDS pandemic, including care for AIDS orphans; adoption as an alternative to expensive, low-success reproductive technologies; and international networks resisting in the name

---

[33] Cahill, *Theological Bioethics*, 18.
[34] Cahill, *Theological Bioethics*, 1–12.
[35] Cahill, *Theological Bioethics*, 43–68.

of social justice the implementations of innovations in human and agricultural genetics.[36] Chapters 3–8 spell out the roles of participatory theological ethics in specific areas, such as decline and dying, national and international health access reform, reproductive and early life, and biotechnology, genes, and justice. Cahill thus has dramatically transformed theological bioethics and its role.

In this book and in her writings, Cahill is very cognizant of the realistic presence of human sin in the world. Total practical success has never been the measure or the expectation of Christian political action. The most Christians can do is to keep trying to bring about greater justice in the healthcare system. However, the contribution of Christian theological bioethics is to set these courageous transformative practices against the horizon of an ultimate, personal power that both judges and sustains human efforts. Collaborative, participatory social action can and must bring about somewhat more just and compassionate sharing of global health resources.[37]

CONCLUSION

This essay has not primarily considered the many topic areas Cahill has discussed in her writings. The focus was on her method with its characteristic emphasis on the "and." Based on this methodological approach, this paper has emphasized five significant and major contributions Cahill has made to reimagining the moral life and the discipline of Christian ethics—1) the primacy of the theological including both moral and dogmatic theology and the importance of the philosophical; 2) a role for the philosophical understanding of human flourishing based on her understanding of Thomism and feminism; 3) the ecumenical and Catholic dimension of her Christian ethics; 4) the social dimension of what has often been treated as merely individual ethics; 5) the importance of both the vision of moral truth and the need for actions to bring about that vision in reality. M

Charles E. Curran is the Elizabeth Scurlock University Professor of Human Values at Southern Methodist University. He has been president of three national societies—the Catholic Theological Society of America, the Society of Christian Ethics, and the American Theological Society. He has been given Lifetime Achievement Awards from the College Theology Society, the Society of Christian Ethics, and Southern Methodist University. His latest books are *60 Years of Moral Theology* (2020) and *The Catholic Theological Sociey of America: A Story of Seventy-Five Years* (2021), both published by Paulist Press.

---

[36] Cahill, *Theological Bioethics*, 69.
[37] Cahill, *Theological Bioethics*, 254.

Journal of Moral Theology, Vol. 11, No. 1 (2022): 37–54

Racial Habitus, Resurrection and Moral Imagination

Ebenezer Akesseh

RACISM AND RACIAL WORLDVIEWS cut across political, economic, and social structures.[1] Racism not only hinders national cohesion and integration, it also reinforces stereotypical tropes and turns people against one another. Those who perpetuate racism thwart the flourishing of their fellow human beings. As Clark et al. point out, "Racial segregation, like all other forms of cruelty and tyranny, debases those who are its victims, those who victimize, and in quite subtle ways those who are merely accessories."[2] The deleterious effects of racism invoke an earnest need to address the persistence of racism within American society and its cultural fabric. This paper discusses how the resurrection of Christ can contribute to mitigating the conscious and unconscious manifestations of structural harm and structural evil associated with racism. I argue that the concept of Christian moral imagination centered on the resurrection offers the Church a framework through which the Christian community and societies can engage racial habitus, which manifests itself, consciously and unconsciously, in the various structures, institutions, and practices that perpetuate racism.[3] In order to address racism, there is the need to explore the "cultural and religious symbols, operative in the imagination and fostered by society," that create false consciousness; thereby implicitly legitimizing and fortifying the walls of discrimination.[4]

The paper begins by positing Pierre Bourdieu's concept of habitus as the conceptual lens with which to explain the notion of *racial habitus*. Since the idea of habitus is premised on the structures and processes that condition behavior, the second part of the paper uses the influence of religion on behavior as the framework for discussing the

---

[1] Though racism transcends geographical boundaries, this paper focusses on racism in North America, especially as manifested between blacks and whites.

[2] Kenneth B. Clark, Gunnar Myrdal, and William Julius Wilson, *Dark Ghetto: Dilemmas of Social Power* (Middletown, CT: Wesleyan University Press, 1989), 67.

[3] My discussion about the Church refers primarily to the Catholic Church. However, it could apply to other churches in analogous ways.

[4] Gregory Baum, *Religion and Alienation: A Theological Reading of Sociology* (Maryknoll, NY: Orbis Books, 2001), 202.

moral and social implications of the resurrection. The third part explores how resurrection can serve as a fruitful nodal point for addressing racial habitus. It argues that the resurrection of Christ presents a counter-narrative that offers a thick ethic of moral imagination that should enable people to work towards racial justice. It proposes three ways through which the resurrection can address racial habitus. First, for the Church to be authentic in its attempts to address racial habitus, she needs to come to terms with her role in fomenting racism and address white privilege that is woven into the fabric of American society. Not only would these help the Church to gain the credibility that would support its attempts to address racism, they would also help Christians who, while condemning acts of racial brutality, are committed to maintaining relationships of white cultural, political, and social dominance to note the ambiguity at play. Second, the resurrection engages our will, decenters our former self and enables us to recenter ourselves in new habits. There is, therefore, the need to engage the will to dislodge racial habitus and in its place shape new habits based on a resurrection ethics which fosters justice and detests racial injustice. Third, since racial habitus operates at the unconscious level and manifests through actions and practices, the practices that can disrupt racism should also aim at the visceral level as well as the actions of people. The Church should use the Eucharist and its social implication to address racial habitus and racism.

HABITUS AND RACIAL HABITUS

According to Pierre Bourdieu, "The structures constitutive of a particular type of environment (e.g., the material conditions of existence characteristic of a class condition) produce *habitus*, systems of durable, transposable *dispositions*."[5] The structures are internalized through largely an unconscious process from birth but become like an "immanent law, *lex insita*," laid down in each agent by his earliest upbringing. In turn, upbringing is the precondition not only for the coordination of practices but also for practices of coordination since the corrections and adjustments the agents themselves consciously carry out presuppose their mastery of a common code.[6] Habitus also "constitutes the precondition of all objectification and apperception" and, therefore, constitutes the prism through which individuals confront their social reality.[7] Additionally, through habitus, collective history and the objective structures are able to reproduce themselves in

---

[5] Pierre Bourdieu, "Structures and the Habitus," in *Anthropology in Theory: Issues in Epistemology*, ed. Henrietta L. Moore and Todd Sanders (Malden, MA: Blackwell Publishing, 2014), 332.
[6] Bourdieu, "Structures and the Habitus," 336.
[7] Bourdieu, "Structures and the Habitus," 339.

individuals who are subjected to the same living conditions. As Bourdieu states,

> The habitus is the product of the work of inculturation and appropriation necessary in order for those products of collective history, the objective structures (e.g., of language, economy, etc.) to succeed in reproducing themselves more or less completely, in the form of durable dispositions, in the organisms (which one can, if one wishes, call individuals) lastingly subjected to the same conditionings, and hence placed in the same conditions of existence.[8]

The weight Bourdieu places on habitus and its importance indicates that it is necessary to pay attention to those aspects of one's culture which consciously condition certain habits and make us act in ways that reproduce the enduring structures of racism and structural injustice.

Sociologist Eduardo Bonilla-Silva applies the concept of habitus in exploring racism. He uses the term *white habitus*, which he explains as "a racialized, uninterrupted socialization process that conditions and creates white tastes, perceptions, feelings, and emotions, and their views on racial matters."[9] According to Bonilla-Silva, "one of the central consequences of white habitus is that it promotes a sense of group belonging (a white culture of solidarity) and negative views about non-whites."[10] In other words, white habitus is a "set of primary networks and associations with other whites that reinforces the racial order by fostering racial solidarity among whites and the negative affect toward racial 'other.'"[11] Bonilla-Silva underscores the social and political implications of white habitus by pointing out that "the universe of the whiteness navigated on an everyday basis by most whites fosters a high degree of homogeneity of racial views."[12] Alex Mikulich reinforces Bonilla-Silva's understanding of white habitus. He notes that "white habitus builds its own prison that is residential, cultural, relational and institutional."[13]

While I find Bonilla-Silva's notion of *white habitus* illuminating, I adopt the term *racial habitus*.[14] Racial habitus enables me to get at the

---

[8] Bourdieu, "Structures and the Habitus," 338.

[9] Eduardo Bonilla-Silva, *Racism without Racists: Color-Blind Racism and the Persistence of Racial Inequality in America* (Lanham, MD: Rowman & Littlefield, 2013), 152.

[10] Bonilla-Silva, *Racism without Racists*, 152.

[11] Bonilla-Silva, *Racism without Racists*, 16.

[12] Bonilla-Silva, *Racism without Racists*, 172.

[13] Alex Mikulich, "White Complicity in US Hyper-Incarceration," in *The Scandal of White Complicity in US Hyper-Incarceration: A Nonviolent Spirituality of White Resistance* (New York: Palgrave Macmillan, 2013), 77.

[14] Sociologists have applied the concept of racial habitus to the discourse of race relations. Jeffrey Sallaz uses the concept of racial habitus in understanding past and

structural and inter-personal dynamics of racism. Racism clearly sets out the parameters and points to what is at stake in conversations on racial injustice. Shawn Copeland notes, "Racism is both an ideology and a set of practices. It does not rely on the choices or actions of a few individuals; rather racism infiltrates, permeates, and deforms institutions."[15] Audrey Smedley and Brian D. Smedley also opine that "race provides the unspoken guidelines for daily interaction between persons" and "often sets the standard and rules for conduct, even though individuals may not always be conscious of this fact."[16] It is essential to pay attention to the insidious forms of racism and how to tackle them because, as Diana Hayes emphasizes, "Rather than the blatant overt racism of prior years, today we are confronted with a more sinister—because less visible—form of covert racism," namely institutional racism.[17]

Institutional racism has deleterious consequences on African Americans. Melvin Oliver and Thomas Shapiro point out that in stark material terms, white and black constitute two nations. Among the many examples they cite are the reluctance of some banks to lend to blacks, the fact that "discrimination follows blacks no matter where they want to live and no matter how much they earn."[18] They also state that "the age and resource patterns for whites and blacks bring several stark differences to light. Black wealth increases over the life cycle and then draws down after 65. While this trend approximates the overall pattern, black assets remain far behind whites in every age grouping."[19] Considering the different scale of effects wrought by Hurricane

---

present racial formation in South Africa (Jeffrey J. Sallaz, "Talking Race, Marketing Culture: The Racial Habitus In and Out of Apartheid," *Social Problems* 57, no. 2 (2010): 294–314). Samuel Perry has applied the concept to interracial evangelical organizations. He argues that "racial conflicts within these organizations are best framed as disputes over moral standards arising out of divergent, racially-constituted, moral dispositions, and second, that these conflicts are worked out via the institutionalization and instilment of white cultural norms, ultimately resulting in the hegemony of white moral standards within the organizations" (Samuel Perry, "Racial Habitus, Moral Conflict, and White Moral Hegemony Within Interracial Evangelical Organizations," *Qualitative Sociology* 35, no. 1 (2012): 89–108). My approach, however, differs from theirs not only because of its emphasis on theology but also because I situate my discussions in a context different from Sallaz's and within a conversation broader in scope than Perry's.

[15] Shawn Copeland, *Enfleshing Freedom: Body, Race, and Being* (Minneapolis: Fortress Press, 2010), 109.

[16] Audrey Smedley and Brian D. Smedley, *Race in North America: Origin and Evolution of a Worldview*, 4th ed (Boulder, CO: Westview Press, 2012), 20.

[17] Diana L. Hayes, "Introduction: We've Come This Far by Faith," in *Taking Down Our Harps: Black Catholics in the United States*, ed. Diana L. Hayes and Cyprian Davis, OSB (Maryknoll NY: Orbis Books, 1998), 5.

[18] Melvin Oliver and Thomas Shapiro, *Black Wealth / White Wealth: A New Perspective on Racial Inequality* (New York: Routledge, 2013), 91.

[19] Oliver and Shapiro, *Black Wealth / White Wealth*, 115.

Katrina on the people of New Orleans in 2005, Bryan Massingale notes:

> Katrina, then, was not just an act of nature. It also was a social phe-
> nomenon that exposed the harsh reality of race-based poverty that ex-
> ists in the United States. Katrina revealed, as no other recent event,
> the tragic confluence of racism and poverty present in our nation – a
> poverty and racism exacerbated by decades of social callousness and
> public neglect.[20]

Similarly, the COVID-19 pandemic has revealed what the Center for Disease Control (CDC) describes as the "long-standing systemic health and social inequities" which "have put many people from racial and ethnic minority groups at increased risk of getting sick and dying from COVID-19." This is because "social determinants of health have historically prevented them from having fair opportunities for economic, physical, and emotional health."[21] In every age category, Black people are dying from COVID at roughly the same rate as white people more than a decade older. In other words, death rates among Black people between 55 and 64 years of age are higher than for white people aged 65–74, and death rates are higher for Blacks aged 65–74 than for whites aged 75–84.[22] According to the South Carolina Institute of Medicine and Public Health, "Black people represent 12.4 percent of the population in the US but represent 23.8 percent of known COVID-19 deaths."[23] As a result of these disparities, Poteat, Millett, Nelson, and Beyrer refer to COVID-19 as "decidedly a racialized disease."[24] They argue that the effects of COVID-19 on Black communities are a manifestation of the anti-black racism entrenched within the American political system.

---

[20] Bryan Massingale, "The Scandal of Poverty: 'Cultured Indifference' and the Option for the Poor Post-Katrina," *Journal of Religion & Society*, Supplement Series 4 (2008): 56.

[21] Center for Disease Control, "Health Equity Considerations and Racial and Ethnic Minority Groups," www.cdc.gov/coronavirus/2019-ncov/community/health-equity/race-ethnicity.html.

[22] Tiffany Ford, Sarah Reber, and Richard V. Reeves, "Race Gaps in COVID-19 Deaths Are Even Bigger than They Appear," June 16, 2020, www.brookings.edu/blog/up-front/2020/06/16/race-gaps-in-covid-19-deaths-are-even-bigger-than-they-appear.

[23] "Data Brief: Newly Released DHEC Death Count Data Shows Disproportionate Impact of COVID-19 on Black Residents in All Regions of South Carolina," *South Carolina Institute of Medicine and Public Health*, July 2020, 1, www.imph.org/wp-content/uploads/2020/07/imph-dhec-brief-covid19-deaths-v.7.pdf.

[24] Tonia Poteat, Gregorio Millett, LaRon Nelson, Chris Beyrer, "Understanding COVID-19 Risks and Vulnerabilities among Black Communities in America: The Lethal Force of Syndemics," *Annals of Epidemiology* 47 (2020): 3, doi.10.1016/j.annepidem.2020.05.004.

RESURRECTION AND MORAL IMAGINATION

These deleterious effects of racism show the need to examine how
a resurrection ethic can address the conscious and unconscious processes which end up becoming "the precondition of all objectification
and apperception" and legitimize the sufferings and hardships endured
by blacks and other minorities. In order to examine how the resurrection can address racial habitus, the paper examines the moral and social significance of the resurrection of Jesus.

Oliver O'Donovan stipulates that the force of the resurrection on
the lives of its witnesses gives it a moral force.[25] In the resurrection of
Jesus, "the moral order was publicly and cosmically vindicated by
God."[26] According to O'Donovan, "Only Jesus has revealed God's final redemptive word about morality."[27] Consequently, "Jesus is not
only a witness to the restored moral order, however indispensable; he
is the one in whom the order has come to be."[28] O'Donovan notes that
the importance he places on the resurrection does not discount the significance of the events that preceded the resurrection, such as the incarnation or the suffering and the death of Jesus, or events that followed the resurrection, such as the ascension or the descent of the
Holy Spirit, because while the former events are grounded in the resurrection, the latter events are "bound-up in the resurrection in a knot
of mutual intelligibility."[29] When the gospel is preached without a resurrection, the cross and the ascension lose their force. The resurrection
also takes us back to the message of the incarnation and directs us
"forward to the end of history when that particular and representative
fate is universalized in the resurrection of mankind from the dead."[30]
The resurrection gives force to the Pentecost event in which "the renewal of the universe touches me at the point where I am a moral
agent, where I act and choose to experience myself as 'I.'"[31] O'Donovan's definitive statements about the resurrection set the tone for
thinking through how belief in Jesus's resurrection must affect our
moral imagination.

Sarah Bachelard points out that for most people an encounter with
the risen Lord resulted in a radical shift in their perception.[32] Examining the resurrection stories, Sarah Coakley affirms Bachelard's stance.
She notes that encountering the resurrection is connected to maturity

---

[25] Oliver O'Donovan, *Resurrection and Moral Order: An Outline for Evangelical
Ethics* (Grand Rapids, MI: Eerdmans, 1994), 15.

[26] O'Donovan, *Resurrection and Moral Order*, 148.

[27] O'Donovan, *Resurrection and Moral Order*, 148.

[28] O'Donovan, *Resurrection and Moral Order*, 150.

[29] O'Donovan, *Resurrection and Moral Order*, 15.

[30] O'Donovan, *Resurrection and Moral Order*, 15.

[31] O'Donovan, *Resurrection and Moral Order*, 15.

[32] Sarah Bachelard, *Resurrection and Moral Imagination* (Burlington, VT: Ashgate,
2014), 46.

of spiritual perception, which involves a process that begins with "an initial 'turning' round, a practice at seeing the world differently and deepening love and communion."[33] The transformation resulting from the resurrection encounter does away with the differences between objectivity and subjectivity. The objectivity of the resurrection "enhances the subjectivity of those who witness it and of those who will profit from such testimony. Conversely, the transformed subjectivity of those who have experienced the self-disclosure of the risen One, and who now know themselves caught up in his risen life, makes them key witnesses to the world-transcending objectivity of what has taken place."[34] A transformed subjectivity situated in the resurrection also involves "distinct but related dimensions of a radical process of de-centering of self and a coming-to-be centered in a new way in Jesus's own relationship with God."[35]

Exploring Rowan Williams's discussion of the resurrection stories of Peter, Mary Magdalene, and the disciples on the road to Emmaus, Bachelard points out that "their selves are now constituted essentially by their relationship to, their being loved by, the risen Jesus."[36] Two implications arise from this relationship, namely, one's relationship to the future and his/her relationship with people. The former implies the notion of missiology, where the disciples receive their identity in response to the call, and the latter implies that this new identity impels them to share their relationship with Christ with another. The missiological implication accentuates that "mission must therefore not only tell the story of Jesus with the purpose of saving souls, but it must also be directed to changing political and economic structures that deny equality and equal opportunities."[37]

Decentering one's self as a result of the resurrection involves embracing forgiveness, reconciliation and conversion as important facets of one's moral life. Forgiveness "involves a costly remembering of our past, its diminutions and its evasions."[38] Reconciliation demands we "repent false perceptions of the moral order and turn to truer ones. The fact that moral illumination does, in its fundamental form, involve conversion—having to unlearn as error what one thought one knew as truth—should alert us to the inadequacy of the accumulative model to express our experience of moral learning."[39] Reconciliation which

---

[33] Sarah Coakley, cited in Sarah Bachelard, *Resurrection and Moral Imagination*, 46–47.

[34] Anthony Kelly, *The Resurrection Effect: Transforming Christian Life and Thought* (Maryknoll, NY: Orbis Books, 2008), 125.

[35] Bachelard, *Resurrection and Moral Imagination*, 47.

[36] Bachelard, *Resurrection and Moral Imagination*, 49–50.

[37] Thorwald Lorenzen, *Resurrection and Discipleship: Interpretive Models, Biblical Reflections, Theological Consequences* (Maryknoll, NY: Orbis Books, 1995), 87.

[38] Bachelard, *Resurrection and Moral Imagination*, 48.

[39] O'Donovan, *Resurrection and Moral Order*, 93.

flows from the resurrection requires we confront our past, embrace the present and press on into the future with a transformed perspective that allows us to plot the trajectories of our lives from the resurrection. Bachelard emphasizes the relationship between reconciliation and resurrection:

> Reconciliation with God and neighbor are not moral norms imposed within the old horizon, as if to be good what I need to be is reconciling, loving and so on. Rather, they constitute a new horizon, a new habitation, a new imaginative framework. We are formed by this new framework such that all moral responsiveness flows through that transformed perspective. We do not see the resurrection, but we see from it. This has implications for normal moral judgment, moral epistemology, and the formation of the moral self.[40]

Since disciples constitute a community, they are able to live and learn how to live the moral and social implications of the resurrection through the support of the community for "Being-with-the-Other is the time and place for being-with-the-crucified-and-risen-One."[41] In other words, the community helps people to embrace the resurrection and its implications for their lives. The process involves "becoming immersed in a habitus – world, a cultural-historical setting, a community of shared beliefs and practices."[42] Brian Robinette argues that the Church as the body of Christ is the referential point of this habitus. Within the body of Christ, the statement "Jesus is risen" gains its meaning and gives birth to a worldview that influences our practices. Robinette adds,

> The affirmation that "Jesus is risen" entails much more than a proposition that might be placed alongside other propositions. Spoken with relative competency, it entails an interpretive framework that gives a distinctive shape to how we understand the world. It constitutes the primary *mythos* by which we live, the *grammar* by which we speak.[43]

The importance of the resurrection becoming the interpretive framework with which we look at the world underscores the difference the resurrection "makes to our imaginative sense of moral life as a whole: the difference it makes to the content and significance of moral concepts; the practice of moral thinking and judgment; [and] the formation the moral self."[44]

---

[40] Bachelard, *Resurrection and Moral Imagination*, 84.
[41] Brian DuWayne Robinette, *Grammars of Resurrection: A Christian Theology of Presence and Absence* (New York: Crossroad, 2009), 26.
[42] Robinette, *Grammars of Resurrection*, 26–27.
[43] Robinette, *Grammars of Resurrection*, 27.
[44] Sarah Bachelard, *Resurrection and Moral Imagination*, 59.

In *Evangelii Gaudium*, Pope Francis offers a reflection on the resurrection which I find applicable for discussions on racial habitus and racial injustice. Pope Francis notes that the resurrection of Jesus holds a vital power which restores life when all seems to be dead (no. 276). Per the logic of the resurrection, newness emerges from darkness and through the storms of history, goodness appears. In other words, human terror is unable to snuff out the seeds of life because as Pope Francis notes, "Christ's resurrection everywhere calls forth seeds of that new world; even if they are cut back, they grow again, for the resurrection is already secretly woven into the fabric of this history, for Jesus did not rise in vain" (no. 278). Christians are, therefore, called upon not to be on the sidelines of the march towards hope but rather to become agents of the newness and to reflect new values which bear fruit even in the midst of darkness. One of the ways by which the Church and her members are to demonstrate the power of the resurrection is by scattering the darkness of persistent injustice and indifference which characterize racism so that authentic and sincere relationships will spring up to replace the hatred and suspicion that sometimes typify racial relationships. The resurrection can achieve this breakthrough not only because the resurrection has permeated the world but also because the resurrection captures our moral imagination.

RESURRECTION AND RACIAL HABITUS

The moral imagination founded on the resurrection of Christ as espoused by O'Donovan, Blanchard, Coakley, Robinette, and Pope Francis discussed above can engage racial habitus at its core and penetrate structures of justice and structural evil since it offers a different narrative that challenges the imagination that grounds racial habitus. The resurrection ethics can, therefore, help communities "to overcome longstanding and deeply entrenched racial antipathies and injustices, poisonous legacies of suspicion, mistrust, fear, animosity, and even hatred that constantly threaten our attempts at intergroup living."[45] It can help us live "and heal the caustic residue of unspeakable harm and violence so as to make new beginning possible."[46] As noted above, the Christian community is the referential point for a habitus rooted in the resurrection. This section, therefore, proposes ways through which the Church can make the resurrection ethic the new *lex insita* that can dislodge the old *lex insita* of racial habitus.

---

[45] Bryan N. Massingale, *Racial Justice and the Catholic Church* (Maryknoll, NY: Orbis Books, 2010), 54.

[46] Massingale, *Racial Justice and the Catholic Church*, 53.

Resurrection, Racial Habitus and Reconciliation

According to Bachelard, "Resurrection ethics is sourced in the experienced reality of the reconciliation of all things in Christ, the reintegration and forgiveness of that which separates us from the source of life, from ourselves and each other and being so transformed into Christ-likeness."[47] She further notes that the Church is the sacramental sign of that reconciliation. Whereas this is true, when it comes to racism, the Church in America needs to embrace its complicity in fomenting racism in order to demonstrate a genuine commitment to fight racism. As Kenneth J. Zanca has amply illustrated, not only did the Church in America support slavery, it was also a slave owning institution and participated in selling slaves.[48] The Jesuits, for example, had slaves who worked on their plantations. Rev. Thomas Mulledy sold 272 men, women, and children in 1838.[49] Also, the Church did not support early attempts at abolition of the slave trade. Actually, "The antagonism between Catholic and Abolitionists won esteem for the Catholic Church in pro-slavery circles."[50]

Looking at its past involvement in the slave trade and the Church's role in perpetuating various forms of racism, one would expect more from the Church in addressing racism and racial habitus.[51] However, the Catholic Church has been critiqued for not doing much in providing a compelling counter-narrative capable of dislodging the racial habitus. Though the Church issued a pastoral letter on racism in 1979 titled *Brothers and Sisters to Us*, in which they strongly condemned racism describing it as a sin that "violates the fundamental human dignity of those called to be children of the same Father,"[52] a report commemorating the 25th anniversary of the pastoral letter on racism revealed what seems like an uncommitted resolve on the part of the

---

[47] Bachelard, "Resurrection and Moral Imagination," 172.

[48] Kenneth J. Zanca, ed., *American Catholics and Slavery, 1789–1866: An Anthology of Primary Documents* (Lanham, MD: University Press of America, 1994), 35–70.

[49] The Georgetown Slavery Archive, slaveryarchive.georgetown.edu/collections/show/1.

[50] Zanca, *American Catholics and Slavery*, 36. It worth nothing that the legalization of chattel slavery is traced to the Catholic Church. In 1452, Pope Nicholas V in *Dum Diversis* gave the kings of Spain and Portugal "full and free permission to invade, search out, capture and subjugate the Saracens, and Pagans and any other unbelievers and enemies of Christ wherever they may be and to reduce their persons into perpetual slavery." This mandate was extended to Africa and the Americas by Pope Alexander VI in 1493. See *Dum Diversis*, cited in Diana Hayes, "Black Catholics in the United States: A Subversive Memory," in *Many Faces, One Church: Cultural Diversity and the American Catholic Experience*, ed. Peter C. Phan and Diana Hayes (New York: Sheed & Ward, 2005), 52; Willie James Jennings, *The Christian Imagination: Theology and the Origins of Race* (New Haven, CT: Yale University Press, 2010), 16–37.

[51] Hayes, "Black Catholics in the United States: A Subversive Memory," 54.

[52] US Catholic Bishops, "Brothers and Sisters to Us," www.usccb.org/committees/african-american-affairs/brothers-and-sisters-us.

Church to combat racism. The report stated that the majority of diocesan bishops and archbishops (82 percent) had not issued statements either individually or jointly on racism, though their pastoral letter recommended it. Pastors also have been largely silent on racism in their sermons, as attested to by the majority of American Catholics who had not heard racism preached at Mass. Citing the National Election Studies (NES), the report stated there has been an increasing divergence of opinions between Blacks and Whites. Additionally, prejudice continues to influence Catholic attitudes towards policy. Affirming the findings of the research committee, Massingale notes, "Despite the bold words of *Brothers and Sisters to Us*, we must conclude that racial justice is not now—and never has been—a passionate matter for most American Catholics." He adds,

> It is difficult not to conclude that Catholic engagement with racism is a matter of low institutional commitment, priority, and importance. If "passion" connotes commitment, involvement, and fervor, the Catholic stance on racism, in contrast, can be characterized as tepid, lukewarm, and half-hearted. Standing against racism is not a core component of Catholic corporate identity.[53]

Massingale further notes that "If the Catholic Church is to be viable, meaningful, and relevant in twenty-first century US society, it must become a proactive force for racial justice."[54] Part of being relevant to the 21st century US society and making standing against racism part of the corporate identity of the Church requires the Church to own up to its past and ask for forgiveness for its role in fostering racism. As noted earlier, the resurrection story underscores the importance of forgiveness and reconciliation and conversion. An important aspect of forgiveness is "a costly remembering of our past, its diminutions and its evasions." Though the Church seems to be late to the dance, it bears mention that in their recent pastoral letter on racism, "Open Wide Your Hearts," the bishops offered an apology for the Church's involvement in racism and its lack of decisive actions in issues of racial justice:

> We, the Catholic bishops in the United States, acknowledge the many times when the Church has failed to live as Christ taught—to love our brothers and sisters. Acts of racism have been committed by leaders and members of the Catholic Church—by bishops, clergy, religious, and laity—and her institutions. We express deep sorrow and regret for them. We also acknowledge those instances when we have not done

---

[53] Massingale, *Racial Justice and the Catholic Church*, 49.
[54] Massingale, *Racial Justice and the Catholic Church*, 101.

enough or stood by silently when grave acts of injustice were committed. We ask for forgiveness from all who have been harmed by these
sins committed in the past or in the present.[55]

Whereas this marks a commendable effort on the part of the bishops,
it is worth pointing out that in asking for forgiveness, the bishops
should have added the structural harm done through the perseverance
of white privilege in the American society because the "Churches are
not separate from the social-historical context that exudes the ideology
of cherished white property."[56] Not only do they not mention the word
in that part of the document, the bishops do not mention white privilege in the 32-page document. The Church missed an opportunity to
address an issue which is woven into the American fabric. An inclusion of white privilege in the apology and a discussion of whiteness
would have opened up a way for whites to examine the taken-for-
granted aspects of racial habitus that are paramount in the American
society. There are countless Whites who "denounce blatant racial injustices, and yet preserve a situation of white social dominance and
privilege."[57] Sister Karen Donahue notes the missed opportunity in the
following statement: "It would have been more helpful and challenging if they [the bishops] had reflected on how racism favors people of
white and makes the white experience the norm."[58]

Engaging whiteness would require the Church to pay attention to
the hopes, sorrows, and despairs of Black Catholics. Listening to such
stories implies attending to what Maurizio Albahari describes as
"delving into the public states of knowing"[59] so as to interrogate the
"actually lived experiences of structural injustice, violence and inequality"[60] in order that "knowledge may produce questions and actions
otherwise muffled by perfunctory self-expression and by structures of
authority and apathy."[61]

Resurrection, Justice and Racial Habitus
    The resurrection influences radical shift in perspectives. It begins
with seeing the world differently and makes the objectivity of the res-

---

[55] USCCB, *Open Wide Your Hearts*, www.usccb.org/resources/open-wide-our-
hearts_0.pdf.
[56] Kelly Brown Douglas, *Stand Your Ground: Black Bodies and the Justice of God*
(Maryknoll, NY: Orbis Books, 2015), 200.
[57] Massingale, *Racial Justice and the Catholic Church*, 30.
[58] Sr. Karen Donahue, "Open Wide Our Hearts – What I Wish the Bishops Would
Have Said," *Sisters of Mercy*, January 21, 2019, www.sistersof-
mercy.org/blog/2019/01/21/open-wide-our-hearts-bishops-racism/.
[59] Maurizio Albahari, "Mediterranean Carnage: Heretical Scholarship and Public Citizenship in an Age of Eloquence," *Anthropological Quarterly* 89, no. 3 (2016): 867.
[60] Albahari, "Mediterranean Carnage," 880.
[61] Albahari, "Mediterranean Carnage," 882.

urrection the overriding perspective that guides a person's moral imagination. It also involves, as Blanchard notes, a radical process of decentering of self and a coming-to-be centered in a new way in Jesus Christ. The process of decentering the self involves taking into account how to dislodge what Bourdieu refers to as "mastery of a common code" produced as a result of history. These are internalized in our habits and have become the lens through which individuals confront their social reality. It also encompasses what O'Donovan describes as unlearning as error what one thought one knew as truth and forming new dispositions and habits.

In order to appreciate how the resurrection is able to dislodge previously held habitus and decenter the self, it is important to appreciate the role of habits and the will in shaping a new ethic of racial justice founded on the resurrection. Citing Aquinas, Jean Porter explains habits as "stable dispositions of innate human faculties, particularly those which are immediately oriented towards action (I-II 49.1,3)."[62] Porter adds that, "Habits are actualizations of the latent potencies natural to something as a creature of a specific kind."[63] Consequently, they are "oriented towards actions and defined by reference to the characteristic kinds of acts that they generate (I-II 54.2)."[64] Like the passions, the will also plays an important role in the formation of habits. The will is "the principle of the voluntary, in virtue of which men and women are responsible agents, held accountable for their acts, and subject to praise and blame, merit and guilt, reward and punishment (I 83.1)."[65] Porter notes that per their operations, "the inclinations of the will are oriented towards actions which bring the agent into relation with something, or someone outside himself (II-II 58.8)."[66] However, the will needs habits in order for it to be properly disposed towards its object.[67] Thus, addressing racism through the resurrection implies a decentering of the person's will through an engagement with Christ's resurrection to enable the will to develop habits that challenge racial bias and structures of racial injustice.

Addressing racism through the resurrection ethic requires paying attention to the demands of justice because "the resurrection of Christ

---

[62] Jean Porter, *The Perfection of Desire: Habit, Reason, and Virtue in Aquinas's Summa Theologiae* (Milwaukee: Marquette University Press, 2018), 15.

[63] Porter, *The Perfection of Desire*, 16.

[64] Porter, *The Perfection of Desire*, 16.

[65] Jean Porter, *Justice as a Virtue: A Thomistic Perspective* (Grand Rapids: Eerdmans, 2016), 73.

[66] Porter, *The Perfection of Desire*, 93.

[67] For a discussion of why the will needs habits and the importance of habits, see Jean Porter, "Why Are the Habits Necessary? An Inquiry into Aquinas's Moral Psychology," in *Oxford Studies in Medieval Philosophy*, vol. 1 (London: Oxford University Press, 2013), 113–36; Jean Porter, "Dispositions of the Will," *Philosophia* 41, no. 2 (2013): 289–300; Porter, *Justice as a Virtue*, 59–113.

is the theological ground for the worth-whileness of the believer's engagement for justice."[68] Lorenzen notes,

> By raising the crucified Christ from the dead, God reveals and enacts,
> as part of his healing and saving activity, his passion for justice. To
> confess that God raised Jesus from the dead implies therefore that
> God's activity cannot be frozen into the past, nor should the word
> "God" be used to validate the ever present status quo. With the resur-
> rection of the crucified Christ, God manifests himself as the One
> whose passion it is to change the world in the direction of justice. Faith
> in the risen Christ therefore makes the believer and the believing com-
> munity sensitive to the recognition of injustice, and at the same time
> it provides the resources for a concrete commitment to justice and its
> implementation. Faith in the resurrection of Christ carries within itself
> the promise and the conviction that history needs to be changed and
> that history can be changed in the direction of justice.[69]

We can, therefore, not separate the resurrection story from discussions
of racial justice. The resurrection perfects the will by disposing it to
act in such a way as to promote right relations with others as well as
form the right dispositions which become the operative framework of
people's moral imagination. For the will to respect the demands of
justice and eschew racism, it is important to form people in the resurrection narrative and highlight its relationship to racial justice. Such
formation must take into account how the virtue of justice is habituated since people's grasp of what it means to be just will always be
tailored to their circumstances, challenges, and opportunities.[70] In
other words, since "our perceptions of other people, like every other
kind of apprehension, are framed in terms of imaginative images, as it
were, paradigms of humanity,"[71] a person should be "trained in such
a way as to respond to all the varieties of humanity that he encounters
with the appropriate moral emotions, in such a way as to be open and
responsive to a rational perception of the due claims of the other" as
required by racial justice.[72]

Resurrection, Eucharist, and Racial Habitus

Christ's resurrection will achieve its purpose of transforming systemic and interpersonal racism if the Church can use "the irresistible
force" of the resurrection (*Evangelii Gaudium*, no. 276) to confront
the racial habitus of her members and members of the communities
through the celebration of the Eucharist because "in the Eucharistic

---

[68] Lorenzen, *Resurrection and Discipleship*, 284.
[69] Lorenzen, *Resurrection and Discipleship*, 279.
[70] Porter, *The Perfection of Desire*, 121.
[71] Porter, *The Perfection of Desire*, 131.
[72] Porter, *The Perfection of Desire*, 131.

celebration we are immersed in the narrative of the Christ's life, death, and resurrection"[73] and "become the body of Christ in the world."[74] Just as racism engages us at the unconscious level the practices that can disrupt racism should also target the visceral level if they are to be effective. Massingale notes that the words and the rites of the liturgy can be powerful ways of dislodging the racial habitus. The Eucharist must form in us alternative value systems other than those grounded in racism so that we can deal with the logic of race relations. According to Massingale, one of the characteristics of Jesus's earthly meals was a table fellowship with all including outcasts and sinners. In his words, "Jesus's meal ministry and his practice of table fellowship seems a deliberate strategy by which he symbolized and made real his vision of radical human equality before God. This stands in fierce opposition to and judgment upon any culture—secular or religious—that excludes or denigrates certain classes or races of human beings."[75] Thus, contrary to the prevailing practice where table fellowship reinforced social differentiation and hierarchical structures, the practices of Jesus established social equality. From this analysis, Massingale argues that our Eucharistic assembly is to reflect the subversive setting of Jesus and stretch our social imaginations in ways that cross racial lines so that everybody will be welcome to the Lord's table. [76] Our celebrations should awaken our awareness to the different manifestations of racism in our society because authentic worship cannot coexist with any form of injustice.[77] As a result, we cannot be complicit in racial injustice and claim to enjoy the fruits of unity celebrated on the altar. The Eucharist should fill us with the passion to take risks in furthering the course of racial justice.

Hayes also argues that the graces we receive from the celebration of the Eucharist must transform the illogical ideologies that set us against each other and heal us of racial differences that divide us, and that empty the Eucharist of its power.[78] Our participation in the Eucharist should help us develop a sacramental worldview which will enable us to reach out in solidarity to people across the racial divide by taking responsibility for the suffering of others. Our sharing in the Eucharist should also lead us to become sacramental signs of God in our communities. Hayes argues further that the Church as a body of Christ must also reflect the implications of the Eucharist by fighting dehumanizing trends in the society. Additionally, the Church should

---

[73] Andrea Bieler and Luise Schottroff, *The Eucharist: Bodies, Bread, and Resurrection* (Minneapolis: Fortress Press, 2007), 133.

[74] Bieler and Schottroff, *The Eucharist*, 131.

[75] Massingale, *Racial Justice and the Catholic Church*, 73.

[76] Massingale, *Racial Justice and the Catholic Church*, 72.

[77] Massingale, *Racial Justice and the Catholic Church*, 73.

[78] Diana Hayes, *Standing in the Shoes My Mother Made: A Womanist Theology* (Minneapolis: Fortress Press, 2010), 77.

think of how the celebration of the liturgy can help us model the love of Jesus and reflect the future glory of Christ through the services it offers to people who live in the alienated spaces of the inner cities.[79]

Like Massingale and Hayes, Copeland argues for the importance of the resurrection in addressing racial habitus and racism by using the Eucharist. Copeland points out the disturbing nature of the convergence of the Eucharist and racism. She posits that the ideology and structures that ground racism in its various forms as well as the actions and practices which perpetuate them stand in opposition to the order of the Eucharist. The "Eucharist relies upon resurrection faith and eschatological imagination."[80] Racism on other hand, "insinuates the reign of sin; it is intrinsic evil."[81] Not only is the Eucharist a countersign to the devaluation and violence directed toward the exploited, despised black body, Copeland also notes that the Greek verb 'eucharistein,' which refers to proper conduct, establishes the ethical implications of what we celebrate in the Eucharist.[82] The Eucharist "forms our social imagination, transvalues our values, and transforms the meaning of being human, of embodying Christ."[83]

Copeland uses the term Eucharistic solidarity to build a robust account of how to deal with racial habitus. As a virtue, Eucharistic solidarity is "a practice of cognitive and bodily commitment oriented to meet the social consequences of Eucharist."[84] Through participation and our sacramental reception of the Eucharist, we are required to make Christ visible by acts of solidarity. This is because we are formed and empowered to establish a new order that counters practices outside and within the Church which negate the symbol of what we become through our Eucharistic celebration. Copeland argues that Eucharistic solidarity can serve as the driving force to help Christian communities confront the challenge of racism because it confronts and disrupts the narrative of slavery and lynching and the unsavory practices carried out against blacks by white racist supremacists and people who share their values. Eucharistic solidarity enables us to "imagine, to hope for, and to create new possibilities."[85] This involves initiating practices which lead to structural and institutional justice.

Eucharistic solidarity makes demands on Christians. It challenges us to the implications and demands of discipleship. It goes beyond just being moved by suffering. According to Copeland, "Commitment to intentional and conscious Eucharistic living initiates a change of direction in the personal and social living of an individual as well as the

---

[79] Hayes, *Standing in the Shoes My Mother Made*, 166.
[80] Copeland, *Enfleshing Freedom*, 107.
[81] Copeland, *Enfleshing Freedom*, 109.
[82] Copeland, *Enfleshing Freedom*, 108.
[83] Copeland, *Enfleshing Freedom*, 127.
[84] Copeland, *Enfleshing Freedom*, 127.
[85] Copeland, *Enfleshing Freedom*, 128.

living of many."[86] It sets the dynamics of love against the dynamics of domination. Since discipleship is embodied praxis, Copeland argues that Eucharistic solidarity demands that we engage in practices that will confront racism even if those practices come at a cost of rejection or loss. As disciples who follow Jesus who himself was rejected by many, we cannot do otherwise if we take the call to discipleship seriously. Copeland's arguments affirm Pope Francis's call that Christians should be agents of newness.

CONCLUSION

In conclusion, "Racism is not merely one sin among many; it is a radical evil that divides the human family and denies the new creation of a redeemed world. To struggle against it demands an equally radical transformation, in our own minds and hearts as well as in the structure of our society."[87] From the recent manifestations of racism and racial tensions in the United States, if the Christian life is indeed a way forward, then it must reemerge as a compelling new invitation to life together so that people can transcend their barriers and think of a life together that unites rather than divides.[88] It is true that "isolation and fear paralyze the capacity to imagine the web of interdependent relationships,"[89] and that "harsh lines of enmity and narrow ideological lenses force people and political decisions into false either-or-frames of reference that belie the complexity of the challenges communities face."[90] However, "The resurrected Jesus described a future for the disciples that would solidify the reconfiguration of kinship and establish the ground for the reformation of the social life in Israel."[91] Consequently, the moral imagination that the resurrection offers emboldens us to face these challenges created by racial tensions and false ideologies.

Moral imagination grounded in the resurrection counters any guiding narrative which is antithetical to justice. The resurrection should help us overcome binary oppositions—black/white, us/them—and enable us to subvert and overturn categories which have been built into our habitus and which have become the operational lens that powerfully mediates our relationships.[92] Racial differences should not lead people to see the "other" as a category to be looked down upon or to discriminate against, but as people created in the image and likeness

---

[86] Copeland, *Enfleshing Freedom*, 127.
[87] US Catholic Bishops, "Brothers and Sisters to Us."
[88] Cited in Jennings, *The Christian Imagination*, 294.
[89] John Paul Lederach, *The Moral Imagination: The Art and Soul of Building Peace* (New York: Oxford University Press, 2010), 172.
[90] Lederach, *The Moral Imagination*, 172.
[91] Jennings, *The Christian Imagination*, 265.
[92] Eugenia Shankles, "The Profession of the Color Blind: Sociocultural Anthropology and Racism in the 21st Century," *American Anthropologist* 100, no. 3 (1998): 676.

of God, redeemed by Christ's death and given new life through the resurrection. Replacing racial habitus with a habitus grounded in a thick resurrection ethic can generate a newness that makes people work for justice because Christ's resurrection "contains a vital power" (*Evangelii Gaudium,* no. 276) that can penetrate racial tensions and heal divisions caused by racial differences. M

Ebenezer Akesseh holds a PhD from Notre Dame with Moral Theology as his area of specialization. He also has a Master of Philosophy (MPhil) degree in Sociology and a Master of Philosophy (MPhil) degree in Human Resource Management, both from the University of Ghana. His interests include issues about justice, African ethics, Catholic social teachings, political theology, virtue ethics, and the relationship between theological ethics and business.

Journal of Moral Theology, Vol. 11, No. 1 (2022): 55–84

$ymbol and Sacrament: Fossil Fuel Divestment and Reinvestment as a Real Symbol of Love

Erin Lothes Biviano

"Joined to the incarnate Son, present in the Eucharist, the whole cosmos gives thanks to God. Indeed the Eucharist is itself an act of cosmic love." – Laudato Si', no. 236.

EUCHARISTIC LOVE FLOWS FROM THE HEART OF the Church into the lives of all the faithful, transforming the matter of daily lives into signs of solidarity and communion. Even the most mundane of all realities—money—partakes of the transformative dynamism of faith when its investment is directed to purposes that serve the common good and is offered as a sacramental act of love of neighbor. In the Catholic tradition, love of neighbor requires both charitable works and social justice, which involves, "above all, the structural dimension of problems and their respective solutions" (*Compendium*, no. 201). Thus, the just commitment of funds through investments—the structural support of the fossil fuel economy—merits theological consideration.

Under sway of secularization, financial issues like investments seem remote from matters of faith and conscience. Yet fossil fuel investments support an energy system that negatively impacts the well-being of billions of persons and damages the vitality of the whole planet. Fossil fuel pollution and climate change desecrate the beauty of God's creation. This massive impact on human and ecosystemic life demands moral consideration.

One response to privatization and secularization is to emphasize universalizable ethical principles; another is centered on the self-identity of the Christian community.[1] Taking the latter approach, I assess the potential of a distinctly Christian and sacramental theology of fossil fuel divestment and reinvestment. Specifically, I argue that the recovery of the sacramental imagination as the proper Catholic lens for viewing the theological meaning of investing has the threefold effect of deepening our spiritual vision of investments in renewable energy

---

[1] David Hollenbach, "A Prophetic Church and the Catholic Sacramental Imagination," in *The Faith That Does Justice: Examining the Christian Sources for Social Change*, ed. John C. Haughey (New York: Paulist Press, 1977), 237.

as sacramental acts of love of neighbor, inspiring the prophetic action of the Church to raise moral awareness in society and driving practical investments that heal the environment.

After a brief outline of the impacts of fossil fuels to establish the urgency and relevance of this topic for theology, I present Catholic social teaching on the environment and note recent Church teachings on energy and fossil fuel use. Next, I consider the potential for revisioning a theology of divestment and reinvestment as a real symbol of love of neighbor within the Catholic sacramental imagination, which is the core of this essay. Fourth, I examine the need for moral witness to raise social awareness of the ethical importance of investments. I then propose that this witness for social justice in the case of fossil fuels is best served by reframing the binary opposition of shareholder engagement and divestment/reinvestment to a relationship of complementarity that engages all modes of advocacy. Finally, I conclude by asserting the practical need for renewable energy at a massive scale and reaffirming the sacramental significance of funding the life-giving energy received by the poor as a gift of covenantal solidarity and stewardship.

As James Gustafson and Gustavo Gutierrez argue, critique gains public relevance only when grounded in the common norms of the faith as well as "experiential engagement in conflicts and struggles of society."[2] This essay emerges from established norms of Catholic socially responsible investing and my experiential engagement with the environmental advocacy and divestment movements. It thus reflects the US Catholic context of my experience. This essay intends to foster a truly catholic "both/and," a bridge-building approach to critical social problems in a spirit of solidarity. Its method and scope are necessarily interdisciplinary, engaging climate policy, impact investment information, as well as Catholic social teaching and sacramental theology. The tone at times departs from traditional dispassionate academic analysis. Climate change is crucifying the earth, a negative contrast experience that demands that urgency intensify the rhetoric. The cry of the earth, the poor, and the future cannot be patronized with rationalism. "Young people demand change" (*Laudato Si'*, no. 13). Nor does this paper review the science of climate change or argue for its authority; this is assumed. Readers are referred to the Intergovernmental Panel on Climate Change[3] and *Laudato Si'* for more fundamental treatment of the science of climate change and its relevance to Catholic faith and every person living on this planet.

---

[2] Hollenbach, "A Prophetic Church," 244.
[3] Intergovernmental Panel on Climate Change, *Climate Change 2014: Synthesis Report; Contribution of Working Groups, I, II and III to the Fifth Assessment Report of the Intergovernmental Panel on Climate Change*, ed. R. K. Pachauri and L. A. Meyer

FOSSIL FUEL IMPACTS: THE CRY OF THE EARTH AND THE CRY OF THE POOR

Why is fossil fuel investment relevant to Catholic moral teaching? Pope St. John Paul II wrote in *Peace with God the Creator, Peace with All of Creation*, "The most profound and serious indication of the moral implications underlying the ecological problem is the lack of *respect for life* evident in many of the patterns of environmental pollution" (no. 7). Climate change must be recognized as a profound and comprehensive life issue, shortening and ending lives all across the globe. Fossil fuels degrade God's creation, drive human-caused climate change, and impact the most vulnerable, raising "the cry of the earth and the cry of the poor" (*Laudato Si'*, no. 49). Climate change is altering growing seasons, crop yields, storm patterns, and coastal dwelling places, leading to hunger and homelessness. The poor are less able to adapt to or recover from storms or drought. Consequently, climate change is creating surges of displaced peoples, estimated to reach 50 to 150 million by 2050.[4] Today, geopolitical strife increases drastically, as migrants crowd borders and internally displaced persons lose their livelihoods. Tomorrow, a hotter planet could have a drastically reduced carrying capacity, supporting only a few billion people, at best.[5] As Pope Benedict XVI emphasized, "If you want to cultivate peace, care for creation."[6]

These physical changes to the earth are clearly documented in the Fifth Assessment Report, the authoritative summary of thousands of scientists sponsored by the Intergovernmental Panel on Climate Change of the United Nations (IPCC). It is likely that global warming will surpass a 1.5°C increase beyond historical average. Transgressing this threshold increases the likelihood that dangerous reinforcement dynamics, whereby warming produces additional warming, will cause climate change to accelerate rapidly and become irreversible.[7] Thus, the urgency of our timeline to act requires bold action to reduce carbon pollution radically. The IPCC has stated boldly that "[g]lobal net anthropogenic CO2 emissions [must] decline by about 45% from 2010 levels by 2030…reaching net zero around 2050."[8]

(Geneva, Switzerland, 2014); Intergovernmental Panel on Climate Change, "Global Warming of 1.5°C," 2019, www.ipcc.ch/sr15/.

[4] John Podesta, "The Climate Crisis, Migration, and Refugees," *Brookings*, July 25, 2019, www.brookings.edu/research/the-climate-crisis-migration-and-refugees/.

[5] Richard Miller, "Deep Responsibility for the Deep Future," *Theological Studies* 77, no. 2 (2016): 439–40.

[6] Benedict XVI, "If You Want to Cultivate Peace, Protect Creation," www.vatican.va/content/benedict-xvi/en/messages/peace/documents/hf_ben-xvi_mes_20091208_xliii-world-day-peace.html.

[7] Intergovernmental Panel on Climate Change, "Global Warming of 1.5°C."

[8] Intergovernmental Panel on Climate Change, "Global Warming of 1.5°C."

The fossil fuels that drive climate change are taking an enormous toll on human health and well-being. Four billion people in developing nations lack energy access. The lack of reliable energy thwarts modern hospitals, safe lighting, effective education, and economic development. Air pollution also destroys tens of millions of tons of crops annually and costs seven million lives due to burning biomass in smoky indoor stoves.[9] The accumulated profits from petrocapitalism have cost dearly in human and ecological suffering. Pope St. John Paul II wrote that "Today, the dramatic threat of ecological breakdown is teaching us the extent to which greed and selfishness—both individual and collective—are contrary to the order of creation, an order which is characterized by mutual interdependence" (*Peace with God the Creator*, no. 8).

The beauty of creation is a revelation of God, desecrated by environmental destruction. In the loss of biodiversity and habitat, we are eliminating life itself and silencing hymns to the Creator (*Laudato Si'*, no. 11). Hearing the cry of the earth and the cry of the poor, the Church has responded with profound magisterial teachings.

CATHOLIC SOCIAL TEACHING AND ENVIRONMENTAL RESPONSIBILITY

"Today the ecological crisis has reached such proportions as to be *the responsibility of everyone*" (*Peace with God the Creator*, no 15; emphasis in original). Explicit Catholic teaching on care for creation has existed at least since the 1972 Vatican delegation to the Stockholm Conference.[10] Subsequent magisterial texts include Pope St. John Paul II's 1990 World Day of Peace Message, Pope Benedict XVI's *Caritas in Veritate*, the US Conference of Catholic Bishops' "Global Climate Change: A Plea for Dialogue, Prudence and the Common Good," and, most definitively, Pope Francis's *Laudato Si'*. These reflections are grounded in the premise of Catholic social thought that Christian faith embraces all of one's actions within the world's social, economic, and political spheres. As *Laudato Si'* emphasizes, "Everything is interconnected" (no. 70*)*.

---

[9] Veerabhadran Ramanathan, "The Two Worlds Approach for Mitigating Air Pollution and Climate Change," in *Pontifical Academies Workshop: Sustainable Humanity, Sustainable Nature, Our Responsibility* (Vatican City: Libreria Editrice Vaticana, 2014), 2.

[10] Marjorie Keenan, *From Stockholm to Johannesburg: An Historical Overview of the Concern of the Holy See for the Environment, 1972–2002* (Vatican City: Pontifical Council for Justice and Peace, 2002); Benedict XVI, *Caritas in Veritate*; United States Conference of Catholic Bishops, *Global Climate Change: A Plea for Dialogue, Prudence and the Common Good*, June 15, 2001, www.usccb.org/issues-and-action/human-life-and-dignity/environment/global-climate-change-a-plea-for-dialogue-prudence-and-the-common-good.cfm.

Increasingly, ecological systems are recognized as interlinked such that the loss of ecological vitality threatens human dignity. Pope Francis writes, "The destruction of the human environment is extremely serious, not only because God has entrusted the world to us men and women, but because human life is itself a gift which must be defended from various forms of debasement" (*Laudato Si'*, no. 5). Furthermore, manifold creatures and flora also give praise to God and remind humanity of their intrinsic worth as beloved by their Creator (*Laudato Si'*, no. 11, 12, 140). Additionally, whatever gifts the earth brings forth are meant for all: "God gave the earth to the whole human race for the sustenance of all its members, without excluding or favouring anyone. This is *the foundation of the universal destination of the earth's goods*" (*Compendium*, no. 171).

The universal destination of goods, the recognition that human dignity depends on a healthy environment, and religious reverence for Creation as God's primordial sacrament are themes of the doctrine of creation that express creaturely interdependence and solidarity. As John Paul II states, interdependence is a "system determining relationships in the contemporary world," and solidarity is the "correlative response as a moral and social attitude....[S]olidarity helps us see the 'other' as our 'neighbor,' a 'helper' (Gen 2:18–20)" (*Sollicitudo Rei Socialis*, no. 38).

Today responsibilities to the neighbor are mediated by energy decisions that have real impacts through shared global economic, social, political, ecological, and climatic systems. Recent Catholic teaching asserts the positive obligation to dismantle structures of the fossil fuel economy and invest in sustainable energy. This obligation reflects the fundamental Catholic obligation of charity and justice, now understood as the need for ecological charitable works and ecological social justice.[11]

According to *Laudato Si'*, "Technology based on the use of highly polluting fossil fuels—especially coal, but also oil and, to a lesser degree, gas—needs to be progressively replaced without delay" (no. 165). Replacing fossil fuels correlates with increasing renewable energies. *Energy, Justice and Peace* states that advanced nations are obliged to develop new sustainable energy technologies.[12] Advanced

---

[11] See Kenneth R. Himes and Daniel R. DiLeo, "*Laudato Si'* in the United States: Reflections on Love, Charitable Works, and Social Justice," *Journal of Moral Theology* 9, special issue 1 (2020): 96–98.

[12] Pontifical Council for Justice and Peace, *Energy, Justice and Peace: A Reflection on Energy in the Current Context of Development and Environmental Protection* (Vatican City: Libreria Editrice Vaticana, 2014), 88. See a summary of this text by Erin Lothes Biviano, "A New Paradigm for Catholic Energy Ethics," *Catholic Moral Theology*, January 28, 2015, catholicmoraltheology.com/a-new-paradigm-for-catholic-energy-ethics/.

countries have "the moral duty of developing the use of the most complex and capital-intensive energy technologies, in order to allow poor countries to feed their development, resorting to simpler and less expensive energy technologies."[13] Developing new energy technologies promotes the universal destination of goods through ensuring clean energy access for all and allows the covenant of solidarity and stewardship to flourish. This development occurs only through investment.

Strong Vatican support for divestment is conveyed in several recent documents. First, the Final Document of the Special Assembly of the Synod of Bishops for the Pan-Amazon Region states: "[W]e embrace and support campaigns of divestment from extractive companies responsible for the socio-ecological damage of the Amazon, starting with our own Church institutions and also in alliance with other churches."[14] The document for implementation of *Laudato Si'*, *Journeying towards Care for Our Common Home: Five Years after* Laudato Si', recommends "practical proposals such as fasting, pilgrimages, seminars, disinvestment or reinvestment campaigns, the financing of joint projects, etc."[15] Additionally, Fr. Joshtrom Kureethadam, head of the ecology and creation sector in the Vatican Dicastery for Promoting Integral Human Development, has called divestment "a moral imperative."[16]

A THEOLOGY OF DIVESTMENT AND REINVESTMENT WITHIN THE CATHOLIC SACRAMENTAL IMAGINATION

The recovery of the sacramental imagination as the proper Catholic lens for viewing the theological meaning of investing has the threefold effect of deepening our spiritual vision of investments in renewable energy as sacramental acts of love of neighbor, inspiring the prophetic action of the Church to raise moral awareness in society, and driving practical investments that heal the environment. I begin with the first and most profound reason for revisioning energy investments.

The Spirituality of Investments within a Sacramental Imagination
The material exchanges that yield profit can and must also be vehicles serving the dignity of the person and the poor. As *Oeconomicae*

---

[13] Pontifical Council for Justice and Peace, *Energy, Justice and Peace*, 111.
[14] "Final Document of the Special Assembly of the Synod of Bishops for the Pan-Amazon Region," *Vatican News*, October 26, 2019, www.vaticannews.va/en/vatican-city/news/2020-02/final-document-synod-amazon.html, no. 70.
[15] Catholic Climate Covenant, *Journeying toward Care for Our Common Home: Five Years after* Laudato Si', catholicclimatecovenant.org/resource/journeying-towards-care-our-common-home, 97, 177-179.
[16] Brian Roewe, "Vatican Official: Church Divestment from Fossil Fuels Is 'Moral Imperative,'" *National Catholic Reporter*, May 20, 2021, www.ncronline.org/news/earthbeat/vatican-official-church-divestment-fossil-fuels-moral-imperative.

et Pecuniariae Quaestiones teaches, all are intended to share in a global economy as allies building the common good:

> [I]n the transmission of goods among persons there is always something more than mere material goods at play, given the fact that the material goods are often vehicles of immaterial goods whose concrete presence or absence decisively determines the quality of these very economic relationships (for example, trust, equity, and cooperation) (no.9).

In the case of energy investments, the material goods that are "vehicles of immaterial goods" are investments in clean energy made out of spiritual solidarity and concern for the well-being of the neighbor. In order to perceive the gift of solidarity in the ordinariness of portfolios and pensions, a new way of seeing, of engaging the imagination, is needed.

Many theologians highlight the power of the imagination to subvert unjust social orders, creatively engaging utopian vision to open spaces of new possibility. Theologian Matthew Eggemeier points to the focus on the creative imagination by Elisabeth Schüssler Fiorenza and Gustavo Gutierrez, on the poetic imagination by Rebecca Chopp and Kathryn Tanner, and on the utopian imagination by Paul Ricoeur. By generating creative visions, the imagination challenges present reality and seeks its actualization in praxis.[17]

Anthony J. Godzieba explores how the Catholic sacramental imagination opens up a view of the possible, a countercultural reality with new potential for greater solidarity and communion. Specifically, Godzieba usefully points to the ethical, critical, and participatory nature of the sacramental imagination. While the specific ecclesial sacraments indeed shape the imagination of the Christian, and are privileged moments of grace, the sacramental imagination here refers to a broader perception of God's presence throughout created reality. The sacramental imagination expresses God's way of being that is both transcendent to and immanent within all creation. The sacramental imagination's "eyes of faith" see grace in all things and also critically examine distorted views of reality, thus releasing the interruptive power of the Christian ethic that calls for discipleship.[18]

---

[17] Matthew Eggemeier, *A Sacramental-Prophetic Vision: Christian Spirituality in a Suffering World* (Collegeville, MN: Liturgical Press, 2014), 6.

[18] Anthony J. Godzieba, "The Catholic Sacramental Imagination and the Access/Excess of Grace," *New Theology Review* 21, no. 3 (2008): 14–26. Godzieba here proposes an interpretation that contrasts with other significant schemas of the sacramental imagination, chiefly David Tracy's schema of the "analogical," or Catholic, imagination and the "prophetic" imagination, which Tracy identifies with Protestantism and the interruptive dynamic of the prophets. Godzieba's view of the sacramental imagination embodies both the analogical and prophetic/interruptive functions of grace.

Godzieba characterizes Christianity as animated by the revelation of God in Jesus Christ, which is the good news that "life *can* be otherwise than an unending cycle of desires and the commodified images that fulfill them."[19] Even discipleship in the market, the daily materiality of portfolios and pocketbooks, can challenge a commodified culture. Within the sacramental imagination, all reality manifests God; every action can be a means of grace. In Jesus Christ, this revelation is disruptive, transcendent, and aflame with resurrection potential.

Godzieba defines the sacramental imagination as a "way of envisioning reality through the eyes of faith that recognizes that the finite can indeed mediate the infinite, that all aspects of created being can mediate grace."[20] Even mundane fiscal choices can mediate a graced response to God. As the Protestant theologian Langdon Gilkey writes, the power of a sacramental religious vision is the "divinely granted capacity to allow finite and relative instruments to be media of the divine, and endow all of secular and ordinary life with the possibility and the sanctity of divine creativity."[21] In today's complex global economy, finite financial instruments play an essential role in the creativity that establishes a sustainable and just economy. As Pope Francis implies, economies should have meaning (*Laudato Si'*, no. 194)! Theology's task is to articulate and reveal the sacramentality of finite reality, then challenge the disciple to respond in a graced way—even in the management of their savings.[22] Persons "must also have the same considerations towards the management of their savings, for instance, directing them towards those enterprises that operate with clear criteria inspired by an ethics respectful of the entire human person, and of every particular person" (*Oeconomicae et Pecuniariae Quaestiones*, no. 33).

As noted, Godzieba's analysis highlights the ethical, critical and participatory nature of the sacramental imagination. Godzieba draws from philosopher Richard Kearney's phenomenological analysis of the imagination to unveil the imagination's ethical function as a vision that penetrates "commodified imagery and 'pseudo-events' where 'reality appears to be a mere shadow.'" Such vision cuts through distorted appearances where "image and reality have dissolved into a play of mutual parody."[23] Kearney's language of commodification echoes that of Matthew Eggemeier, who likewise speaks of a sacramental vision that resists reducing creation to a commodity to be exploited. "[A] retrieval of the sacramental spirituality of finding God in all things—

---

[19] Godzieba, "The Catholic Sacramental Imagination," 21.

[20] Godzieba, "The Catholic Sacramental Imagination," 16.

[21] Langdon Gilkey, *Catholicism Confronts Modernity: A Protestant View* (New York: Seabury Press, 1975), 196–197.

[22] Godzieba, "The Catholic Sacramental Imagination," 17.

[23] Richard Kearney, "Ethics and the Postmodern Imagination," *Thought* 62 (1987): 43, in Godzieba, "The Catholic Sacramental Imagination," 18.

specifically in the beauty of creation—serves as an alternative to the market reduction of the world to a commodity for industrial use."[24]

Kearney's evocation of parody aptly describes the distorted rhetoric of fossil fuel corporations claiming to uphold the functioning of the world and serve the poor while systematically undoing nature's established patterns and destroying the livelihoods and health of the poor. For example, oil companies in Nigeria have extracted billions of dollars of profit while offering no local access to the gas that is outright wasted through flaring.[25] Local communities are starved for energy while wading in the oil that flows from weekly spills over their farmlands and fishing grounds.[26] To support this farce through oil investments is a mockery of justice. For Kearney, imagination both unmasks this parody and reveals the call of the other suffering energy poverty and environmental destruction and the cry of the earth that demands an ethical response. Furthermore, imagination brings hope: "Renouncing the pervasive sense of social paralysis, the poetic imagination would attempt to restore man's faith in history and to nourish the belief that things can be changed."[27]

Thus, the Catholic sacramental imagination's second, critical dimension penetrates false projections of reality and creates a new awareness of reality that highlights its ethical obligations. Godzieba tellingly employs a phrase used by climate scientists to describe the untenable situation of continuing with emissions at the current rate: "business-as-usual." He writes, "The poetic imagination is thus critical in its own right: it judges the status quo, the 'business-as-usual' situation of the present as inadequate." Imagination breaks free of the "technological and ethical quagmire of the postmodern context," the oil-soaked Anthropocene, to envision reality anew, awakened by the cry of the earth and the poor.[28]

Third, the performative, embodied aspect of the sacramental imagination signals the imperative to participate in the new ethical reality. According to Godzieba, the sacrament "is not a thing to be defined or a text to be decoded, but rather a performance to be experienced, a praxis demanding our participation."[29] Hence, a sacramental theology

---

[24] Eggemeier, *A Sacramental-Prophetic Vision*, 10.

[25] Edward Osang Obi, "Creational Solidarity Strengthens the Weakest Link: Energy Ethics and Climate Change in Sub-Saharan Africa," in *Light for a New Day: Interfaith Essays on Energy Ethics*, ed. Erin Lothes (Highland Park, NJ: GreenFaith, 2016), 19.

[26] Dionne Searcy, "Nigeria Finds a National Crisis in Every Direction It Turns," *New York Times*, July 17, 2016, www.nytimes.com/2016/07/18/world/africa/nigeria-niger-delta-buhari-oil-militants.html.

[27] Kearney, "Ethics," 44, cited in Godzieba, "The Catholic Sacramental Imagination," 19.

[28] Kearney, "Ethics," 44, cited in Godzieba, "The Catholic Sacramental Imagination," 19.

[29] Godzieba, "The Catholic Sacramental Imagination," 17.

of investment is not only critical insofar as it judges the status quo, but performative and participatory. A critical new way of seeing enlarges the disciple's sense of ethical obligations and calls for praxis. "Thinking otherwise is the catalyst for acting otherwise."[30] Heeding the ethical obligation revealed by the sacramental imagination means participating in acts of solidarity, including investments that express solidarity through healing the earth and building healthy energy access for the poor.

A "Real Symbol"

Bernard Prusak turns to Jesuit theologian Karl Rahner to deepen the meaning of symbolic reality behind the actions of daily life. Prusak writes, "In contemporary reflection on the sacraments there is a renewed understanding of what Rahner calls 'the natural depth of the symbolic reality of all things.'"[31] Rahner's classic articulation of a Catholic theology of symbol points to the symbol's power as reality, not mere sign or image: "A symbol is not something separate from the symbolized.... On the contrary, the symbol is the reality... which reveals and proclaims the thing symbolized, ... being its concrete form of existence."[32] A symbol is the fullest expression of the thing, its self-realization.

That a symbol must necessarily express itself to "attain [its] own nature" is almost self-evident in the case of love and solidarity.[33] The very ontological reality of the thing (in this case, love of neighbor) must be expressed to come to existence: "The being is known in this symbol, without which it cannot be known at all."[34] Love, like faith, without works is dead.

The Christological and anthropological depth of a theology of the symbol is far outside the scope of this paper.[35] Yet it can be noted that humanity is fulfilled in love of neighbor, a love that is united to love of God. As James Keenan observes, "[T]he love of God makes possible the love of self. And these together make possible the love of neighbor."[36] The fullest expression of the symbol of the human person is the person together with her "intertwined relationships: with God, with our neighbour, and with the earth itself" (*Laudato Si'*, no. 66). In Rahner's summation: "[T]he whole incalculable mystery of man is contained and exercised in this act of love of neighbour"—in the act

---

[30] Godzieba, "The Catholic Sacramental Imagination," 20.

[31] Karl Rahner, "The Theology of the Symbol," in *Theological Investigations*, vol. 4, trans. Kevin Smyth (New York: Crossroad, 1966), 239.

[32] Rahner, "The Theology of the Symbol," 251.

[33] Rahner, "The Theology of the Symbol," 224.

[34] Rahner, "The Theology of the Symbol," 231.

[35] Rahner, "The Theology of the Symbol," 243.

[36] James Keenan, *Moral Wisdom: Lessons and Texts from the Catholic Tradition*, 2nd ed. (Lanham, MD: Rowman & Littlefield, 2010), 21.

of love of the other, one's love for the Thou is united and brought to achievement.[37]

Thus, love is expressed and constituted by action; it is really actualized by commitments such as refusals to fund polluting energy and decisions to fund clean energy. These are not empty symbols; they are real actions grounded in the financial economy *and also* moral expressions of love of neighbor and God's creation. Hence the "symbol" of divestment constitutes a real symbol of the love of neighbor.

The "symbol" of divestment and reinvestment is the reality that reveals a concrete commitment to a new economic and environmental future for the beloved earth and the beloved neighbor. The investment of funds in renewable energy heals the earth by reducing pollution and is a real gift of the blessings of health, education, and work powered by clean energy. One can no longer dismiss divestment and reinvestment as symbolic actions as if "symbolic" connotes "for show" or "pointless." Reclaiming the profound theological meaning of a symbolic action reveals the love motivating actions like divestment, and the concrete outcome of divestment is clean air and water, gifts as essential for life as bread to eat and water and wine to drink.

Accordingly, Prusak goes on to underscore the sacramental depth of Jesus's "ordinary," purportedly symbolic actions that in fact actualize justice. "Jesus understood the power of symbolic action, such as breaking and sharing bread and drinking wine together at a meal .... His symbolic gesture powerfully actualized the reign of a merciful and loving God searching for, welcoming, and celebrating with those who were lost."[38] While Prusak speaks of the symbolic gesture of sharing bread, the specific action of the Eucharistic sacrament, he also conveys that discipleship includes the transformation of the disciple's imagination. Like Godzieba, Prusak emphasizes the participatory nature of the sacrament. The conversion Jesus had as his goal is not the eucharistic conversion but the conversion of the disciples into the Body of Christ. "The eucharistic bread exists to be broken and shared."[39] Likewise, the gifts of the earth should advance the common good of all and honor God's creation. The sacramental imagination, when inspiring the disciple by its critical and ethical vision, invites one to leave the altar and participate in the world in a spiritual sense of "symbolic" sharing in solidarity.

Eggemeier shows how the sacramental imagination, so sensitive to beauty, is complemented by a prophetic imagination which perceives

---

[37] Karl Rahner, "Reflections on the Unity of the Love of Neighbor and the Love of God," in *Theological Investigations*, vol. 6, trans. Karl-H. and Boniface Kruger, (New York: Crossroad, 1966), 242.

[38] Bernard P. Prusak, "Explaining Eucharistic 'Real Presence': Moving beyond a Medieval Conundrum," *Theological Studies* 75, no. 2 (2014): 254–255.

[39] Prusak, "Explaining Eucharistic 'Real Presence,'" 256.

and protests against suffering. Together both the sacramental and prophetic imaginations develop the critical vision needed to denounce injustice and conceive of a new world. "Thus, while these two forms of imagination diverge in the ways they name reality, from a Christian perspective the sacramental and prophetic imaginations are held together because both are grounded in a commitment to seeing the real."[40] The prophetic imagination sees the idolization of commodified nature and the desacralization of God's creation and denounces this reality; the sacramental imagination looks to the already-incoming new reality of clean energy and sustainable lifeways and celebrates their life-giving grace.

Divestment and reinvestment are thus visible signs of invisible realities: the visible reality of conferring funds to build a healthy and sustainable economy motivated by the invisible commitment to life on our common home. Conversely, business-as-usual investments manifest the invisible reality of the power relationships that pervade energy inequality, which are plainly visible in energy poverty, pollution, disproportionate climate impacts, and ecological debt. The sacramental and prophetic imaginations see these realities clearly.

In their divestment announcement in August 2018, the Irish Catholic Bishops' Conference rejected the rhetoric that dismisses symbolism:

> Our announcement, whilst modest in terms of financial resources, *is more than just symbolic*. It is about joining the growing social movement, led by young people across the world, calling for the realignment of our financial policies to safeguard their future. It makes good sense and it is the least we can offer our future generations.[41]

The language of "offering" coheres with the ancient grammar of sacramentality, in which a gift of resources makes manifest a deeper love. Divestment is an offering of solidarity with the young people of this world in intergenerational justice, a witness to love of neighbor, and a gift that is "more than just symbolic."

Interpreting this solidaristic love together with Rahner's theology of the symbol, divestment as a "symbol" *is* the visible reality of love for our common home and all its families of life. To view divestment as a real symbol of solidarity and love mediated through a concrete offering of the means of life and health (funds for clean energy) places divestment within the fundamental material grounding of Catholic

---

[40] Eggemeier, *A Sacramental-Prophetic Vision*, 13.
[41] Irish Catholic Bishops Conference, "Statement by Bishop William Crean Announcing the Decision of the Bishops' Conference to Divest from Fossil Fuels," August 24, 2018, www.catholicbishops.ie/2018/08/24/statement-by-bishop-william-crean-announcing-the-decision-of-the-bishops-conference-to-divest-from-fossil-fuels/; emphasis added.

faith, vision, and ethics: the sacramental imagination. Participating in the sacrament of offering one's investments to build up a sustainable economy is a "symbolic" action and a real gift, one that enables all to partake in the covenantal sharing of neighbor love and earthly resources.

A Covenantal Economy of Solidarity and Stewardship

The moral agent's participation in the sacramental economy through personal financial choices is set within the economy of love and creativity as detailed in the doctrine of creation. All creation is part of a sacred communion called to solidarity and praise. As Pope Francis writes,

> The creation accounts in the book of Genesis contain, in their own symbolic and narrative language, profound teachings about human existence and its historical reality. They suggest that human life is grounded in three fundamental and closely intertwined relationships: with God, with our neighbour and with the earth itself. (*Laudato Si'*, no. 66)

This cosmic sacramental economy of intertwined relationships is described by Nigerian theologian and divestment advocate Fr. Edward Obi, OP, as a threefold dynamic uniting creation and the Creator, who has created and redeemed the creation for wholeness.

> This wholeness, which can be actioned by a notion of "fellow-being," is an essential sacramental signification of God's original plan for creation, namely, the salvation of *all* through the universal access of *all* to God's goodness.... It can be realistically structured in a triangular, dialogical relationship of covenant: God with creation—in divine provision; creatures among themselves—in solidarity; and creation unto God—in thanksgiving. This dialogical relationship is Sacramental in essence.[42]

The sacramental economy originates in the creation of the cosmos by God, gifting the earth with goods for our provision and salvation. This economy continues in communion among fellow creatures who share a covenant of solidarity, of mutual help, and of responsibility. The cycle returns to God via the response of stewardship and creaturely praise. In this covenant, we again see the unity of love of God and neighbor: "According to St John, we are loved by God (Jn 15:12) and

---

[42] Edward O. Obi, "Economic Justice as a Gauge of Sacramental 'Fellow-Being,'" in *Celebrating the Sacramental World: Essays in Honour of Emeritus Professor Lambert J. Leijssen*, ed. Kekong Bisong and Mathai Kadavil (Leuven: Peeters, 2010), 187.

by Christ so that we may love one another (Jn 13:34)."[43] Thus, a sacramental view of investing places finance within the biblical moral vision of creation and perceives the pragmatic exchange of needed investments within the covenantal, sacramental economy of God's providence, neighborly justice, and creaturely praise and gratitude. Financial creativity is an unexpected but essential way to express covenantal solidarity, which is humanity's duty within a sacramental economy of creation.[44]

The sacramental realization of love of neighbor enacted by redirecting funds to clean investments, for the sake of a stable climate and fruitful earth, is no less symbolic than providing funds to buy bread for the hungry. It is the actual reality of love of neighbor and future generations and all living families of the earth.

I have explored the potential of viewing energy investments through a sacramental imagination, the core theme in my thesis that the recovery of the sacramental imagination has the threefold effect of deepening our vision of energy investments as sacramental acts of love of neighbor, raising moral awareness in society, and driving practical investments. I now turn to the second theme, the power of divestment and reinvestment to awaken that sacramental vision when it is lacking.

INVESTMENTS AS PROPHETIC ACTIONS RAISING MORAL AWARE- NESS

The market is a legitimate human institution if directed to the common good, a teaching established by multiple magisterial statements. As *Oeconomicae et Pecuniariae Quaestiones* teaches, "Every human reality and activity is something positive, if it is lived within the horizon of an adequate ethics that respects human dignity and is directed to the common good…including financial markets" (no. 8). Pope Emeritus Benedict XVI teaches in *Caritas in Veritate*: "Every economic decision has a moral consequence" (no. 37) and "Investment always has a moral, as well as economic, significance" (no. 40). Pope John Paul II writes that "[i]t is the task of the State to provide for the defence and preservation of common goods such as the natural and human environments, which cannot be safeguarded simply by market forces" (*Centesimus Annus*, no. 40). Protecting the environment serves the common good and justifies expenses: "When making use of natural resources, we should be concerned for their protection and consider the cost entailed—environmentally and socially—as an essential part of the overall expenses incurred" (Pope Benedict XVI, 2010 World Day of Peace Message).

---

[43] Rahner, "Reflections on the Unity of the Love of Neighbor and the Love of God," 234.

[44] Erin Lothes Biviano, "Catholic Energy Ethics: Commitments and Criteria," *Relations: Beyond Anthropocentrism* 6 (2018): 143–152.

Thus, Pope Francis builds on papal precedent when he emphasizes that "[p]rofit cannot be the sole criterion to be taken into account" (*Laudato Si'*, no. 187). Investing in any corporation in order to maximize profit is specifically forbidden by *Laudato Si'* (no. 109). Consequently, Catholic investment guidelines exclude investments in abortion, contraception, or weapons on a moral basis, regardless of fiduciary concern for lost profitability resulting from divestment therefrom.

The Bishops' Investment Guidelines

The US Catholic bishops' *Socially Responsible Investment Guidelines* enshrine the fundamental message that our investments need to be ethically shaped. Individual investors are complicit in the actions of polluting corporations. The concept of social evil recognizes that "countless specific human actions with varying degrees of responsibility...give rise to social structures and practices imbued with selfishness and evil."[45] Investments are one of these structures with which many cooperate more or less knowingly and also serve as a pathway for social change.[46]

Within these guidelines, divestment and reinvestment are acknowledged among multiple tactics for social change. The first principle of socially responsible investing according to the US bishops is "do no harm." The second is "active corporate participation" through exercis-

---

[45] Robert W. McElroy, "Pope Francis Makes Addressing Poverty Essential," *America Magazine*, October 8, 2013, www.americamagazine.org/church-poor.

[46] Is the investor truly responsible for corporate pollution when his aim is to safeguard his investments and retirement? It may be argued that the investor's object is to fund a retirement account; ExxonMobil's object is to buy oil rigs. While investors may not directly intend to purchase oil rigs, they are nonetheless funding extractive equipment through their investments, and such funding is indistinguishable from ExxonMobil's purchasing of oil rigs. A fossil fuel company's business is extraction and profit, and one's investments enable extraction and the subsequent profit (or loss). This is immediate material cooperation. See Thomas R. Kopfensteiner, "The Man with a Ladder," *America*, November 1, 2004; James F. Keenan and Thomas R. Kopfensteiner, "The Principle of Cooperation: Theologians Explain Material and Formal Cooperation," *Health Progress*, April 1995, www.chausa.org/publications/health-progress/article/april-1995/the-principle-of-cooperation. In fact, David Cloutier shows that for investors, it is reasonable "to expect a return on investment, but *to intend to maximize* such return is to share in the intention of fossil fuel companies, and so to formally cooperate with their means of attaining this maximization" (David Cloutier, "Fossil Fuel Divestment," unpublished conference paper, Divest/Invest Conference, Dayton, Ohio, November 5–7, 2015). M. Cathleen Kaveny expands the framework of the principle of cooperation by adding the "mirror image" concept of the appropriation of evil, which specifies incorporating the fruits of another's immoral action into his own act. See "Appropriation of Evil: Cooperation's Mirror Image," *Theological Studies* 61 (2000): 280–313. Cloutier and Kaveny both consider gravity, remoteness, alternate means to an end, and other distinctions that cannot be addressed here. But in short, the *cooperation with or appropriation of the evil of* global life-threatening environmental degradation *must be very remote or prudentially justified, and it is neither.*

ing shareholder responsibilities. The third principle embraces "positive strategies (promote the common good)."[47] As the bishops note regarding the first principle, "This strategy involves two possible courses of action: 1) refusal to invest in companies whose products and/or policies are counter to the values of Catholic moral teaching or statements adopted by the Conference of bishops; 2) *divesting from such companies*" (emphasis added).[48]

Fossil fuel companies whose products pollute and whose policies intend aggressive expansion stand counter to Catholic moral teaching, which states that these products must be "progressively replaced without delay" (*Laudato Si'*, no. 165). Using fossil fuels is a tolerated "lesser evil" until the energy economy completes the essential transition to a renewable economy. Holding corporate policy opposing this energy transition counters *Laudato Si'*, *Energy, Justice and Peace*, and the global bishops' conferences' statement calling for a transition to 100 percent renewable energy.[49] All of these Catholic documents give testimony to the vision of a new economy that is not yet achieved but is indeed possible with present technologies. Possibility becomes reality through commitment to the proposals generated by a creative imagination willing to relinquish present structures and commit intellectual resources to framing concrete new proposals for a better world.[50]

Francis asks, "Is it realistic to hope that those who are obsessed with maximizing profits will stop to reflect on the environmental damage which they will leave behind for future generations?" (*Laudato Si'*, no. 190). The fossil fuel companies' intractable opposition to change is specifically identified by the US bishops' investment guidelines as grounds for divestment: "Investments of this type may be tolerated, so long as the Conference engages in active participation *and there is a reasonable hope of success for corporate change*."[51] No time line for reasonable change is given by the bishops, suggesting

---

[47] United States Conference of Catholic Bishops, *Socially Responsible Investment Guidelines*, November 12, 2003, www.usccb.org/about/financial-reporting/socially-responsible-investment-guidelines.

[48] Currently, these guidelines are under revision, see Brian Roewe, "Review of US Bishops' Investment Guidelines is Underway," *EarthBeat*, May 19, 2021, www.ncronline.org/news/earthbeat/review-us-bishops-investment-guidelines-underway.

[49] Coopération Internationale pour le Développement et la Solidarité (CIDSE), *Statement in Lima on the Road to Paris* (2015), www.cidse.org/catholic-bishops-statement-in-lima-on-the-road-to-paris/.

[50] International Energy Agency, *Net Zero by 2050* (Paris: IEA, 2021), www.iea.org/reports/net-zero-by-2050. It is hard to exaggerate the importance of this far-seeing document from a formerly conservative think-tank representing oil producers.

[51] USCCB, *Socially Responsible Investment Guidelines*. Emphasis added.

that prudence should heed the science that calls for immediate action.[52] Achieving successful corporate change within the fossil fuel industry has been the hope of environmental advocates for decades. Yet their prayers, coalitions, and campaigns have stumbled before intensely strategic and incredibly well-funded opposition from fossil fuel companies.

The intractable opposition of fossil fuel companies is key among the criteria employed by many faith communities when discerning divestment. Rev. Fletcher Harper, executive director of the international interfaith environmental coalition GreenFaith, articulates the criteria for divestment as intractable opposition to change; large-scale, systematic harm; and the need for religious communities to reject complacency, redefine society's moral code, and spur an appropriate disgust for corporate-sponsored ecocide.[53] These criteria reflect the power and purpose of the sacramental-prophetic imagination: to reject destructive structures such as those of petrocapitalism and open new possibilities for society.

The Intractable Resistance of Fossil Fuel Companies as a Condition Calling for Divestment

Between 1990 and 2015, Exxon, Chevron, and ConocoPhillips prevented the passage of *all* 113 climate-related resolutions submitted to them; as sponsors withdrew the resolutions, the companies convinced regulators the resolutions should be withdrawn or the companies campaigned against them.[54] When shareholders voted 62.3 percent in favor of a proposal to publish risk assessments of climate-related scenarios at the May 2017 Exxon shareholders meeting, this *nonbinding* resolution was opposed by management. What the vote truly showed is that *shareholders* wish for climate change action—not ExxonMobil.[55] ExxonMobil suppressed its own reports about climate change for decades, Harvard researchers conclude, systematically misleading the

---

[52] Prudence is the governing theme of the bishops' document, USCCB, "Global Climate Change: A Plea for Dialogue, Prudence, and the Common Good," June 15, 2001, www.usccb.org/resources/global-climate-change-plea-dialogue-prudence-and-common-good.

[53] Fletcher Harper, "Divest and Reinvest Now! The Religious Imperative for Fossil Fuel Divestment and Reinvestment in a Clean Energy Future," *GreenFaith*, greenfaith.org/take-action/divest-and-invest-now/.

[54] Elizabeth Douglass, "Exxon's Gamble: 25 Years of Rejecting Shareholder Concerns on Climate Change," *InsideClimate News*, June 8, 2015, insideclimatenews.org/news/16112015/exxons-gamble-25-years-rejecting-shareholder-concerns-climate-change/.

[55] "ExxonMobil Gives in to Shareholders on Climate Risk Disclosure," *Fortune*, December 12, 2017, fortune.com/2017/12/12/exxon-mobil-climate/.

public since 1977.[56] The Global Climate Coalition, a prominent lobbying group, refuted climate science against the findings of its own experts.[57] Its members included ExxonMobil, Chevron, and the American Petroleum Institute.[58]

Alarming evidence shows that, far from shifting to a new, renewable business model, ExxonMobil intends to be the last oil company pumping profits from the earth, heedless of the climate impact. ExxonMobil's chief executive officer, Darren Woods, has stated his intention to increase profits from oil and gas to become three times what they were in 2017, reaching $23 billion in 2025. The goal is not simply to maintain production but to increase it through pumping vast new projects in the United States, Brazil, and Guyana.[59] The most powerful and insidious way that oil companies suppress the otherwise inevitable acceleration of a low-carbon economy is through corporate lobbying. *The Guardian* reported official US documents showing ExxonMobil pressured President George W. Bush not to ratify the 1997 Kyoto Protocol.[60]

American citizens concerned about climate change also have little political power against the massive wealth of oil companies deployed in the US Congress. The oil and gas industry spent an incredible $125.6 million on lobbying during 2018, which compares to all lobbying by all sectors in 2018 of $1.5 billion.[61] Lobbying paid off, as industry-funded senators urged President Trump to withdraw from the Paris Climate Agreement.[62] Analysis of corporate behavior that influences climate change perceptions shows that the five companies with the greatest "opposition to Paris Aligned Climate Policy" are Koch Industries (worst), Southern Company, ExxonMobil, Chevron, and

---

[56] Geoffrey Supran and Naomi Oreskes, "Assessing ExxonMobil's Climate Change Communications, 1977–2014," *Environmental Research Letters*, August 12, 2017, iopscience.iop.org/article/10.1088/1748-9326/aa815f/meta.

[57] Andrew C. Revkin, "Industry Ignored Its Own Scientists," *The New York Times*, April 23, 2009, www.nytimes.com/2009/04/24/science/earth/24deny.html.

[58] Amy Westervelt, "How the Fossil Fuel Industry Got the Media to Think Climate Change Was Debatable," *The Washington Post*, January 10, 2019, www.washingtonpost.com/outlook/2019/01/10/how-fossil-fuel-industry-got-media-think-climate-change-was-debatable/.

[59] "Bigger Oil," *The Economist*, February 9, 2019, 17.

[60] John Vidal, "Revealed: How Oil Giant Influenced Bush," *The Guardian*, June 8, 2005, www.theguardian.com/news/2005/jun/08/usnews.climatechange.

[61] Center for Responsive Politics, "Industry Profile: Oil & Gas," www.opensecrets.org/federal-lobbying/industries/summary?cycle=2018&id=E01.

[62] All twenty-two signatories received contributions from oil and gas PACs totaling $4,095,071 over five years. See US Senator James M. Inhofe et al., "Letter to President Donald J. Trump," www.inhofe.senate.gov/imo/media/doc/Paris%20letter.pdf. Jeffrey Sachs, "Oil and Gas Industry Has Way Too Much Control Over Congress," *CNN*, April 16, 2019, www.cnn.com/2019/04/16/opinions/energy-industry-too-much-power-congress-sachs/index.html.

Valero Energy.[63] In December 2020, ExxonMobil agreed under pressure from shareholders to reduce the emissions intensity per barrel of oil and gas produced but is not making any changes to its business model to prepare for a clean energy transition. A senior analyst of investment sustainability concluded there is nothing that "should change an investor's level of concern about Exxon's climate strategy."[64]

Despite the outrageous claims of some energy companies that they exist to provide the poor with energy, the poor need *energy*, not fossil fuels. Countless energy extraction projects cause intense harm to the poor while denying them access to the fuels that are removed from their lands.[65] As Pope Francis states, "Civilization requires energy, but energy use must not destroy civilization!"[66] In sum, the disinformation campaigns, predatory denial of climate science and fossil fuel impacts, exploitative profiteering from human suffering and ecocide, political pressuring, amid active efforts to *expand* the extraction of fossil fuel, represent intractable opposition to change—not a "reasonable hope for corporate change."

Such strategies contradict an economy oriented to the common good and the preferential option for the poor, a covenantal economy in which "[p]rofit and solidarity are no longer antagonists" (*Oeconomicae et Pecuniariae Quaestiones*, no. 11). Instead, these corporate actions exemplify a situation where "mere profit is placed at the summit of the culture of a financial enterprise, and the actual demands of the common good are ignored, [and] every ethical claim is really perceived as irrelevant" (*Oeconomicae et Pecuniariae Quaestiones*, no. 23).

Not every company is as intractably opposed to the clean energy transition, and many (especially European companies) are indeed acquiring solar and wind assets and becoming renewable energy companies. But there is no justification for funding those companies that reject the energy transition, nor for those whose transition plans are too slow for climate safety. What decades of exploitation and pollution

---

[63] "Corporate Carbon Policy Footprint: Physical Carbon Emissions May Be Only Part of the Pictures—Introducing the 50 Most Influential," InfluenceMap, September 2017, influencemap.org/site/data/000/299/CPF_Report_Aug_2017.pdf, 6.

[64] Nicholas Kusnetz, "Exxon Pledges to Reduce Emissions, But the Details Suggest Nothing Has Changed," *Inside Climate News*, December 15, 2020, insideclimatenews.org/news/15122020/exxon-mobil-pledge-emissons-net-zero/.

[65] The Nigerian oil crisis exemplifies such postcolonial exploitation, see Cyril Obi and Temitope B. Oriola, "Introduction: The Unfinished Revolution; The Niger Delta Struggle Since 1995," in *The Unfinished Revolution in Nigeria's Niger Delta*, ed. Cyril Obi and Temitope B. Oriola (New York: Routledge, 2018).

[66] "Address of His Holiness Pope Francis to Participants at the Meeting for Executives of the Main Companies in the Oil and Natural Gas Sectors, and Other Energy Related Business," June 9, 2018, www.vatican.va/content/francesco/en/speeches/2018/june/documents/papa-francesco_20180609_imprenditori-energia.html.

have instead shown is indeed an obsession with profits and refusal to change, at the cost of ecological health, a moral failing that investors cannot duplicate. There exists a significant moral hazard of cooperating with fossil fuel companies who demonstrate intractable resistance to the common good and ongoing intention to profit maximally by increasing the prospecting, extraction, and sale of fossil fuels. What should the conscientious investor do?

THE CURRENT DEBATE OVER ENGAGEMENT AND DIVESTMENT

In response to the dilemma of funding fossil fuel infrastructure through investment portfolios, conscientious investors have intensely debated the merits of shareholder engagement with fossil fuel companies as opposed to divestment and reinvestment. This debate is critical because it has direct bearing on the effective transformation of our global energy system, which currently drives climate change and impacts the entire family of life. Here, I review the arguments on both sides.

The Argument against Divestment: Investors' Concerns and Commitment to Engagement

To both profit-minded investors and shareholders committed to engagement, divestment is often seen as risky, hypocritical, futile, and "symbolic." The perceived risk of reduced returns contradicts an investor's fiduciary responsibility and the future security of her family, community, or corporation. This is an extremely important point to hundreds of Catholic money managers for parishes, dioceses, and religious communities who are penurious or indeed bankrupt. It is no small fear to worry about sustaining these organizations, maintaining diocesan payroll and keeping parishes open, and caring for aged clergy and religious. Some might justify a portfolio including oil as prudentially protecting against risk, judging it indefensible to risk a parochial school's operation, a couple's retirement, or an endowment's future by investing entirely in green energy.

The argument from hypocrisy views divestment as a claim to a false sense of moral purity by those who continue to drive and fly. This argument buttresses a general sense that environmental idealists are unaware of the actual impacts of real-life choices, given their focus on protest actions. The charge of hypocrisy recognizes green zealots who, counter-productively, advertise their heightened eco-conscience.

Futility, or even ignorance, is another objection to divestment. Market watchers observe that other investors will purchase the fossil fuel stocks sold by divestors, rendering their actions futile. Again, the rhetoric and hopes of divestment advocates seem unsuited for "the real world."

Finally, engaged shareholders do not want to lose their voice in corporate decision making for the sake of a "symbolic" protest, as they value the ability to influence boards on a wide range of issues important to Catholic social teaching (instead of the single issue of fossil fuels). As legal scholars observe, while investors have a moral responsibility to limit their complicity in the fossil fuel economy, divestment tactics may lack influence without financial sanctions against the industry. "Moreover, the movement does not engage sufficiently with the systemic qualities of finance capitalism that must also be reckoned with in order to address broader patterns of environmental unsustainability."[67]

The Argument for Divestment and Reinvestment: Practical Need and Moral Witness

First, regarding risk, today there are new risks to being invested in fossil fuels. Coal values have fallen so steeply that divesting from coal is common sense.[68] Furthermore, oil faces similar devaluation due to the situation of "stranded assets." As international accords and public sentiment move away from the assumption that fossil fuels should continue to power society, fossil fuel companies are forced to write off their reserves and effectively lose their assets and thus returns. For example, in 2017 ExxonMobil wrote off 4.8 billion barrels of reserves due to falling oil prices, nearly 20 percent of their reserves.[69] In 2020, ExxonMobil wrote off $20 billion of assets.[70] Overall, since 2014 Exxon has lost $184 billion of its value, or a 41 percent loss.[71]

Notably, according to Francis G. Coleman, former executive vice president at Christian Brothers Investment Services, lower returns are not inevitable with socially responsible investing. "Absolutely, definitively, without question, that is not true," Coleman said. "I can say without a doubt, without equivocation, that is false."[72] At the same time, some divestment advocates view potential loss as part of the cost of discipleship.[73]

In addition, new definitions of fiduciary responsibility are emerging that may define investments in fossil fuels as risky and imprudent.

---

[67] Benjamin J. Richardson, "Divesting from Climate Change: The Road to Influence," *Law & Policy* 39 (2017): 325–48.

[68] Jeff Desjardins, "The Fall of Coal in Three Charts," *Visual Capitalist*, July 1, 2016, www.visualcapitalist.com/decline-of-coal-three-charts/.

[69] "Bigger Oil," *The Economist*, February 9, 2019, 19.

[70] Kusnetz, "Exxon Pledges."

[71] Matt Egan, "Exxon's Market Value Has Crumbled by $184 Billion," *CNN Business*, February 5, 2020, www.cnn.com/2020/02/05/business/exxonmobil-oil-stock/index.html.

[72] Dan Stockman, "Sisters Lead the Way in Mission Investing That Influences Corporate Policy and Advances Social Good," *Global Sisters Report*, May 23, 2016, www.globalsistersreport.org/news/trends/sisters-lead-way-mission-investing-influences-corporate-policy-and-advances-social-good.

[73] Harper, "Divest and Reinvest Now!"

Scores of climate change lawsuits are already underway.[74] Catholic universities and hospitals are not immune to claims that their investments affect students' and patients' well-being as much as the education or health care they are providing.[75] Catholic institutions cannot employ utilitarian arguments to claim large returns are justified by polluting investments. Nor can they avoid the fact that polluting investments are contributing to a diminished future for their students or patients.

Second, divestment supporters argue there is no hypocrisy in continuing to drive or fly while such travel remains largely unavoidable, if one also commits to prayer, ecological conversion, parish creation care ministry, energy efficiency, lifestyle changes, and political advocacy. Like a first moral act grounding further virtuous habits, taking the clear action of divestment creates moral energy for further actions.[76]

Third, though others may repurchase oil stocks, divestment is not futile because it frees enormous funds for reinvestment in renewable energy instead. Since balanced portfolios are always the goal, funds should be directed to diversified positive economic sectors (health care, communications, technology, manufacturing, clean energy, etc.). Whatever proportion of funds does go into the energy sector would support renewables instead of fossil fuels. Renewable energy has particular need for the funds liberated by divestment as wind and solar cannot access some of the capital and tax breaks available to fossil fuel corporations.[77] To date, the divestment movement has shifted $14.5 trillion to such essential and practical investments in renewable energy.[78] A stunning major divestment includes the recent commitment of the New York State pension fund, a highly conservative and well-

---

[74] Columbia Law School Sabin Center for Climate Change Law and Arnold & Porter, "U.S. Climate Litigation," climatecasechart.com/us-climate-change-litigation/. This database contains an astounding number of climate change cases.

[75] Erin Lothes Biviano, Daniel DiLeo, Cristina Richie, and Tobias Winright, "Is Fossil Fuel Investment a Sin?" *Health Care Ethics USA*, January 23, 2018, www.chausa.org/publications/health-care-ethics-usa/archives/issues/winter-2018/is-fossil-fuel-investment-a-sin. Boston College is currently under investigation by the Massachusetts Attorney General for investments that contradict its mission at the urging of a student coalition.

[76] Nancy M. Rourke, "A Catholic Virtues Ecology," in *Just Sustainability: Technology, Ecology, and Resource Extraction*, ed. Christiana Z. Peppard and Andrea Vicini (Maryknoll, NY: Orbis Books, 2015), 194.

[77] Travis Bradford, Peter Davidson, Lawrence Rodman, and David Sandalow, "Financing Solar and Wind Power: Insights from Oil and Gas," The Center on Global Energy Policy, March 2017, 7–9, www.energypolicy.columbia.edu/sites/default/files/Financing%20Solar%20and%20Wind%20Power.pdf.

[78] "Go FossilFree.org," gofossilfree.org/divestment/commitments/.

regarded fund.[79] Faith communities are the single largest subgroup of divestors.[80]

Most important, fossil fuel divestment is never futile and is especially powerful because it *stigmatizes fossil fuel expansion, production, and consumption.* Divestment is a moral interruption to the status quo that shifts the social narrative around fossil fuels and has the potential to move legislators away from accepting the support from fossil fuel companies that ties their hands regarding fossil-free legislation. As such, divestment is a key expression of the sacramental imagination that envisions a new future and prophetically challenges the forces that oppose it.

REFRAMING THE BINARY OPPOSITION OF ENGAGEMENT AND DIVESTMENT

Given this debate, what practical principles should guide institutions deliberating over the right mix of justice strategies such as divestment or shareholder engagement? Shareholder engagement and divestment both offer the moral witness of an "interruptive" sacramental-prophetic vision. Both are strategies that seek to enact the possibilities of justice envisioned by faith. I reject the opposition of engagement and divestment and reframe the binary opposition of shareholder engagement and divestment/reinvestment to a relationship of complementarity that engages all modes of advocacy.

Significant witness can occur through shareholder engagement. Many Catholic institutions are members of the Interfaith Center for Corporate Responsibility (ICCR) and have advanced workers' rights, immigration, women's rights, life issues, peace, and justice through engagement. Shareholder engagement is, however, particularly challenged to succeed against the fossil fuel industry for two reasons. First, there is a distinction between *advocating for corporate change in process* and *advocating for corporate change in product.* Changes that improve the fairness, safety, health, and empowerment of workers are process changes that a corporation can accept while making the same product. Yet it is inherently challenging for a company to comply with requests to put themselves out of business by ceasing to produce their product. Some oil companies have done just that, investing in solar and wind with other greenhouse gas reduction goals. Notably, these

[79] Anne Barnard, "New York's $226 Billion State Pension Fund Is Dropping Fossil Fuel Stocks," *New York Times*, December 9, 2020, www.nytimes.com/2020/12/09/nyregion/new-york-pension-fossil-fuels.html.

[80] For a list of Catholic divestors, see Global Catholic Climate Movement, "Who Is Divesting and Why?" catholicclimatemovement.global/leaders/.

are largely European companies.[81] Second, the *pace of change* fostered by shareholder engagement does not match the actual need for a faster societal shift to renewable energy. The urgency of this essential shift cannot be overstated. The "carbon budget," or amount of fossil fuels that can be burned and stay below a certain temperature, runs out alarmingly soon. As analysts state, "If we assume that emissions remain constant, the 1.5°C budget runs out sometime in 2025, while the 2°C budget runs out sometime in 2035."[82]

In Bill McKibben's famous calculation, three numbers matter. The first is 2, as in the 2°C temperature rise limit. Next is 565 gigatons of carbon, the amount of carbon that can yet be released into the atmosphere and stay below 2°C. Finally is 2,795, the amount of carbon already contained in the proven coal and oil and gas reserves of the fossil fuel companies and oil-rich state oil firms. As McKibben grimly points out, 2,795 is *five times higher* than our "permissible" budget to reach the uncomfortably warm 2°C world.[83] Thus, there are less than five years to reach an abrupt cessation of fossil fuel use, yet emissions continue to rise.[84] Many faith-based investment houses have been conducting business-as-usual shareholder engagement for over twenty-five years *with the result of society existing in the current climate crisis situation.*

Faith-based groups may choose to continue to dialogue through multiple shareholder campaigns. Different persons find various forms of engagement meaningful, and these diverse ministries should be respected. Furthermore, positive investment, or impact investing, "is another way to do Catholic ministries in the world: using our financial resources to drive social change."[85] But it is not adequate *solely* to dialogue with fossil fuel companies. All must seize and deploy the greatest capital we have: the moral capital launched by refusing to

---

[81] As You Sow, "Chevron Corporation: Paris Aligned Business Plan," December 18, 2018, www.asyousow.org/resolutions/2018/12/18/chevron-corporation-paris-aligned-business-plan.

[82] James Morrissey and Nicolas Maennling, "Leaving Fossil Fuels in the Ground: Who, What, and When?," *Columbia Center on Sustainable Investment*, October 14, 2016, blogs.ei.columbia.edu/2016/10/14/leaving-fossil-fuels-in-the-ground-who-what-and-when/.

[83] Bill McKibben, "Global Warming's Terrifying New Math," *Rolling Stone*, July 19, 2012, www.rollingstone.com/politics/politics-news/global-warmings-terrifying-new-math-188550/.

[84] In fact, business-as-usual emissions are increasing at a rate of 0.1 percent, when what is needed is an 8.5-percent annual decrease in emissions. See Morrissey and Maennling, "Leaving Fossil Fuels in the Ground."

[85] Elizabeth Eisenstadt Evans, "Impact Investing Moves Money from 'Do No Harm' to Promoting Social Good," *National Catholic Reporter*, January 18, 2020, www.ncronline.org/news/people/impact-investing-moves-money-do-no-harm-promoting-social-good. Impact investing has been the focus of three major Vatican conferences that will continue biennially, see Vatican Impact Investing Conference, www.viiconference.org/.

fund and profit from the expansion of fossil fuel infrastructure—the moral capital of divestment.

Climate-focused investors need retain only $2,000 of shares to maintain the right to conduct shareholder engagement. Additional shares are not needed to vote on proxies and file resolutions, which, notably, are generally advisory, meaning the company is not obliged to act on them.[86] An investor would need to command 1 to 3 percent of a company's total stock to have special persuasive powers—and all of ExxonMobil's ICCR investors in the United States would not total 1 percent of their stock.

Divestment does not abandon dialogue but continues the dialogue beyond the boardroom to broader society and the public square, where such discourse is essential and sadly needed.[87] Divestment aims to convert the public as much, if not more, than the fossil fuel company by summoning investors, consumers, and "people in the pews" to think more deeply about the moral meaning of fossil fuel dependence and act in their own lives to reduce that dependence and support clean energy policies. Divestment seeks to draw others into the politics of imagination. The audience of divestment is much larger than the board of directors.

To leave $2,000 invested in fossil fuels and reinvest the rest in fossil-free energy, represents a deliberately diverse strategy and a more ethically nuanced approach. This approach employs engagement *together with* divestment/reinvestment, thus reframing the binary opposition and recognizing the complexities within this situation. This dual method also follows the bishops' urging "to hold a minimal position in those companies."[88]

What, then, is the rationale for leaving the rest of one's portfolio in fossil fuel–invested funds? Religious communities have enormous potential to question fossil fuel dependency and courageously redefine moral investment behavior for society. Catholic hospitals, Catholic universities, diocesan investment committees, and other Catholic institutions have significant moral influence among Catholics and in the public square.[89] Indeed, a call for divestment increasingly emerges from the highest levels of Church authority. A 2020 report from a Holy See Interdicastery Table on Integral Ecology calls for Catholics to

---

[86] Faith-based investment professional, anonymous, personal communication, May 26, 2017.

[87] I thank Eli S. McCarthy, PhD, Georgetown University, Program on Justice and Peace, and director, Justice and Peace, Conference of Major Superiors of Men, for this insight.

[88] United States Conference of Catholic Bishops, *Socially Responsible Investment Guidelines*.

[89] Global Catholic Climate Movement, "Jeffrey Sachs Encourages Catholic Organizations to Divest," June 16, 2016, catholicclimatemovement.global/jeffrey-sachs-divestment.

"shun companies that are harmful to human or social ecology, such as abortion and armaments, and to the environment, such as fossil fuels."[90] Fossil fuel divestment is recognized as a *Laudato Si'* goal in "*Laudato Si'*: Special Anniversary Year Plan."[91] The bishops' conferences of Belgium, Ireland, Austria, the Philippines, Greece, Luxembourg, and Malta have already divested, along with scores of other Catholic institutions. The University of Dayton was the first US Catholic university to divest, resulting from conversations among its board members wishing to express their Catholic and Marianist mission and commitment to environmental stewardship. Seven years later, the endowment is fully divested, and reports show its returns are similar to or marginally better than projected returns had the school not divested.[92]

If desired, with a retained $2,000 worth of shares, Catholic investors can vote as a matter of course on all shareholder initiatives. Christian investment services have a responsibility to create options for portfolios divested from fossil fuels that maintain relationships with faith-based shareholder engagement.[93] Such fossil fuel screens and impact investing methods are not novel strategies to wealth management professionals.[94] The bishops' guidelines should be updated to reflect the above-mentioned Vatican documents and to include specific calls for transitioning from fossil fuels.

Evidence for the power of divestment to influence society's moral code exists, first, in the effectiveness of past divestment campaigns (such as those targeting the government of South Africa) and, second, in financial managers citing divestment as a protest that is shifting investment trends. Jim Cramer, a CNBC analyst, writes that oil and gas

---

[90] Philip Pullella, "Vatican Urges Catholics to Drop Investments in Fossil Fuels, Arms," *Reuters*, June 18, 2020, www.reuters.com/article/us-vatican-environment/vatican-urges-catholics-to-drop-investments-in-fossil-fuels-arms-idUSKBN23P1HI.

[91] Dicastery for Promoting Integral Human Development, *Laudato Si' Special Anniversary Year*, May 24, 2020, 8, www.humandevelopment.va/content/dam/sviluppoumano/documenti/FINAL%20EN%20-%20Laudato%20si'%20Anniv%20Year%202020-2021.pdf.

[92] Brian Roewe, "How the University of Dayton Divested from Fossil Fuels—and What Happened to Its Bottom Line," *National Catholic Reporter*, July 14, 2020. Georgetown, Seattle University, and Creighton University have also pledged full or partial divestment.

[93] Resources include GreenFaith's Divest and Invest Now movement at greenfaith.org/programs/divest-and-reinvest, and The Catholic Impact Investing Collaborative (CIIC), at www.catholicimpact.org/. See also "Ethical Investments in an Era of Climate Change: A Guide to Reviewing Environmental and Social Governance of Catholic Investments" at catholicclimatemovement.global/wp-content/uploads/2017/11/GCCM_Tr%C3%B3caire-Catholic-Toolkit.pdf.

[94] Despite complications such as commingled mutual funds, one manager estimates that a large institution might require five years at most to manage a portfolio's transition. John O'Shaughnessy, Catholic Investment Impact Collaborative, personal communication, November 20, 2017.

stocks are no longer "investible" due to trends driven by environmentally conscious younger investors. "[W]hen lots of money managers refuse to own your stocks, those stocks go lower," Cramer said.[95] Climate finance researchers have studied the correlation of the stock value of two hundred major fossil fuel companies with multiple divestment announcements and observe short- and long-term effects on negative returns.[96] Shell has also stated the impact of divestment on its operations.[97]

While many faith communities are leaders in sustainable investment, some Church communities also need an interruption to their practices. Since *Laudato Si'*, Catholic investors might be expected to show more concern about their investments' environmental impact. Yet one Catholic investment manager took an unofficial client poll in 2016 and found that over half had not yet discussed divestment.[98] Understandably, these groups (largely institutions and religious communities, not parishes) have pressing issues like declining membership and community members who will outlive the financial resources to support them. The manager observed that many of his clients are doing the investment work for their organization somewhat reluctantly. He frequently hears, "I wish I were back in the classroom/migrant center/campus ministry office." This striking insight suggests that many clients may not fully recognize the moral meaning of investing or at least that they trust their advisors to implement traditional Catholic screens and engagement. Add the relative novelty of climate change, and they do not question the impact of supporting fossil fuels in their portfolios. Notably, neither do the outside managers hired by many Catholic investment firms, who are required to impose traditional Catholic screens while values such as fossil fuel screens are left to the managers' discretion.

While investments may not have the satisfaction of person-to-person ministry, it is critical today to acknowledge and engage the enormous moral and financial power of faith-based investments. Seeing through a sacramental imagination where "everything is connected" (*Laudato Si'*, no. 70), one may perceive that transferring funds to support the life-sustaining need for clean energy is a sacramental offering

---

[95] Tyler Clifford, "Investors Should Sell Oil Stocks on Any Rumored OPEC Deal," *CNBC*, March 9, 2020, www.cnbc.com/2020/03/09/jim-cramer-investors-should-sell-oil-stocks-on-any-rumored-opec-deal.html.

[96] Truzaar Dordi and Olaf Weber, "The Impact of Divestment Announcements on the Share Price of Fossil Fuel Stocks," *Sustainability* 11, no. 11 (2019): doi.10.3390/su11113122.

[97] "Shell Annual Report Acknowledges Impact of Divestment Campaign," 350.org, June 22, 2018, 350.org/press-release/shell-report-impact-of-divestment/.

[98] Faith-based investment professional, anonymous, personal communication, July 20, 2017.

of love of neighbor and a moral witness for change before a society all too complacent as climate change accelerates.

THE PRACTICAL NEED FOR REINVESTMENT IN CLEAN ENERGY AT A MASSIVE SCALE

Divestment and reinvestment are positive and practical solutions to the crisis of dirty energy because reinvested funds can purchase clean energy. Clean energy is needed at a massive scale to meet the planet's lower emission goals to stabilize climate and reduce the intense impacts of climate change. *Global society must invest trillions of dollars in renewable energy.* Yet there is an investment gap of a trillion dollars a year, as spending by fossil fuel companies outpaces investments in renewables and oil subsidies foolishly continue.[99] Globally, enormous reserves of oil and gas exist.[100]

Given the crisis, it is unconscionable to invest any funds in fossil fuel infrastructure beyond the $2,000 to maintain shareholder voting status when resources are desperately needed to build renewable infrastructure. Renewable energy systems are dropping phenomenally in cost and availability, rapidly rising to the challenge of powering the world.[101] Reinvesting is a pragmatic decision to invest in the transition to a decarbonized economy and actualize the option for the poor. Developing complex, renewable energy takes place only through investment—individual, institutional, and societal investments. This task falls to humanity because "our vocation to protect God's handiwork is essential to a life of virtue; it is not an optional or a secondary aspect of our Christian experience" (*Laudato Si'*, no. 217). Reinvesting is an act of courageous hope as well. Halting emissions rapidly might allow atmospheric CO_2 to decline to 350 parts per million at century's

---

[99] Mark Fulton and Reid Capalino, "Investing in the Clean Trillion: Closing the Clean Energy Investment Gap," CERES, January 15, 2014, www.ceres.org/resources/reports/investing-clean-trillion-closing-clean-energy-investment-gap. See also Janet Redman, "Dirty Energy Dominance: Dependent on Denial," *Oil Change International*, October 2017, priceofoil.org/content/uploads/2017/10/OCI_US-Fossil-Fuel-Subs-2015-16_Final_Oct2017.pdf.

[100] Morrissey and Maennling, "Leaving Fossil Fuels in the Ground."

[101] Silvio Marcacci, "Renewable Energy Prices Hit Record Lows: How Can Utilities Benefit from Unstoppable Solar and Wind?" *Forbes*, January 21, 2020, www.forbes.com/sites/energyinnovation/2020/01/21/renewable-energy-prices-hit-record-lows-how-can-utilities-benefit-from-unstoppable-solar-and-wind. See also Ram Manish et al., "Global Energy System Based on 100% Renewable Energy," Lappeenranta University of Technology and Energy Watch Group, April 2019, energywatchgroup.org/wp-content/uploads/EWG_LUT_100RE_All_Sectors_Global_Report_2019.pdf.

end.[102] New research shows the hope that warming will slow markedly once emissions cease.[103]

Thus, divestment is a practical diversion of funds to build a clean energy economy, a response to the cry of the earth and those suffering energy poverty, and an act of Christian hope. "Every gesture of our liberty, even if it appears fragile and insignificant, if it is really directed towards the authentic good, rests on Him who is the good Lord of history and becomes part of a buoyancy that exceeds our poor forces" (*Oeconomicae et Pecuniariae Quaestiones*, no. 34). With this hope, taking action through divestment and reinvestment constitutes a moral interruption to the intractable opposition of the fossil fuel economy to a new future, an interruption inspired by the sacramental imagination.

CONCLUSION

The decision to divest is not a judgment of guilt on the developed industrial nations for their ingenuity, nor condemnation of industry built on fossil fuels before knowing the impacts of greenhouse gases. With this knowledge, however, continued investment places us in what Willis Jenkins identifies as a wicked problem and "the greatest peril of climate change: that the accidental powers of humanity generate problems that exceed our moral imagination and defeat our abilities to take responsibility."[104]

Reclaiming the power of the sacramental imagination can awaken the responsibility to enable investments to be the fullest expression of solidarity they can be, ending complicity with fossil fuels and offering one's resources as the visible sign of compassion for the earth and the poor. Recognizing that "everything is interconnected," investments in the renewable energy economy are concrete acts of love of the neighbor experiencing energy poverty and of the ecosystem facing ecocide. This paper has re-visioned divestment and reinvestment as the powerful actuality of transferring funds to purchase and invest in renewable energy, a gift constituting an actual present economic change and a gift best understood as having the sacramental character of a real symbol.

Young people are asking those who hold the reins of power to alter their course.[105] This demand is a cry from the hearts of the generation

---

[102] Keith Kloor, "The Eye of the Storm," *Nature Climate Change* 1 (2009): doi.org/10.1038/climate.2009.124.

[103] Bob Berwyn, "Many Scientists Now Say Global Warming Could Stop Relatively Quickly after Emissions Go to Zero," *Inside Climate News,* January 3, 2021, insideclimatenews.org/news/03012021/five-aspects-climate-change-2020/.

[104] Willis Jenkins, *The Future of Ethics: Sustainability, Social Justice, and Religious Creativity* (Washington, DC: Georgetown University Press, 2013), 17.

[105] World Youth Day 2019, *Our Manifesto*, January 27, 2019, 5.3, laudatosigeneration.org/our-call/.

that will endure, and is enduring, the most impacts resulting from decisions made by others. It is the moral challenge of the generations that have held power to reverse the fossil fuel economy and fund a clean, healthy, renewable, inclusive, and sustainable economy. In so doing, this generation, like Simon of Cyrene, might lift the weight of a crucified earth off future generations so that they live to see instead earth's renewal and share in eucharistic thanksgiving for the gifts of God's creation. M

Journal of Moral Theology, Vol. 11, No. 1 (2022): 85–106

Guns and Practical Reason: An Ethical Exploration of Guns and Language

Mark Ryan

THERE IS NO SHORTAGE OF WORDS AND RHETORIC being offered up in relation to the topic of guns, much of it directed to the political standoff regarding how to respond to gun violence.[1] Yet the debate over guns in America, especially as it concerns putting in conversation the positions of "gun people" and "non-gun people,"[2] barely scratches the surface of substantive convictions held on both sides about the place of guns in our lives. A critical reason for this is that the language and rhetoric of the debate suppresses such convictions, keeping the discussion shallow and antagonistic. This, I argue, is in part due to the inadequate ethical conceptions—conceptions of practical reason—that frame the debate.

A richer discussion between gun and non-gun persons might be modeled by contrasting two conceptions of practical reason. One of these conceptions is characterized by the insistence that the relation of means to ends can only be instrumental, such that the "means" we take up in pursuit of our ends are indifferent to the ends themselves. In so doing, it overlooks the rootedness of practical reason in social practices. The other conception views at least some means as constitutive of the ends themselves. It further recognizes the integral relationship between practical reason and social practices. I borrow terms used by Charles Taylor in an essay titled, "Explanation and Practical Reason," to elaborate this distinction between two ways of conceiving practical reason.

One can bring out the way guns only make sense to us within social practices by examining their character as artefacts or instruments that

---

[1] President Biden recently called gun violence in America an "epidemic," taking advantage of a metaphor made apropos current events ("Remarks by President Biden on Gun Violence Prevention," The White House, April 8, 2021, www.whitehouse.gov/briefing-room/speeches-remarks/2021/04/08/remarks-by-president-biden-on-gun-violence-prevention/).

[2] I elect for these terms rather than the more common "pro-gun" and "pro-control" or "anti-gun" for reasons I hope will become clear in the course of my paper. In short, while the typical terms fit a conception of the gun debate as the attempt to gain ground in a zero-sum political game, the latter captures better the way guns are bound up with deeper moral convictions.

mediate our relationship to our environs. Drawing on Matthew Crawford's work on tools and their place in social practices, I illuminate how guns as mechanical instruments help shape a world of experience first of all for gun people, and secondarily, in ways both contrasting and complementary, for non-gun people.

Both Crawford's theorizing about human awareness mediated by instruments and Taylor's about different conceptions of practical reason are employed in this essay to reflect upon examples drawn from my own experience of guns in the context of my relationship with a brother-in-law, "Joe." Joe is a committed gun person, while I am a quintessential non-gun person. We are thus examples of two different "life worlds" with respect to guns. The encounter with Joe provided an opportunity to dig beneath the superficiality of the popular terms of America's gun debate, and I use this ethnographic approach in the service of greater ethical clarity.

As data, my conversations with Joe can be correlated with sociological work on the nature of public debate about guns in American life, works buttressing my claim that American gun debates are morally shallow, when not positively distortive in nature. These conversations also help us see that a problematic conception of practical reason funds the muteness about substantive convictions in popular gun discourse.[3] Furthermore, what I argue to be a superior conception of practical reasoning to the one I believe more typically frames the discussion, and which Taylor calls "*ad hominem*" practical reasoning, shows why and how a personal encounter with guns and interpersonal dialogue flowing from such an encounter has legitimacy in an ethical evaluation of guns, especially when the ultimate purpose is to indicate how a shallow debate about guns might be deepened.

After an opening discussion of the paper's orientation as an exploration in moral psychology, there follows a brief presentation of sociological evidence for the claim that gun discourse in America is impoverished and a deeper look at Charles Taylor's two conceptions of practical reason. I next move on to present two examples drawn from my encounters and subsequent discussions with "Joe" about guns, examining these in light of Taylor's and Matthew Crawford's theories. I finally deepen the exploration of ethics in relation to language by turning briefly to Rowan Williams's theory of language and art. Williams's theory complements the discussion of practical reason in relation to language that has gone before and sheds light especially on the problem of how to move forward into a language supportive of richer

---

[3] For example, on the role of narratives crafted to attach blame and identify heroes in the gun debate within social media, see Melissa Merry, "Constructing Policy Narratives in 140 Characters or Less: The Case of Gun Policy Organizations," *The Policy Studies Journal* 44, no. 4 (2016): 373–395.

dialogue. At the same time, Williams's work discloses a theological backdrop to the issues of language within the gun debate.

GUNS, LANGUAGE, AND MORAL PSYCHOLOGY

We have truncated our ethical discussions of guns in America for reasons that are morally significant. The character of our language about guns both suppresses much of what might be said about the significances guns have for us and gives rise to distorted speech about how guns figure in our lives. While this paper focuses on diagnosing the causes of this impoverishment, in doing so it points toward a way of enriching our talk about guns.

"Guns don't kill people; people kill people," is currently a slogan employed by advocates of gun rights in order to deflect attention from the prominence of guns in the mass shootings whose frequency numbs us to the loss of life. Yet it also reflects a presupposition that underlies both sides of the debate over guns as popularly conceived: our tools and other technologies do not possess goodness or badness in themselves; it all depends on how someone uses them.

The belief that guns in themselves must be morally neutral, I claim, rests on a moral psychology and concomitant account of practical reason, the deliberation toward bringing about a human good through action. This moral psychology, in turn, funds the impoverishment of the language we use to speak of guns' significance in our lives. According to this psychology, an interior, non-bodily, capacity, such as the solitary "will" of the existentialists, is related to the body as to a tool through which it realizes its ends.

This picture of the human agent underwrites a complementary conception of the agent's practical reasoning. Just as the body becomes passive, neutral, so, with regard to practical reason, all "means" are morally indifferent to the ends sought. This psychology makes credible the claim that guns are "mere means" and that guns as such can bear no moral scrutiny at all. Indeed, it is related to a whole way of thinking often called "instrumentalism." Theologian Brad Kallenberg locates instrumentalism, together with reductionism and standardization, among the effects of "technopoly," or the ascendancy of technology in our culture.[4] He defines instrumentalism as the claim that no physical artifact has inherent moral or political properties. The only thing that can make an artifact good or bad is the use to which it is put. This implies that we should be able to make moral judgments about our actions and activities with no attention to the tools and other technologies so routinely used within them.[5]

---

[4] For a helpful discussion of instrumentalism, see Brad Kallenberg, *God and Gadgets: Following Jesus in a Technological Age* (Eugene, OR: Cascade Books, 2011), 15–20.
[5] For a compatible concept to instrumentalism or technopoly, consider Pope Francis's "technocratic paradigm," (*Laudato Si'*, no. 106).

Instrumentalism can only evaluate the means to an end as effective or ineffective. We are thus limited in what we can say about means to such adjectives as "efficient" or "inefficient." Yet as integral to the actions we perform to bring about certain ends, tools such as guns begin to enter into how we see the ends themselves. Eventually, it is through our most commonly adopted means that we come to understand the ends we seek. Recognizing that means may be inseparable from the good we seek to bring about implies that we can and should say more about them. They are worthy subjects of moral discourse and imagination, and the failure to see how some means deeply inform how we conceive our ends results in a kind of moral inarticulacy. It results in an impoverished form of speech.

A SOCIOLOGICAL PERSPECTIVE ON THE LANGUAGE OF THE GUN DEBATE IN AMERICA

The debate about guns in our society suffers from linguistic impoverishment. Lisa Fisher provides a historical and sociological perspective on this impoverishment. [6] She argues that our public debate has features designed to emphasize the divide between opposites at the extremes, while at the same time overshadowing any common ground within Americans' convictions regarding a reasonable place for guns to occupy in our way of life. These fully articulate positions at the extremes are highly refined rhetorically to promote their aims. The scripts employed reflect a simplified and essentialized message, boiled down to strategic talking points. [7] They employ a rhetoric of hostility, indeed of war, as each side proclaims itself to be "under siege" by their opponents. They are constructed, in other words, to win ground in an arena of power politics. In this mechanistic vision of public debate and politics, the only virtue is effectiveness in vanquishing one's opponents. Thus, the form of the debate sustains the strictly divided positions, making the ideas of open exchange and transformation unthinkable.

It is not hard to see that by participation in such gun discourse one naturally adopts a form of practical reasoning akin to what Charles Taylor calls "apodictic." Skill in reasoning is measured by one's ability to marshal appropriate means to achieve a goal that is "given," which is to say not itself material for reflection. It is hardly the sort of practical deliberation where truth or wisdom is thought to reside beyond any one individual's grasp, thus necessitating genuine dialogue,

---

[6] Lisa Fisher, "The Social Construction of Polarization in the Discourse of Gun Rights vs. Gun Control," in *Understanding America's Gun Culture*, ed. Craig Hovey and Lisa Fisher (Lanham, MD: Lexington Books, 2018), 1–30.

[7] Fisher, "The Social Construction," 1.

or common deliberation.[8] Noting how scholars themselves have become implicated in a dynamic that naturalizes polarization, Fisher recommends the undertaking of studies that would,

> examine the language and meaning construction employed on both sides of the debate to understand more about how it is that areas of agreement are downplayed and areas of disagreement are emphasized, as these social processes lend to continued perceptions of divisiveness and detract from the ability of those on both sides of the issue to engage in meaningful dialogue about guns in American society.[9]

My own approach seeks this goal by critically attending to the conceptions of practical reasoning underlying our discourse about guns.

My use of ethnography to illustrate the distinctions between forms of practical reasoning aims to address key features of the gun discourse identified by Fisher. The polarized discourse Fisher describes presents the other side as an enemy to be vanquished. Each side envisions its opposite as a one-dimensional subject, incapable of nuance or sympathy with those with whom it finds itself in conflict. The flip side of this flattened view of one's opponent is the perhaps uneasy feeling that one's own agency has been reduced to choosing strategic means of realizing one's own, already fully evident, desires. As a result, one's own self becomes less porous to genuine encounter with the other and less able to experience the kind of self-transformation such encounter may bring.

The ethnographic experience I present seeks to re-open this closed discourse by embodying a different kind of conversation in a few, related respects. First, given the extended family connections that link Joe to me, it can be fairly said that we both had a stake in the conversation's quality. As we met and discussed guns in his home, the common good of the family surrounded our dialogue. This contrasts to the zero-sum politics noted above.

Second, the thick description characteristic of ethnography allows one to consider the gun person's identity in light of his life-world, or environment as mediated by those things that matter to him. In some contexts, guns represent something very much like what Alasdair MacIntyre calls a "practice," where socially established activities generate a sub-community of discourse within the broader human form of life. Thick description contrasts with the polarized gun rhetoric that

---

[8] Indeed, Fisher concludes ("The Social Construction," 25) that "the conversation is dominated by the most vocal advocates on both sides of the issue, who are most committed to their positions, most likely to step forward to argue and advance their respective cause and less likely than more moderate voices to concede ground in the debate, which only underscores the polarization."

[9] Fisher, "The Social Construction," 4.

sees the opponent one-dimensionally, as simply an enemy to be conquered.

Third and related, the ethnographic approach allows for this encounter on guns to occur amidst the affections of an ongoing friendship. It is in the nature of true friendship that each of the friends undergoes transformation as the relationship endures over time. As Aristotle pointed out, the self of a true friend is in a real sense in the hands of her friend.[10] Only through the contemplation of a friend may we know ourselves. Conversation within a friendship thus contrasts with the politicized discourse described above wherein the self is both thinned out and walled in within its narrow political identity. For all of these reasons, the ethnography I present complements the philosophical analysis.

TWO WAYS OF CONCEIVING OF PRACTICAL REASON ACCORDING TO TAYLOR

Charles Taylor helps us see clearly how different conceptions of practical reason are inextricably linked together with moral psychological considerations. In "Explanation and Practical Reason," Taylor delineates and contrasts two conceptions of practical reason, "apodictic" versus "*ad hominem.*"[11] Apodictic practical reasoning according to Taylor is an offshoot of the epistemological tradition that privileges a procedural conception of reason and embraces naturalism, an ontological picture that denies the relevance of the good, or of incommensurably "higher" aims and values in human life. When it comes to moral debate, apodictic reasoning presumes the full self-consciousness and self-clarity of the interlocutors, debates—if they are to count as "rational"—will possess self-evident, fully explicit criteria for adjudicating differences, and parties will immediately recognize conditions of defeat. All this implies that moral argument takes place in a neutral field, something like a properly refereed soccer match, so that the judgment of one side as victorious will be absolute ("2-0") rather than more or less.

There are problem with this conception, Taylor avers. For one, it easily spawns moral relativism when one becomes conscious of the more plodding and protracted nature of real moral debate. For another, naturalism's projection of a neutral field of moral argument turns out to be deceptive. While naturalism's proponents seem to have eschewed the human dimension of higher goals and desires—positing a neutral field—they are actually just failing to acknowledge them in

---

[10] Aristotle, *Nichomachean Ethics*. trans. Martin Ostwald (London: Pearson, 1999), Book VIII.
[11] Charles Taylor, "Explanation and Practical Reason," *Philosophical Arguments* (Cambridge, MA: Harvard University Press, 1997), 34–60.

open speech. They have, in other words, followed a way of inarticulacy. Taylor in fact connects this moral inarticulacy, a source of apodictic practical reasoning, with the cultural phenomenon of instrumentalism.[12]

Ad hominem practical reason, by contrast, does not presuppose an imagined field of neutrality but begins with our deep commitments, or "strong evaluations" in Taylor's language. For the "self-interpreting animals"[13] Taylor believes us to be, the full and practical outworking of these deep commitments is not readily visible to us through individual introspection. We are, like Augustine said, puzzles to ourselves. An implication is that practical reasoning will often be embedded within interpersonal relationships, such as a mature or a budding friendship, where commitments are discovered and indeed transformed through time. Furthermore, Taylor claims, our moral commitments are never just ours, as our obsession with the priority of the individual may mislead us to believe. Rather, they reside within our practices, which locate us in relation to other agents. Therefore, it is in relation to our inescapable social practices that our accounts of these commitments are to be tested for faithfulness. Rather than the following of a specific procedure, the essence of practical reason is found in the attempt to answer the question, "What makes the best sense of our communal forms of life?"[14]

---

[12] In the conclusion (chapter 25) of *Sources of the Self*, Taylor discusses instrumentalism at length. He offers a reading of instrumentalism, and the controversies surrounding it, as a frame for interpreting the tensions characteristic of the modern western identity. See Charles Taylor, *Sources of the Self: The Making of the Modern Identity* (Cambridge, MA: Harvard University Press, 1989), 499–512. Further, for an important representation of Taylor's thesis tying together practical reasoning under the modern (i.e., "apodictic") conception we have been discussing with a habitual inarticulacy with regard to the higher values that motivate us, see Taylor, *Sources of the Self*, 75–90, and especially, 86–87. Tellingly, the chapter title where these pages appear is, "The Ethics of Inarticulacy."

[13] See the essay of this name in Charles Taylor, *Human Agency and Language: Philosophical Papers 1* (Cambridge, UK: Cambridge University Press, 1985), 45–76.

[14] Naturalism's presence in ethics is detectable in moral theories that claim all evaluative terms can be reduced to "descriptive" terms. Taylor argues, however, that many evaluative terms, e.g., "courage," have no descriptive equivalents, meaning that "we cannot grasp what would hold all their instances together as a class if we prescind from their evaluative point. Someone who had no sense of this point wouldn't know how to 'go on' from a range of sample cases to new ones." The connection of moral understanding and linguistic ability is clear here. A few pages later, Taylor goes on to make clear the relation of practical reason to a kind of fluency in the moral language implicit in our practices. "What needs to be said [in refutation of naturalist moral theories] can perhaps best be put in a rhetorical question: What better measure of reality do we have in human affairs than those terms which on critical reflection and after correction of the errors we can detect make the best sense of our lives? 'Making the best sense' here includes not only offering the best, most realistic orientation about the good but also allowing us best to understand and make sense of the actions and feelings of ourselves and others. For our language of deliberation is continuous with

The examples to which I now turn to defend my thesis illustrate both dimensions of practical reason: its embodied and social character and its setting within interpersonal relationships over time. The first example comes from a family gathering and helps refute instrumentalism. The story illustrates the claim that it is not sufficient to think about tools like guns as mere instruments, as one's repeated use of particular tools contributes to the production of a world of meaning. The second demonstrates the tension in the contemporary gun debate between, on the one hand, an instrumentalist understanding of guns, and, on the other, one that acknowledges their place in a socially established way of life.

EXAMPLE 1: UNCLE JOE'S GUN INTERRUPTS A FAMILY GATHERING

Typically, our inchoate understandings of the meanings of artefacts come into view only when we encounter them in unexpected places. On Christmas vacation of 2016, my wife, three children and I had come to the home of my mother-in-law where all five of my brothers and sisters-in-law had gathered for the holiday, ten adults and eight children in all. On this particular night, several first cousins were there visiting with their families. This meant the number of small children was multiplied, and since one of these cousins was recently married, a new spouse was in the mix.

The main floor of this house has space enough for three centers of activity. The dining room had two board games going atop its mammoth table, each with about five players participating, the room just off the kitchen serves those wanting to focus on conversation and catching up, while the large living room provides two activity centers: kids might gather to watch TV or to play on one side, while several adults converse or play a game on the other. This is more or less how we had arranged ourselves on this night.

Even happy families are not perfect, but this kind of gathering has always felt to me like a safe haven from the competitive world. With no goal external to being together, you can let your guard down and enjoy each other. The presence of new members—the aforementioned husband of my wife's cousin—made it also an occasion for broadening our affections.

Now in the midst of this social, familiar activity, out of the corner of my eye I spied a handgun. We were in the part of the living room opposite the TV. Joe, my sister-in-law's husband, was carrying it in the small of his back. Sitting on a high stool caused the handle to protrude upward and out from its concealment in his jeans. The positioning looked uncomfortable, and I imagine letting it come up and show

---

our language of assessment, and this with the language in which we explain what people do and feel" (Taylor, *Sources of the Self,* 54, 56–57).

itself was a fair trade for a bit of relief. Or did Joe mean to let us see it?

The sight stopped me in my tracks, and I absented myself from his vicinity, craving space to process. Safe in the bathroom I tried to get a handle on my feelings, or at least recover my composure. My emotions changed from shock to anger. As I have already mentioned, guns represent a foreign world to me; it was as though I had been somehow tricked into playing on unfamiliar turf: something in the rules that constitute the relations we had been enjoying had suddenly changed. The anger I felt was born of my sense of powerlessness to respond. Was this an intentional "move" on Joe's part? If so, what did it mean? I found myself fantasizing about "fighting back" with the only weapon available to me: words. Joe never went to college, so I felt some advantage when it comes to verbal sparring. Perhaps I could "cut him down to size" in return for surreptitiously placing himself in what I took to be the "high place" of social authority. Clearly, I had already interpreted his game in an uncharitable light.

But why the "high place"? The term suggests a hierarchical social setting, yet my earlier description of family gatherings suggested that they lack such jockeying for power that is constitutive of other social events. That is what makes them so joyous. Some other dimension of, or intrusion upon, the gathering was being revealed here—something in contradiction with the simple joy described above. But what to make of it?

I can now see how some of the terms I grasped at to interpret Joe's gun were supplied by American culture wars—terms whose ubiquity can infect even moments of simple joy, causing one to feel on one's guard against signs that one's largely unreflected political sensibilities are being challenged. But here I wish to focus on a different and more basic question. How might my immediate response to Joe's gun reveal something about the social significance of guns for us? That is, how are guns embedded within and productive of worlds of shared meanings?

RECLAIMING THE BODY: THE WORLD OUTSIDE YOUR HEAD

In his recent book *The World Beyond Your Head: On Becoming an Individual in an Age of Distraction*, Matthew Crawford explores the nature of human attention.[15] He focuses especially on how, through bodily engagement in our physical surroundings, we come to be a certain kind of self or agent inhabiting a world that answers to our abilities. He is especially interested in how tools extend our bodies into the environment, shaping those environments in terms of the significances

---

[15] Mathew Crawford, *The World Beyond Your Head: On Becoming an Individual in an Age of Distraction* (New York: Farrar, Straus and Giroux, 2015), 45–68.

they hold for us. Tools can open up a world to our perception by training us to attend to our environments differently. Ultimately, Crawford's work helps us to see tool use as formative, in the sense of shaping what the user recognizes as valuable and thus leading her to inhabit
a particular world of significances.

Crawford's insights shed light on the particular joy I have experienced in the course of my relationship with Joe. Joe is handy, having
formerly worked as cabinet-maker and now as an operator of heavy
equipment. Being an intellectual, I have enjoyed talking to him about
topics where either he is more of an expert—construction, car and mo-
torcycle mechanics—or brings a non-academic perspective, such as
the politics of the workplace, and even theology. I have found that,
seeing the world as a craftsman, Joe has an intimacy with aspects of
the built environment I lack and a wonder about the physical world
that I have not.[16] I once stood mesmerized in his workshop amongst a
great variety of tools, all impeccably ordered, a library of sorts. I find
Joe's perspective frequently illuminates me, while remaining to a degree strange. The variety of topics on which I have found our discussions fruitful further implies that Joe's formation as a craftsman is not
merely of local importance—not just limited to interactions with and
knowledge of physical artefacts—but informs his thinking about the
other subjects as well.

Because of his familiarity with the world of tools and craftsman-
ship, Joe provides me with a window into a world different from my
own. We exist in more or less the same physical surroundings, but his
skill development—the shaping of his attention, Crawford would
say—has made him more discerning of this world under certain aspects. Of course, this also means that we live, to an extent, in different
worlds. If tools account for part of the way the world appears to us, it
would follow that Joe's love of guns—their handling, firing, even
building his collection of them—creates a real if not unbridgeable distance in the worlds we inhabit.

Crawford's work also calls attention to the way worlds of experience are worlds "for us," shared worlds that we inhabit as social animals. He asks us to consider the typical, institutional painted walls
such as the ones in the library where he sits working on his book. What
color are they? Well, who's asking? Perhaps the occasion is an art
class, and the instructor asks his students this question in order to get
them to see as a painter sees. Such looking would ultimately find, depending on the time of day, various shades created by patches of light
and shadow. But why, in ordinary circumstances, if a patron were

---

[16] On a recent family outing, Joe and I hiked into the rain forest on the Olympic Pen-
insula. As I soaked in the awesome fir trees silently, he found myriad forms of life,
from the forest floor to heights of the canopy, worthy of attention—and photographs.

asked the color of the walls in the reading room, would she automatically respond, "They're beige!"? It is because, Crawford explains, our ordinary perceptions are mediated by familiarity with social conventions. One such convention is the way contracted painters come in with buckets full of a single color and roll it on.[17]

When I saw the gun and holster in the small of Joe's back I was for a moment, jarred and disoriented. It wasn't only the object *qua* object that grabbed hold of my attention; indeed, I already knew what guns look like. It was also that this gun was out of place. I have been formed to look at guns as belonging in a particular context, one that couldn't be made to align with the "safe haven" of our family gathering. My own social training has led me to understand the fitting context for guns to involve police officers and soldiers, not ordinary citizens and most definitely not family members on the occasion of a holiday get together. Furthermore, the way I was trained to think of guns is rooted in my identity which is equally socially constructed. My shock and even anger on this occasion had much to do with this challenging of how I was trained to look at things. I was socially disoriented. Thus, my reaction was not simply to challenge Joe's judgment, but to bring the rest of society's judgment to bear on Joe's actions. I wanted to express that Joe's behavior was out of sync with what "we" take to be normal.

Thus, if Joe's familiarity with guns has led him to be able to perceive the world under certain aspects that are not "on my radar screen," it is nevertheless equally true that he and I live in a shared world, one constituted in part by social practices. Our knowledge of guns is always already mediated by their inclusion in such practices. While we participate in different social practices, one in which Joe and I both participate is that of family. What's more, this combination of difference and commonality frames the challenge of our discussion of guns and their significance. It indicates both the difficulty and the unavoidability of negotiating the stakes we had in simply being present at the family gathering.

Both aspects of this encounter—the way the use of tools is world-shaping and how worlds so shaped are unavoidably social—weigh against the claims of instrumentalism. That guns *qua* tools have a place within world-shaping practices so that their meanings are never merely private but also part of a socially negotiated space implies that instrumentalism misrepresents their significance.

---

[17] As Crawford notes, to see the blotches of distinct shades is in fact to dig underneath normal perception. Individuals who see the shades, as an artist does, have in fact gone through a sort of training, the first stage of which is to "un-see" in the normal way. A popular picture suggests to us that perception is rightly understood by beginning with static images recorded by the retina. These images are then somehow arranged to form the composite image we report when asked. This loses sight of the connection between seeing and *training*. Crawford, (*The World Beyond Your Head*, 143–144).

Still, what determines whether, or to what extent, the negotiations of our differences in a world that Joe and I are destined to inhabit together becomes the occasion of joy or consternation? The decisive factor would seem to be our openness to each other, across these differences.

EXAMPLE 2: CONTINUING THE DIALOGUE WITH UNCLE JOE ON GUNS

After a year or two of reflecting on the night of the family gathering in light of some academic research on gun culture, I engaged Joe in a direct discussion of guns. When I asked Joe for research purposes to teach me the basics of guns in the summer 2019, he surprised me a bit by the enthusiasm of his "yes." He apparently relishes the opportunity to give newbies a proper introduction, even those he would rightly surmise to be highly suspicious of guns and gun ownership such as myself. In addition to being highly disciplined in his approach, I found him to be deeply knowledgeable about the physics of guns. He asserted, moreover, that the goal of such training is to be found in the employment of guns for sport and implied that when people start shooting at each other the world has, in effect, been turned upside down. I know that he practices target shooting and other gun skills, and he was drawing on many previous experiences of teaching this course in gun basics when I entered his "classroom" (i.e., his dining room).

Our session began with Joe behooving me to use the term "firearm" rather than "gun," and the importance of proper vocabulary re-surfaced throughout. He pointed out that what I was tempted to call a "bullet" was actually the "cartridge," and what I wanted to refer to as the "handle" was the "grip." He was further adamant to distinguish the oft-misused "clip" from the "magazine." Clearly, for him, proper terminology closely correlates with proper understanding, as one cannot hope to arrive at the latter without developing good linguistic habits. I further came to see that the goal of this part of the lesson was to prod me to attend to the gun as a machine, a physical artifact, and to remove the mystique guns have for such as me. In this case, what we were handling was a CZ 9mm pistol. The technically correct terminology promotes a sense of sober realism about guns. With this comes a sense of seriousness and respect. Yet I wondered what kind of moral myth about guns Joe presumed I had been clinging to.

In line with his seriousness about guns, I found that Joe's approach to his guns was characterized by strict discipline. This was reflected in the first stage of the lesson where Joe presented me with a yellow card with the four basic rules of "Gun Safety" printed on it. They include, "1. All guns are always loaded; 2. Never point the gun at anything you are not willing to destroy; 3. Keep your finger off the trigger until your sights are on the target; 4. Be sure of your target and what's beyond it." That he had these cards ready to hand testifies to Joe's commitment to "basic firearms training" as well as his seriousness about guns. For Joe it is possible, and necessary, to keep guns within a rule-governed arena.

Joe's demeanor through the lesson was not only serious and precise but also warm and welcoming. I mentioned above that I was a "newbie" to be brought into greater understanding of guns. The pace of the lesson was measured, a clear sign of his intention to provide a comfortable and caring learning environment. Joe is a natural teacher, one who meets students where they are and provides space and encouragement for growth. There was also a sense in which Joe was trying to ease the newcomer's fear of guns as such and convert it into a respect that would permit a greater intimacy with them. Finally, Joe intimated that he saw himself as a kind of emissary from the community of gun owners to an outsider. My fear of guns was partly responsible for my suspicion of the gun owner community. His warmth, then, was equivalent to an act of diplomacy. Indeed, he was offering his welcome on behalf of the gun community.

PRACTICAL REASON, LANGUAGE, AND INARTICULACY IN OUR SPEECH ABOUT GUNS

Moral debate about guns has been hampered by the influence of instrumentalism. Instrumentalism, moreover, shapes our conception of practical reasoning by dichotomizing the agent into "body" and "mind," indeed making of the body little more than an instrument to do the will's bidding. Flowing from this comes a conception of practical reason where means are never recognized as constitutive of the end but merely more or less efficient ways to bring it about. Instrumentalism furthermore removes the human agent from the matrix of shared, social understandings. As a result, the arena of practical reasoning is imagined as a neutral playing field populated by equal (and equally transparent) players, the frictionless minds of modern epistemology. Contrast this with actual situations of dialogue where socially established practices, permeated by shared understandings, set boundaries for what can reasonably be claimed.

In a sense, both of these approaches are present in my gun lesson with Joe. The instrumentalist or apodictic approach can be discerned in the way Joe speaks of guns primarily as neat, if dangerous, mechanical devices, and the social practice approach can be found in the way Joe clearly viewed our encounter as an opportunity to welcome me into the new family of gun-people as well as an occasion to generate good will across the divide between gun-people and non-gun people. But, as I will argue, the inability to identify, to name, this tension between instrumentalist and non-instrumentalist understandings is precisely one of the factors holding the debate back.

Speaking the Language of Mechanism

Turning back to the experience of my firearms instruction with Joe, a first area to consider is the self-conscious attentiveness to language characteristic of Joe's approach to guns. Joe was careful to call each component of a gun—or, rather, a "firearm"—by its proper name. The technical character of such terms—"grip" and "cartridge"—mediates viewing guns as mechanisms, and the mechanical viewpoint carries a sense of seriousness and objectivity. The aura of objectivity was, I believe, one reason for Joe's being particular about words. Of special interest here is how such mechanical discourse about guns informs discussions of their social import.

Joe is impressively articulate about how a gun works; he sees, we might say, the "telos" of a gun qua mechanical instrument quite clearly. When the gun is understood, that is, in terms of its mechanical function—i.e., what it "does" and how—one ought to praise Joe's knowledge. His articulate knowledge at this level, as displayed in my account of our dialogue above, links guns themselves to a broader family of mechanical instruments in which he situated them. For instance, broaching the topic of highly dangerous contraptions in general, he spoke of how guns contrast with explosives and generally to chemical substances that in combination are highly dangerous. Guns, mechanically speaking, he suggested are better compared with other propelling devices such a sling-shots, even the human arm and hand "loaded" with a rock, than with explosives. He spoke as an engineer. Joe did not altogether avoid acknowledging the power of guns, reflected in their effects upon targeted objects. Yet he used relatively cold terms in this regard, such as the verb "destroy" within his rule #2, "Never point the gun at something you are unwilling to destroy." The dramatic difference between destroying, say, an empty coffee can versus a human head is left unuttered.

This assumes that what a gun is "for" is circumscribed by its character as mechanical instrument. Where the limits of this mode of speech about guns become apparent is where the meaning of guns goes beyond the mechanical to the social. If I place the discussion of the mechanical similarities of guns to slingshots and even to a human arm in the context of two gun collectors conversing about design, or maybe about the history of gun engineering, we may rightly admire the savvy on display. Yet Joe's insistence on the relevance of gun mechanics to another kind of discussion—namely, the discussion we once had about whether we needed more rigorous legal restrictions to protect us from gun violence—ought to unsettle. To be clear, in this latter context Joe's reference to the mechanics of guns as being like human hands and unlike explosive devices, diverts attention from their use as effective killing machines. Indeed, any frank review of the history of guns would reveal that the objective of killing other humans is evident within their design as mechanical instruments.[18] Joe as much as admitted this when he explained to me the basic difference between handguns and rifles from a performance perspective, the former maximizing maneuverability for short range skirmishes and the latter accuracy at a distance.

What is left out of Joe's knowledgeable speech about guns as mechanical artifacts? Precisely the social significance of the degrees of lethality just about any impartial observer might note as she considers "artifacts" from semi-automatic handguns to sling-shots to a human hand throwing a rock or a punch. Joe would admit that violence or destruction is a possible end found in each of these "instruments" but remained curiously muted about the markedly disparate potential for degree and intensity of harm "built into" the gun. His refusal leads further to a failure to attend seriously to the varied motivations that might cause persons to want to acquire guns (of various kinds); guns remain a mere curiosity, a hobby, for Joe. In sum, Joe's knowledge of guns as mechanical artifacts, then, fails to also see guns in terms of their social "ends."

Joe is impressively articulate about how a gun works, identifying the "telos" of a gun qua mechanical instrument quite clearly. When the gun is understood merely as a mechanical artifact, Joe's erudition is laudable. But, again, this assumes that the gun's telos is exhausted by its character as mechanical instrument. Yet the telos of the gun as a *social* artifact discloses another and quite different arena in which the task of making linguistic sense of guns is correspondingly distinct. To grasp the gun's social telos requires another kind of linguistic skill and awareness. Indeed, what seems to be needed is a kind of bifocal vision or ability to move between the mechanical and social where necessary.

Some unconscious motivation seems to be pressuring Joe to suppress the incommensurable, and differently complex, set of questions that necessarily accompany speech about guns as socially meaningful objects. The failure to note the transition from mechanical to moral vocabularies bespeaks a motivated suppression of unquestionably relevant material for moral consideration. What does this suppression have to do with the underlying ethical structures I identified earlier in this essay? The moral psychology of instrumentalism provides ground for thinking of guns primarily as mechanisms, as morally neutral tools. Instrumentalism thus funds the popular moral rhetoric—"guns don't kill people; people kill people"—that aids and abets this discursive

---

[18] For an illuminating account of how gun makers adapted their production and marketing strategies to capitalize on emergent fears about crime and social unrest, see Evan Osnos, "Making a Killing: The Business and Politics of Selling Guns," *New Yorker*, June 26, 2016, www.newyorker.com/magazine/2016/06/27/after-orlando-examining-the-gun-business.

suppression by lending an aura of moral legitimacy to those who speak this way. The apodictic conception of practical reason that fails to acknowledge its own grounding in social practices and sees all means as equally arbitrary steps to attain an end can thus be seen as an undercurrent within Joe's attentiveness to terminology, or his favoring in these circumstances the language of mechanics for a discussion of guns.[19]

Our concepts are thus helpful in diagnosing what is hampering the debate. A questionable model of practical reasoning is intimately related to an importantly incomplete understanding of what our guns mean for us. Apodictic practical reasoning captures the mechanical aspects of guns but in a language that obscures the wider context of human goods that are indeed relevant. Yet the same discussion between Joe and me, in other respects, tacitly acknowledged the social dimension of guns.

Welcome to the Family

An additional facet of my gun lesson with Joe to reflect on in the light of our ethical tools is suggested by the warm and welcoming tone of the encounter. I noted above the generous attitude Joe adopted as teacher. He shared with me later that day his prayer that my mind may have been brightened by his teaching and that, if he had succeeded in changing my ill opinion of guns, I might, in turn, represent them to my students in a good light. One dimension of this welcome goes beyond the student-teacher relationship to signify Joe's offering me an introduction to, if not an induction into, a community that provides its

---

[19] A similar point is illustrated by a related discussion Joe and I had about the design of certain firearms. I found Joe to equivocate in his answer to the question of whether firearms are "meant for destruction." For instance, we were going over safety rules—specifically the rule never to point the gun at anything you are not willing to destroy—when the topic of people shooting guns at one another came up. Joe pretended the idea of people using guns against other people to be strange and abhorrent, an anomaly. Yet I noted that much of our discussion of the functionality of rifles—which provide excellent accuracy—versus handguns—superior in maneuverability—seemed to presuppose self-defense or attack with regard to other people as the backdrop (at least the paradigmatic backdrop, as certain sports can be imagined to likewise value these qualities in distinct guns). Like the example of a preference for mechanical language, the discussion of design I believe reflects the pressures toward inarticulacy coming from the first conception of practical reason. A motivation, and consequence, for Joe's equivocation regarding gun design might again be a desire not to have to attend to the violent motivations that might naturally lead persons to acquire guns. Put differently, were Joe not held captive by the instrumentalist conception of practical reasoning, such that guns figure as mere instruments, might he not see that handguns especially have certain "will," certain ends, embedded within their design—such that their features cannot be adequately described without value-rich vocabulary: the willing of ends that, if he must acknowledge them, he would be sure to find worrisome?

members with a distinctive social identity. Joe saw his task as to "familiarize" me with guns, both in the sense of overcoming ignorance and supplanting alienation with friendship.

Gun ownership stands in constitutive relationship with a certain socially generated identity. Evidence for this is that Joe enjoyed talking about what made the paradigmatic gun owner an exemplary person. That is, our lesson about guns naturally led to the issue of the kind of discipline a gun owner ought to cultivate. An avid movie watcher, Joe enthusiastically acknowledged the aptness of my allusion to Karate Kid to illustrate the claim that with the acquisition of superior destructive power comes the obligation for superior discipline. On the other hand, Joe's go-to example of gun wielders lacking the requisite discipline, and thus tarnishing the image of gun users in the minds of the ignorant, were kids in the "inner city" whose ostentatious displays of bravado were tell-tale signs of failure to embody the character befitting of a gun owner.

In a similar vein, an MA student of mine for whom guns have been part of the furniture of the world since early childhood responded to a writing assignment by describing marksmanship as a MacIntyrean practice,[20] making reference to how the ethos of a shooting range is cooperative, requiring and developing trust among marksmen that they will exercise heightened vigilance and care for each other's safety, animated by a practitioner's tacit grasp of the purpose behind the rules of behavior established for the shooting range. He went on to describe how marksmen recognize select experts as embodying the highest standards of excellence within the practice, the habits of mentorship commonly found in order to train new members of the community, and a shared history outlining how the practice has evolved over time. He concluded that marksmanship named a community where virtues are developed.

How do we make sense of such testimonies that guns are connected to morally formative communities? *Ad hominem* practical reasoning makes clear how our habitual means, including tools, are part of the moral picture. They are not merely instrumental to, but also *constitutive of*, the ends themselves. Furthermore, ethics is not restricted to evaluating the allegedly solitary will. The moral agent is an embodied agent, actively involved in the surrounding world. How one engages the world shapes how one knows it and how one is disposed to act within it. Thus, on this conception of practical reasoning the moral life is viewed as one of ongoing formation, where our actions and our characters inform each other with an ultimate end, a "telos," providing direction for the journey.

---

[20] For Alasdair MacIntyre's now classic definition of a practice, see *After Virtue: A Study in Moral Theory* (Notre Dame, IN: University of Notre Dame Press, 1982), 187.

In an email exchange, Joe and I had broached the issue of "mistakes" made by armed individuals, on this occasion a police officer's shooting of an unarmed young person. I suggested that simply holding a gun affects what appears "relevant" to a situation, shaping one's instantaneous answer to the question, "what is going on?" In support of my suggestion, I attached a psychological study linking the mere holding of a gun to the misperception of objects as threatening in one's visual field. Joe was unwilling to even enter such a discussion. Rather, he shut it down directly by simply noting that I seemed to be moralizing gun ownership. "You seem to be suggesting guns are bad." My suggestion, implying that the gun-to-gun wielder relation is a two-way street, would of course challenge the moral freedom of the instrumentalist's disembodied will, a key feature of this moral psychology.

As the gun lesson demonstrates, correlative to the social identity of the gun owner is an idea of proper discipline, both as a means to and a reflection of socially recognized moral character. Yet, the pressure to view guns as mere tools subverts the very idea that there is a kind of moral character proper to a gun owner. For in our discourse, the former serves to keep guns out of the moral equation, and this puts all of the discussion of practices and histories connected with guns off limits. In sum, a kind of cognitive dissonance should arise for anyone who attempts to think at one time both along instrumentalist and moral community lines. Our conceptual tools have helped us to unearth two modes of understanding that exist side by side within our discourse about guns. One mode involves seeing guns primarily as mechanical instruments or human artifacts. Another mode views them first and foremost as a part of the way "we" live, as implicated in a moral community. It seems that our ability to readily name and identify this tension within our speech about guns is critical, a necessary condition for that bifocal vision mentioned above. For, as we have seen, it is possible to muddle along unawares of this contradiction in our thinking and dispositions toward guns.

One reason a participant in this debate might have for failing to acknowledge this tension has to do with the attractiveness of the ideals of freedom and self-transparency held out by the apodictic model of practical reasoning. A symptom of the ubiquity of instrumentalism in our lives is that we idealize a "freedom" that is predicated on the ability to raise ourselves above the social practices and common understandings in which our lives are lived. This conception of freedom makes sense against a historical background focusing on western politics and science. On one hand, gaining freedom from traditional political authorities whose power was legitimated by traditional beliefs required a new epistemology where the individual would take responsibility for what and how she believes.[21] On the other, the success achieved by modern science through de-personalizing the forces of nature led moral philosophers to aspire to a similar objectivity, resulting ultimately in an impersonal "morality." These two forms of freedom feed the picture of moral freedom as self-transparency and disengagement reflected in instrumentalism.

Put differently, to engage in *ad hominem* practical reasoning is to risk exposing one's commitments and facing the fact that by virtue of these one is always already bound to others. Learning to acknowledge the limits of our control over our identities exposes us to certain risks, foremost perhaps that of becoming vulnerable to transformation. Once opened in this way, there is no clear limit to what one may discover to be implicated in the construction of our identities. Openness to *ad hominem* dialogue about guns in America could easily broach the issues of how our histories of racial and gender injustice have shaped our identities. In my reference to discipline above, I noted that Joe used the term "inner city" as short hand for undisciplined gun owners. Yet, antiracist studies point out that the term "inner city" has become a kind of code—the meaning of which we perhaps hide even from ourselves—for African Americans. Thus, when considered in light of practical reason that recognizes constitutive means, racism too becomes a relevant, perhaps inescapable, subject matter when it comes to our guns. We become thus not only vulnerable to one another but vulnerable in relation to our own histories.[22] A greater awareness of the problem has the potential to be the beginning of a richer dialogue.

Before concluding, I turn to a short consideration of the work of Rowan Williams to address the question of language's relation to risk and transformation. Williams's contribution becomes relevant when it becomes clear that to move forward into a richer dialogue between gun people and non-gun people requires a willingness of the participants to risk exposure and change at a personal level.

ROWAN WILLIAMS ON LANGUAGE AND GRACE
Rowan Williams's work on language and art allows us to address the roots of our resistance to the kind of risk implied by *ad hominem*

---

[21] For a brief and helpful summary of this history, see Matthew Crawford, "How We Lost Our Attention," *The Hedgehog Review* 16, no. 2 (2014): hedgehogreview.com/issues/minding-our-minds/articles/how-we-lost-our-attention.

[22] For an ethnographic study that presents guns in the context of de-industrialization, race, and gender, see Jennifer Carlson, *Citizen Protectors: The Everyday Politics of Guns in an Age of Decline* (Oxford: Oxford University Press, 2015). See also Jennifer Carlson, "The Equalizer? Crime, Vulnerability and Gender in Pro-Gun Discourse," *Feminist Criminology* 9, no. 1 (2013): 59–83.

practical reasoning.[23] It permits us to address the question, "Why is it that human beings use language to protect ourselves?" In other words, Williams finds a tension within human language use itself. To explain this, he finds it necessary to distinguish two forms of linguistic behavior, which roughly map onto Taylor's apodictic and *ad hominem* conceptions of practical reasoning. "Description" names the use of language to map one's surroundings for orientational and practical purposes. It is akin to the instrumental character of apodictic reasoning. The trouble comes when Description becomes reductionism, the willful limiting of reality to what fits my own purposes or interests, manifesting an underlying craving for control. We saw elements of this in Joe's speaking about guns as mechanisms. "Representation," by contrast, sees language use as participation in a reality truly other than the self, such that "the known object is active in the knowing subject beyond the knowing subject's full grasp." [24] Representational uses of language, for examples of which Williams turns to the arts and especially novels, have the capacity to enlarge the self as they transfigure the world. Just as Taylor's apodictic practical reason mirrors Williams's Description by presuming the full availability of the good in human consciousness, so Taylor's *ad hominem*, likening practical reasoning to bringing inchoate evaluations into greater articulacy, resembles Williams's Representation. Both have role for self-discovery within relationships lived out over time.

According to Williams, our craving for Description's predictability stems from a profound fear that our sense of self and world is under threat. In the case of my relationship with Joe, this fear manifests as the willingness to suppress the tension created by embracing by turns an instrumentalist and a community focused understanding of guns, rather than grappling with it, since to do so would require deeper examination of the sources of one's identity. Williams, in a lecture on the *Gilead* novels of Marilynne Robinson, notes that the resistance to give up control gives rise to and finds protection in a "moral" identity that invokes a sense of membership in a community of other "good people" of the most toxic sort.[25] This too maps onto some aspects of

---

[23] Williams' most prolonged treatment of language use can be found in his Gifford Lectures; Rowan Williams, *The Edge of Words: God and the Habits of Language* (London: Bloomsbury, 2014).

[24] Language as Representation, Williams writes, "absorb[s] the life of what is encountered at a level that makes it possible both to recognize and to represent that life in another form" (Williams, *Edge of Words*, 60).

[25] Williams elaborates that what he means by an identity based upon "goodness" is one where the "I" or "We" defines itself on the basis of what I/we do right, graces of our behavior. The emphasis lies on what the I/We have done, in order to be or become the virtuous sort of people we are, whether the reference be to one's individual moral heroism, one's refined upbringing/education, or one's family's honor. For the good Christian folks of Gilead, it is sometimes about accounting for the way they have been "blessed." Williams calls this phenomenon, and the identity based upon it, "toxic

Joe's invocation of a gun community, as when he ritually extended a welcome to me to begin to join such a community through our gun lesson and subsequent discussions. Of course, it must be said that toxic community construction can and does easily come into being among non-gun people as well.

So, argues Williams, we find ourselves in the paradoxical position of having to turn to language in order to free ourselves from the effects of language. What is needed is that use of language that shows us the associations through which we are always already implicated in the lives of others. Here, Williams turns to novels as exemplary. The conversion required by reading such good literary works, he argues, involves learning to see the other, the one we have identified as a threat, as in fact a source of grace. I add that only such an insight, the kind that what Williams calls "Christian literary witness" may provide, is likely to get us to take the risk required for a deeper, a transformational, debate about guns. In short, language as Representation means seeing our own deeper participation in reality as precisely what would save us.

What, then, are the implications of the distinction between language as Description and as Representation for Joe and me? On one hand, I have noted some resemblance between the "gun community" to which Joe welcomed me and the protective, insular life that flows from Description and Instrumentalism at their worst. This is most apparent when a simplistic binary of bad guys and good guys is used to define boundaries, but it often comes in more subtle versions. Yet there is too the possibility that this very sense of communal identity includes the resources for deeper social searching, a fruitful awareness of its own implicatedness in the reality of its human other. Further, the temptation is equally present for non-gun people to write off gun people using definitions that are equally deceptive in their clarity. Representation, on the other hand, reminds us of the need for a language that displays the shared character of our world, which for us both I am afraid means facing our painful histories, including their elements of race and gender injustice.

---

goodness." It is sustained by a repression of how the I/We is implicated in lives of those others against whom it defines itself. Thus, Williams names the purpose of Christian literature like Robinson's novels as "to reconnect goodness to reality." Rowan Williams, "Address to 2018 Theology Conference at Wheaton College," YouTube, www.youtube.com/watch?v=R58Q_Q3KEnM&t=2311s. Portions of the program were published in *Christian Century*. See, "Faith, Imagination, and the Glory of Ordinary Life: Marilynne Robinson and Rowan Williams in Conversation," *Christian Century*, March 25, 2019, www.christiancentury.org/article/interview/faith-imagination-and-glory-ordinary-life.

CONCLUSION: A MORE SELF-AWARE DIALOGUE

Our debate about guns in America is stymied. I have argued that the study of ethics can help us diagnose silences and distortions in the debate and help point a way forward. In particular, a critique of the ethical concepts undergirding our discussions of guns helps us to see that these concepts both suppress much of what might be said in regard to guns and give rise to a certain tension between, on one hand, an instrumental reading of guns and, on the other, a social understanding of them. In this paper, I have explored how a conception of practical reason shaped by instrumentalism (or "apodictic practical reason") funds this tension, as well as why *ad hominem* practical reasoning allows us to name it, a first step toward a richer debate. Finally, I briefly treated the work of Rowan Williams on language as shedding light on the risks of self-exposure that must be accepted if we are to move forward into the richer discussion about the place of guns in our common life toward which *ad hominem* practical reasoning points. ■

Mark Ryan received his PhD in Religious Ethics at the University of Virginia (2006). He has been nurtured in his work by the thought of Alasdair MacIntyre, Stanley Hauerwas, and Rowan Williams. He has been teaching moral theology and business ethics as a Lecturer at the University of Dayton since 2014 and serves as a member of the Catholic and Marianist Identity Committee of the School of Business Administration at the University of Dayton.

Journal of Moral Theology, Vol. 11, No. 1 (2022): 107–130

Aquinas's Unity Thesis and Grace: Ingredients for Developing a Good Appetite in a Contemporary Age

Megan Heeder

CONTEMPORARY AMERICAN SOCIETY IS pervaded by images of thinness such that one's perception of one's beauty and value are often linked to how skinny one is. Numerous women (and men) struggle with society's focus on thinness and its impact on their perception of themselves and their bodies. This struggle has been an area of focus for moral theologian Beth Haile who turns to Aquinas's conception of virtue, connatural knowledge, and grace as she engages the moral theological tradition to suggest how women might respond to the consequences of living in a society supremely focused on thinness. While Haile's work is groundbreaking and visionary, the burgeoning storm of social media in the eleven years since her dissertation's publication necessitates returning to Haile's work both to plumb its riches and consider how it might be implemented in and expanded for a contemporary age.

In this paper's first section, I survey the eating disorder landscape in the United States. Next, I analyze the strengths and potential for growth in Beth Haile's Thomistic treatment of eating disorders in the contemporary age. The third part of the paper reviews current literature on Aquinas's unity thesis which offers a response to the contemporary age's challenges. Aquinas's thesis presents the virtues as growing together, moderated by prudence, in the larger context of God's grace. Attending to the collective growth of the virtues provides a way to respond to the difficulties and effects of living in a society hyperfocused on thinness as a marker of beauty. The final section of the paper applies the unity thesis contextualized in grace to the process of navigating eating disorders in a contemporary context, particularly as a response to the challenges presented by thin-ideal images present on the internet and social media. Examples in this paper's fourth part illustrate the role of unified virtue and grace in women's struggles with eating disorders.

EATING DISORDERS IN THE US

Current statistics indicate that around thirty million people of varying ages and genders suffer from an eating disorder in the United States.[1] Specific types of eating disorders occur at distinct rates. Anorexia (the most deadly eating disorder) impacts somewhere between 1 percent to 5.2 percent of young women.[2] Both anorexia and bulimia have been found to present life-long struggles for about 5 percent of the population.[3] While often viewed as less severe or threatening, nonspecified eating disorders occur frequently and present particular challenges. Nonspecified eating disorders (including less-severe forms of

[1] "Eating Disorder Statistics," ANAD (National Association of Anorexia Nervosa and Associated Disorders), anad.org/education-and-awareness/about-eating-disorders/eating-disorders-statistics/.

[2] In "Eating Disorders," in *Child and Adolescent Psychopathology*, ed. Theodore Beauchaine and Stephen Linshaw (New York: Wiley, 2012), 715–738, Eric Stice and Cara Bohon determine that between 0.9 percent and 2.0 percent of females and 0.1 percent to 0.3 percent of males will develop anorexia at some point in their lives. Subthreshold anorexia occurs in 1.1 percent to 3.0 percent of adolescent females. In "Epidemiology and Course of Anorexia Nervosa in the Community," *American Journal of Psychiatry*, 164, no. 8 (2007): 1259–1265, doi: 10.1176/appi.ajp.2007.06081388, Anna Keski-Rahkonen et. al arrived at more conservative findings (with a more limited definition of what constitutes an eating disorder), suggesting that anorexia nervosa presents itself among young women at a rate of between 0.3–0.4 percent and among young men at a rate of 0.1 percent. In "The Prevalence and Correlates of Eating Disorders in the National Comorbidity Survey Replication," *Biological Psychiatry* 61, no. 3 (2007): 348–358, doi: 10.1016/j.biopsych.2006.03.040, James Hudson, Eva Hiripi, Harrison G. Pope, Jr., and Ronald C. Kessler asked 9,282 English-speaking Americans about a range of mental health conditions, including eating disorders (maintaining a broader definition of eating disorders). The study found that 0.9 percent of women and 0.3 percent of men had anorexia during their life. In "An 8-Year Longitudinal Study of the Natural History of Threshold, Subthreshold, and Partial Eating Disorders from Community Sample of Adolescents," *Journal of Abnormal Psychology* 118, no. 3 (2010): 587–597, doi: 10.1037/a00164, Eric Stice, C. Nathan Marti, Heather Shaw, and Maryanne Jaconis followed 496 adolescent girls from age 12 to 20 and found that 5.2 percent of the girls met criteria for DSM-5 anorexia, bulimia, or binge eating disorder. When the researchers expanded their criteria for eating disorders to include nonspecific eating disorder symptoms, a total of 13.2 percent of the girls were found to have suffered from a DSM-5 eating disorder by age 20. It is worth noting that likely due to cultural expectations and pressures, women are more often diagnosed with eating disorders than men, and subsequently this paper will focus on the experience of women with eating disorders. However, NEDA's website indicates that from 1999 to 2009, the number of men hospitalized for an eating disorder-related cause increased by 53 percent. Researchers seem to believe this increase is indicative of a greater acceptance of the occurrence of eating disorders among men, as opposed to eating disorders quantitatively increasing among men. It has been noted that diagnosis often occurs later for men because sociocultural stereotypes classify eating disorders as a "woman's disease." Further statistics on this topic can be found on NEDA's website.

[3] "Eating Disorders," Cleveland Clinic, www.clevelandclinicmeded.com/medical-pubs/diseasemanagement/psychiatry-psychology/eating-disorders/.

anorexia that may fall below the typical diagnosis threshold, binge-ing/purging, over-exercising paired with calorie restriction for medi-cally-unnecessary weight loss, use of laxatives, etc.) persist at a rate of about 5 percent for both youth and adults.[4] The diagnosis of a non-specified eating disorder is often considered to be less extreme than a diagnosis of anorexia, bulimia, or other eating disorders, yet studies find that those with nonspecified eating disorders experience in-creased anxiety compared to those diagnosed with anorexia. Nonspec-ified eating disorders persist for a lifetime for about 5 percent of the population and constitute 50 percent of eating disorder diagnoses.[5]

Preoccupation with weight and body image begin at a very early age in the US. By the time young girls turn six, they begin to express concern about their weight or body shape: 40-60 percent of girls in elementary school (ages 6–12) are concerned about their weight or about becoming too fat.[6] While studies involving social media's influ-ence on body dissatisfaction are limited, magazines' influence on body image has been well-documented. Of the elementary school-age girls who read magazines in the US, 69 percent say that the pictures influ-ence their concept of the ideal body shape and 47 percent say that the pictures make them want to lose weight.[7] While recognizing the com-plexity of factors that influence the development of eating disorders, the best-known environmental contributor to the formation of eating disorders is the sociocultural idealization of thinness.[8] The thin-ideal is particularly prevalent on the internet and in social media, and young people use both at rapidly increasing rates. The Nielsen Company, a US-based global marketing and research firm that tracks media habits and internet-use trends across the world, found that the average Amer-ican spends upwards of eleven hours a day using media—which is

---

[4] Daniel Le Grange, Sonja Swanson, Scott Crow, and Kathleen Merikangas, "Eating Disorder not Otherwise Specified Presentation in the US Population," *The International Journal of Eating Disorders* 45, no. 5 (2012): 712, doi:10.1002/eat.22006. Sub-sequent citations in this paragraph draw from this study unless otherwise noted.

[5] While the effects of eating disorders on self-identity and confidence are serious, eating disorders' consequences go beyond a loss of confidence, struggling to moderate eating, and/or body dissatisfaction. Eating disorders' mortality rate is higher than any other mental illness, except that of opiate addiction. About every sixty-two minutes someone dies as a direct result of an eating disorder. Young people between the ages of fifteen and twenty-four with anorexia have ten times the risk of dying compared to their same-aged peers. About 5-10 percent of those struggling with anorexia die within ten years of contracting anorexia nervosa and 18–20 percent of those struggling with anorexia will die after twenty years of struggling with the disease. Without treatment, up to 20 percent of people with serious eating disorders die. With treatment, the mor-tality rate drops to 2–3 percent. All data is taken from NEDA and ANAD.

[6] "Statistics & Research on Eating Disorders," NEDA (National Eating Disorder As-sociation), www.nationaleatingdisorders.org/statistics-research-eating-disorders.

[7] NEDA, "Statistics & Research on Eating Disorders."

[8] NEDA, "Statistics & Research on Eating Disorders."

more than the average time one spends sleeping or working each day.[9] Youth in America (ages 8–18) spend at least half of their screen time on internet mobile devices.[10] Young people ages 13–18 spend about nine hours a day using entertainment media, and teenagers ages 8–12 average six hours a day on entertainment media.[11]

Several correlational studies have researched the relationship between the use of social media and body image concerns. Studies on pre-teen girls and high school females found that users of Facebook report "more drive for thinness, internalization of the thin-ideal, body surveillance, self-objectification, and appearance comparisons than do non-users."[12] When pre-teen girls, female high school students, and undergraduate women increase the time that they spend on Facebook, their reported propensity to diet is increased, as is each of the side-effects mentioned above.[13] Similar tendencies have been found in studies done with men as well.[14] Studies also found that "elevated appearance exposure on Facebook (e.g., posting, viewing, and commenting on images) was associated with greater weight dissatisfaction, drive for thinness, thin-ideal internalization, and self-objectification among female high school students."[15] However, correlative studies do not establish whether the Facebook users who participated in the abovementioned studies are more concerned with their body image as a result of their Facebook use, or if people who are more concerned with their body image spend more time on Facebook as a result.[16]

Longitudinal studies on social media's effect on body image are collectively inconclusive. One study found that greater social media use among male and female high school students predicted more body dissatisfaction and more conversations about appearance with their peers 18 months after the study took place.[17] In this study, body dissatisfaction did not predict social media usage, which points to social media's negative impact. A second study of female college students supported the prior study's findings, indicating that when users engaged in maladaptive Facebook usage (which constituted seeking negative social evaluations and engaging in social comparisons on the

---

[9] NEDA, "Statistics & Research on Eating Disorders."

[10] NEDA, "Statistics & Research on Eating Disorders."

[11] NEDA, "Statistics & Research on Eating Disorders." NEDA references Common Sense Media, Inc., (2015) as the source of these statistics. These amounts vary by race, income, and gender, and do not include the use of media in school or doing homework.

[12] Jasmine Fardouly and Lenny R. Vartanian, "Social Media and Body Image Concerns: Current Research and Future Directions," *Current Opinion in Psychology* 9 (2016): 1, doi:10.1016/j.copsyc.2015.09.005.

[13] Fardouly and Vartanian, "Social Media and Body Image Concerns," 1.

[14] Fardouly and Vartanian, "Social Media and Body Image Concerns," 1.

[15] Fardouly and Vartanian, "Social Media and Body Image Concerns," 2.

[16] Fardouly and Vartanian, "Social Media and Body Image Concerns," 2.

[17] Fardouly and Vartanian, "Social Media and Body Image Concerns," 2.

platform), it correlated to increased body dissatisfaction four weeks later.[18] In addition, a study on orthorexia (disordered eating patterns due to an individual's obsession with healthy eating) found that those who used Instagram presented more symptoms than those who did not. [19] However, in contrast to both of the aforementioned studies, other research tracking high school females' use of different social media platforms like blogs, Twitter, Facebook, and online games, did not identify a relationship between social media use and body image concerns, even in a six-month follow up.[20] This study indicates that not all social media platforms impact users' body image concerns equally, and platforms should be evaluated individually.

A 2017 study evaluated social media use and its impact on both body image and eating disorders. The study found that problematic use of social networking sites (which the study's authors identify as dependence on social networking) is related to body image, self-esteem, and eating disorder symptoms/concerns.[21] Behavior like lurking on others' pages without posting on them, or commenting on people's profiles, were found to be connected to increased body image concerns which are in turn linked to people's desire to change how they want to look by engaging in disordered eating habits or eating disorders.[22] The total time users spend on social media is also related to an increase in eating disorder symptoms and concerns.[23] The researchers also point to a 2013 study which noted that when young adult Facebook users seek out negative evaluations and engage in social comparison online, they experienced an increase in negative eating pathology like bulimic symptoms or overeating.[24] In sum, while the influence of social media and online images on young people's body image in contemporary American society is not certain, it is likely.[25]

THE PERVASIVE THIN-IDEAL AND CONNATURAL KNOWLEDGE

Beth Haile's virtue-ethics approach to eating disorders provides a foundation for considering social media's impact on body image and eating disorders. Research from a variety of perspectives points to a spiritual or moral sense, both personal and societal, that lies at the core

---

[18] Fardouly and Vartanian, "Social Media and Body Image Concerns," 2.

[19] Rosie Jean Marks, Alexander De Foe, and James Collett, "The Pursuit of Wellness: Social Media, Body Image, and Eating Disorders," *Children & Youth Services Review* 119 (2020): 3, doi:10.1016/j.childyouth.2020.105659.

[20] Fardouly and Vartanian, "Social Media and Body Image Concerns," 2.

[21] Sara Santarossa and Sarah J. Woodruff, "#SocialMedia: Exploring the Relationship of Social Networking Sites on Body Image, Self-Esteem, and Eating Disorders," *Social Media + Society* 3, no. 2 (2017): 1.

[22] Santarossa and Woodruff, "#SocialMedia," 1, 7.

[23] Santarossa and Woodruff, "#SocialMedia," 6.

[24] Santarossa and Woodruff, "#SocialMedia," 2.

[25] Marks, De Foe, and Collett, "The Pursuit of Wellness," 3.

of eating disorders and makes a virtue ethic response in the context of grace appropriate. Haile references Michelle Mary Lelwica's *Starving for Salvation: The Spiritual Dimension of Eating Problems Among American Girls and Women*, in which Lelwica argues that a preoccupation with thinness and food is driven by a desire for fulfillment—a desire that is, at its root, spiritual.[26] Lelwica's work, among that of scholars from various fields (psychology, sociology, medicine, etc.), indicates that the behavioral manifestation of eating disorders or subthreshold symptomatology points back to "the *underlying desires and dispositions from which those behaviors emerged.*"[27] Additional sociological research links eating disorders with a (misguided) morality: Simona Giordano indicates that the impulse to be light or thin can be aligned with a moral desire to be good.[28] Lelwica's work identifies a core element of eating disorders as a search for (spiritual) fulfillment in response to an underlying disposition or desire. When one places Lelwica's findings into conversation with Giordano's work, striving for thinness appears to be a response to a moral desire to attain goodness.

The work of anthropologists Richard O'Connor and Penny Esterik indicates that the moral dimension of eating and food is not solely present in those struggling with eating disorders, but is a part of society at large. Haile focuses on O'Connor and Esterik's argument that, for those struggling with anorexia, restrictive eating goes beyond an effort to be beautiful and constitutes an effort to be good—a claim that agrees with Giordano's finding.[29] O'Connor and Esterik go on to classify people with eating disorders as "misguided moralists." However,

---

[26] Beth Haile, "A Good Appetite: A Thomistic Approach to the Study of Eating Disorders and Body Dissatisfaction in American Women" (PhD diss., Boston College, 2011), 6–7. Future references to Michelle Mary Lelwica's work will be taken from Haile's presentation of it in her dissertation. In addition to Lelwica's *Starving for Salvation* (Oxford: Oxford University Press, 2002), her recent *Shameful Bodies: Religion and the Culture of Physical Improvement* (New York: Bloomsbury Academic, 2017) is another source of insight into this dilemma. Hannah Bacon (*Feminist Theology and Contemporary Dieting Culture: Sin, Salvation and Women's Weight Loss Narratives* (New York: T & T Clark, 2019)), Jessica Coblentz ("Catholic Fasting Literature in a Context of Body Hatred: A Feminist Critique," *Horizons* 46, no. 2 (2019): 215–245, doi: 10.1017/hor.2019.55), and Lisa Isherwood (*The Fat Jesus: Christianity and Body Image* (New York: Seabury Books, 2008)) have each contributed important research in this area since the publication of Haile's dissertation, but pursuing the nuances of their specific contributions is beyond the scope of this essay.

[27] Haile, "A Good Appetite," 7. Author's emphasis. Haile explores the work of scholars and researchers from the fields mentioned here, but the constraints of space do not permit a further articulation of their findings.

[28] Haile, "A Good Appetite," 63. The citations of Giordano's work represent Haile's presentation of it in her dissertation.

[29] Haile, "A Good Appetite," 63. The further descriptions of the moral aspect of eating disorders in this paragraph come from Haile's presentation of O'Connor and Esterik's work, 63–64.

the dispositions of those struggling with eating disorders reflects a so-cietal attitude or morality surrounding food and eating habits, not something unique to those with eating disorders. Society's moral dispositions regarding food are expressed in the moral language that is used to talk about exercise and eating. Avoiding fat and exercising are perceived as virtuous, while eating and gaining weight are vicious. Other examples of moral food language are expressed in statements most of us use thoughtlessly: "sinning" with a delicious, decadent dessert, "confessing" binges or breaks in diets, or "being good" when one makes healthy choices when faced with a range of meal options. It is clear that the moral dimension of food and body image resonate not only in the experiences of those struggling with eating disorders, but in larger societal attitudes that arise from the idealization of thinness.[30]

Society's attitude about thinness drives body dissatisfaction (beginning at age eight) and behaviors that strive to bring bodies into conformity with society's skinny ideal.[31] Haile brings together the work of Lelwica, Giordano, O'Connor, and Esterik in the following statement: "Disordered attitudes and behaviors towards food in people with eating disorders and other forms of disordered eating are rooted more fundamentally in a disordered view of one's body."[32] Haile's next move is to identify the external factors that contribute to a disordered perception of the body.

Addressing the influence of images and the media on how one views the body requires an exploration of the "thin-ideal" and its internalization. Psychosocial literature's term for the broad societal internalization of thinness as desirable is "thin-ideal internalization." Thin-ideal internalization measures the extent to which the media's ideal of thinness has been adopted by an individual.[33] Research indicates that after women view images of ultra-thin women, if they are of an average or above-average weight, their body dissatisfaction and self-esteem are negatively impacted. The same study indicates that a high degree of thin-ideal internalization is one of the best predictors of the onset and maintenance of eating disorders.[34] The aforementioned research, among other studies, led Haile to conclude that "there is an empirical connection between exposure to certain images, specifically what is referred to as thin-ideal images of women, and increases in body dissatisfaction and eating disorder symptomatology."[35] While other societal expectations exist for men's bodies,

---

[30] The author would like to again note the contributions of Bacon, Coblentz, and Isherwood to this conversation, but due to space cannot attend to the intricacies of their arguments here (see footnote 26 for more detailed references to their work).

[31] Haile, "A Good Attitude," 69.

[32] Haile, "A Good Appetite," 8.

[33] Haile, "A Good Appetite," 8.

[34] Haile, "A Good Appetite," 8.

[35] Haile, "A Good Appetite," 8.

women experience social pressure to achieve an unrealistic thin-ideal, prompting many of them to turn to exercise, dieting, and other methods of dealing with their body dissatisfaction. For some women, societal expectations of extraordinary thinness contribute to the development of an eating disorder, which can also be linked to other factors (genetics, perfectionism, childhood experiences, etc.).[36] A study referenced in a 2020 literature review supports the idea that the thin-ideal influences the formation of eating disorder behavior by indicating that the risk of disordered eating is higher in countries where body-type ideals have been internalized.[37] Haile's claim that the thin-ideal's influence on women's self-esteem, body dissatisfaction, and the subsequently increased risk of developing eating disorders aligns with the research reviewed in this paper's first section, and both combine to form a formidable portrait of the contemporary challenges associated with thin-ideal internalization, social media, and body image/eating disorder concerns.

Haile presents Thomistic virtue ethics as a helpful theological hermeneutic for the societal idealization of thinness and its manifestation in individuals who struggle with body dissatisfaction and eating disorders. She argues that a Thomistic approach is well-suited to exploring eating disorders in the context of a thin-idealized society because virtues are "firm and stable dispositions to do the good" or the "interior principles underlying acts."[38] Thus, a virtue ethic approach compels one to focus less on manifested behaviors and more on the interior life of the individual struggling with eating disorders or eating disorder behavior.[39] Haile notes that adopting a Thomistic ethic imparts a "moral maximalism" in which every action a moral agent does or does

---

[36] Haile, "A Good Appetite," 69. It is worth noting that the scholarly discussion regarding the factors that predispose individuals to struggle with eating disorders is complex and multi-faceted. Haile offers a more thorough presentation of these factors in her dissertation, but due to space I will not elaborate on this fascinating interdisciplinary research here.

[37] Marks, De Foe, and Collett, "The Pursuit of Wellness," 3.

[38] Haile, "A Good Appetite," 7.

[39] Haile does not ignore the social sin that contributes to the development of the thin-ideal and the effect it has on women. However, in order to focus on what a Thomistic virtue ethic approach contributes to a moral assessment of eating disorders, she acknowledges the multi-fold aspects of sin at work in the development of the thin-ideal and chooses to focus on the internal life of the individual, and how one might respond to the sociocultural forces at work in their daily lives. On page 211, she recognizes that "a virtue-based approach to morality must examine the social and environmental forces which facilitate or hinder the development of virtue," and goes on to discuss the issue of structural sin, problems with the current socialization of US women, etc. See 217–219 of Haile's dissertation for her assessment of the thin-ideal as a result of social sin, particularly the way in which society and the media view and use women's bodies, and her call for social conversion on p. 229. Also see Daniel J. Daly, "Structures of Virtue and Vice," *New Blackfriars* 92 (2011): 341–357.

not perform matters.[40] "Operating within a teleological moral frame-work, the goodness or badness of any act for Aquinas depends on how conducive that act is in achieving its due end (*telos*), and on how con-ducive the end of the action is towards the ultimate end of the human agent, which Aquinas (like Aristotle) takes to be happiness (*eudemo-nia*)."[41] In Aquinas's ethic every act is evaluated by how successfully it achieves its end and how well that end contributes to the ultimate goal of the human person: flourishing, or *eudemonia*.

However, a moral paradox exists when one applies this end or *te-los*-based reasoning to eating disorders. One can be aware that an act contributes to an end that is not good, yet continue to desire to engage in that behavior and achieve that end. Such a paradox exists in those struggling with eating disorders. One can know that the act of engag-ing in eating disorder behavior does not contribute to one's flourishing yet continue to desire to engage in its unhealthy patterns. Haile notes that the distinctiveness of Aquinas's moral theory in responding to this conundrum is located in its illustration of "how the ability to 'reason well' is dependent on the extent to which a person's personality (that is, the complex behavioral, emotional, and mental features of a unique individual) is rightly ordered."[42] Like the problem of addiction, stud-ying eating disorders and eating-disorder behavior raises "a general problem as to how individuals can so consistently behave in a way they know to be unhealthy and unreasonable, both in their desire to conform to a thin-ideal and in the behaviors in which they engage to reach this goal."[43] Haile notes that women without a diagnosable eat-ing disorder experience extreme body dissatisfaction and engage in behaviors symptomatic of eating disorders, "even when rationally they acknowledge that this ideal is not healthy, beautiful, or realistic."[44] Thus, Haile determines that eating disorders and body dissatisfaction do not result from "deficient or erroneous knowledge, but rather, a matter of erroneous or deficient desires."[45] Identifying desire as a pri-mary (misguided) force in women's eating disorder behavior leads to the question of how to address it. Lacunas in knowledge are often rec-tified by education. Yet forming right-desire is much more difficult than educating women on the impact of eating disorder behavior on the body or the influence of the thin-ideal, especially for women whose valuation of goodness and worthiness have become tied to achieving an unhealthy weight. As women seek to (re)form their de-sires through therapy, support from friends and family who want to

---

[40] Haile, "A Good Appetite," 15.
[41] Haile, "A Good Appetite," 14.
[42] Haile, "A Good Appetite," 11.
[43] Haile, "A Good Appetite," 11.
[44] Haile, "A Good Appetite," 11.
[45] Haile, "A Good Appetite," 11.

see them healthy, and spiritually formative disciplines, one is prompted to consider what else from the Christian theological tradition can aid their recovery.

Haile presents Aquinas's conception of connatural knowledge as a possible response to women struggling to align their desire for thinness with their knowledge that being too thin is not healthy. Haile cites a study indicating that "[o]ver half of American girls and undergraduate women report being dissatisfied with their bodies. Research has identified body dissatisfaction as one of the most important variables in predicting eating disorder onset and maintenance."[46] This research indicates the gravity of and need for a reasonable response to the thin ideal's impact on American women and prompts Haile's turn to Aquinas's conception of connatural knowledge. Haile describes Aquinas's understanding of connatural knowledge as "the mode of cognition based on the appetitive inclination toward an object of desire, allow[ing] us to expand the scope of knowledge beyond the activity of the intellect and appreciate the critical role of the emotions [and human experience] in moral knowledge."[47] Haile notes the interconnectedness of reason, emotion, and sense experience as she observes:

> In connatural knowledge, reason, emotion, and sense experience are connected in a single intuitive apprehension. Connatural knowledge is in a sense, a more powerful form of knowledge than the intellect's knowledge of concepts because it unites the knower with the object known: [quoting Aquinas, I-II, Q. 28, art. 1, ad. 3] "Knowledge is perfected by the thing known being united, through its likeness, to the knower. But the effect of love is that the thing itself which is loved, is, in a way, united to the lover, as stated above. Consequently the union caused by the lover is closer than that which is caused by knowledge."[48]

In other words, connatural knowledge is the knowledge of love which prompts us to desire that which is connatural to us.[49] Haile reminds her reader that in Aquinas's understanding of connaturality, the more one acts on one's inclinations to possess that which one desires, the more permanent and stable one's inclinations (or habits) become. Both good and bad objects and desires can become connatural to a person.[50] Connatural knowledge helps us understand how women can know that they are too thin, or that they desire to be too thin, and yet continue

[46] Haile, "A Good Appetite," 12. Citing F. Johnson and J. Wardle's "Dietary Restraint, Body Dissatisfaction, and Psychological Distress: A Prospective Analysis," *Journal of Abnormal Psychology* 114 (2005): 119–125.
[47] Haile, "A Good Appetite," 10, 135.
[48] Haile, "A Good Appetite," 18–19.
[49] Haile, "A Good Appetite," 19.
[50] Haile, "A Good Appetite," 19.

the behaviors which they hope will align them with the "beauty" of the thin-ideal.

Aquinas's theory of connatural knowledge also aligns with the aforementioned scientific data tracing the thin-ideal's impact on women's body dissatisfaction. Fardouly and Vartanian's previously-mentioned research review of social media's effect on body image indicates that many users of social media (predominantly Facebook) experience higher drives for thinness, greater internalizing of the thin-ideal, and more frequent comparisons of their bodies to their peers' physiques and diet.[51] The 2020 study "The Pursuit of Wellness" also shows that the risk of disordered eating is higher in countries in which the internalization of body-type ideals has taken place.[52] These studies, among others, lend scientific support to Haile's application of Aquinas's theory of connatural knowledge to eating disorders and body image.

Yet it is important to note that connatural knowledge is not deterministic for Aquinas. A dialogue between the intellect and the appetite or passions permits judgment to occur; whatever one perceives, or what society values and upholds does not necessarily or automatically become connatural to the person. While our human appetite drives what we desire (to be unnaturally thin, in this example), the intellect helps guide the appetite, and the intellect cannot make a judgment without the appetite's influence.[53] Haile summarizes Aquinas's assessment of the relationship between human appetite or passion and the intellect by stating that, "The passions point the will towards the concrete goods that allow it to realize its final good, happiness. Thus, the will is dependent on the passions, and both are dependent on knowledge."[54] Knowledge is the foundation of the will and the appetite which allows both the intellect and the passions to the formed, not merely determined by societal influences.

Echoing Haile's articulation of Aquinas, Jean Porter describes the interdependent relationship of the intellect and will as best "understood as two moments in one process by which the rational creature grasps her proper good (or perhaps a similitude of the same) and acts accordingly."[55] When the appetite is attracted to an apparent good, it becomes a source of judgment for the intellect. This mode of judgment is distinct from "the intellect's rational discursive way of judging."[56]

---

[51] Fardouly and Vartanian, "Social Media and Body Image Concerns," 1.

[52] Marks, De Foe, and Collett, "The Pursuit of Wellness," 3.

[53] Haile, "A Good Appetite," 145.

[54] Haile, "A Good Appetite," 147.

[55] Jean Porter, "The Unity of the Virtues and the Ambiguity of Goodness: A Reappraisal of Aquinas's Theory of the Virtues," *Journal of Religious Ethics* 21, no. 1 (1993): 149.

[56] Haile, "A Good Appetite," 163.

However, "Aquinas's moral theory helps us to realize that greater intellectual awareness about the nature of these images and their potential dangers is not the solution." Rehabilitating the appetite requires a
re-habituation, or training the appetite to desire other goals wherein a
richer truth and meaning are found. This process is not merely an intellectual one and takes place in the context of grace.

Haile applies Aquinas's understanding of connatural knowledge to
the experience of women exposed to and influenced by thin-ideal images. As women view images of beautiful, too-thin women, they desire to become like them:

> A woman diets and exercises, and may even starve herself and purge
> largely because she experiences a certain affinity with the thin-ideal
> she is bombarded by on a day-to-day basis. Based on her appetite, she
> knows that what these images offer is desirable—that extreme thin-
> ness is what makes a person beautiful—even if she rationally knows
> the opposite. This inclinational knowledge shapes how she acts. The
> more she exposes herself to these images, the more stable her inclina-
> tion to desire them, and the more consistently she acts to conform her-
> self to them.[57]

Simply put, the more a woman aspires to conform to the thin-ideal that
surrounds her, the more it becomes connatural to her. This paradox is
difficult to understand, prompting many people to wonder how one
can know that the women they see are too thin, unhealthily so, and yet
desire to look like them. However, the desire to be thin paired with
actions that enact that desire (dieting, over-exercising, etc.) exist sim-
ultaneously with the realization that the goal, desire, and behavior are
unhealthy.[58] A significant portion of women who struggle with body
dissatisfaction know that thin-ideal images are not real, nor conducive
to body satisfaction, health, or flourishing, yet still desire to conform
to them. The desire for thinness, which often correlates to beauty and
goodness, is difficult to either ignore or re-habituate.

Haile's central proposition to address the challenge presented by
the thin-ideal is that women should moderate their interaction with
magazines to avoid seeing harmful images. She suggests media fasts,
focusing on fashion magazines as something women struggling with
body dissatisfaction and eating disorders can and should avoid.[59] Haile
concludes that "By examining the exposure to a thin-ideal of human
beauty, we have seen that every action, even the most seemingly mundane and ordinary like looking at fashion magazines, are *moral* actions
and contribute to overall happiness of the moral agent."[60] To combat

---

[57] Haile, "A Good Appetite," 22–23.
[58] Haile, "A Good Appetite," 128.
[59] Haile, "A Good Appetite," 251.
[60] Haile, "A Good Appetite," 226.

images' negative influence and the ease with which they become connatural to women, women should avoid the images. As previously indicated, current research supports Aquinas's philosophical claim on which Haile's suggestion is based. Haile notes that "Studies do indicate that reduced exposure to media promulgating a thin-ideal may result in reduced body dissatisfaction and disordered eating symptomatology."[61] However, the act of disassociating oneself with images that surround and pervade one's life is difficult, as is persevering in that avoidance and re-habituating one's desires. Haile explains:

> One of the misconceptions this dissertation is trying to challenge is that one can always change one's behavior simply by changing one's beliefs, or developing more informed beliefs. We have seen that Aquinas in his conception of connatural knowledge does not support this opinion—our action is largely determined by our loves, in addition to our rational commitments to moral principles. Additionally, the empirical evidence on thin-ideal internalization and body dissatisfaction supports the Thomistic thesis regarding the importance of affective knowledge. Simply knowing that an image is unrealistic or contrary to flourishing is not sufficient to prevent being affected—both in attitude and action. Change of behaviors requires a change of heart.[62]

In addition to the dilemma Haile articulates, a further challenge exists. The social media and internet age presents an obstacle to Haile's suggestion that women avoid magazines that feature thin-ideal images or go on media fasts to avoid their becoming connatural. Ad generators are able to identify users' age and gender based on their searches and social media profiles, almost ensuring that women of all ages will be presented with thin-ideal images. Women are also likely to encounter sponsored profiles on Instagram, Twitter, or Facebook that feature photos of ultra-thin women designed to capture attention and generate interest in a diet, new fashion, fitness routine, or other good or service. In short, thin-ideal images are all but impossible to avoid. Along with the development of the virtues in unity, something more is needed for changing one's heart, re-habituating desire, and becoming more virtuous in viewing one's body or avoiding eating disorder behavior.

For Aquinas, the re-habituation of desire is guided and assisted by the Holy Spirit's grace. Grace is the means by which one becomes connatural with God's charity.[63] Grace from the Holy Spirit "disposes a person on an affective level to divine things according to her ultimate *telos*, which is union with God."[64] Haile explains that the "fulfillment of the perfection of the rational creature cannot be achieved by means

---

[61] Haile, "A Good Appetite," 185.
[62] Haile, "A Good Appetite," 244.
[63] Haile, "A Good Appetite," 26.
[64] Haile, "A Good Appetite," 118.

of a rational creature's natural internal capabilities—something from without is needed, which Aquinas identifies as the infusion of divine grace, by which the creature is rendered capable of 'a kind of participation in divinity.'"[65] Grace makes it possible to both desire and be a part of God's goodness and being.

The creature's perfection does not exclude natural happiness. Rather, Haile describes Aquinas's conception of happiness and its alignment with the *telos* of an individual in the following manner: "Supernatural happiness does not replace natural happiness, but rather, profoundly affects the way in which natural happiness can be achieved in this life. Through its orientation towards a higher goal than 'optimal flourishing,' the human appetite pursues things which are not only conducive to health and happiness, but also conducive to union with God."[66] Both the perseverance required to pursue the "higher goal" of optimal flourishing and the means to progress toward that goal come through the Holy Spirit's aid. In addition to the help of the Holy Spirit, Haile notes the role that the virtues' embodied practice plays. "One does not learn moderation or balance only by conceptualizing or theorizing what moderation and balance consist in; rather, one learns moderation and balance also through practice. We learn by doing."[67]

In summary, this essay's first section reviews the research on eating disorders' pervasiveness, the rate at which young people use media, and social media's influence on body satisfaction in young people. This research collectively presents a challenging picture for the contemporary world. Haile responds to these challenges by presenting a response to the growing societal idealization of thinness through Aquinas's virtue ethics, particularly his recognition that humans can know something is wrong (like society's thin-ideal) and still desire it. To address wrongly-ordered desire in regard to the thin-ideal, Haile focuses on Thomas's presentation of the concept of connatural knowledge by which one becomes "connatural" with what one sees. However, counteracting an unhealthy connaturality requires a re-habituation of the appetite, which itself necessitates grace in cooperation with virtue, and Aquinas's unity thesis and treatment of grace can build on Haile's laudable turn to Thomistic virtue theory.

AQUINAS'S UNITY THESIS

Aquinas's conception of a virtue is radically distinct from the myriad ways that contemporary society conceives of it. Jean Porter articulates Aquinas's understanding of a virtue as a "habitual qualification of one of the intellectual or desiderative faculties of the human soul,

---

[65] Haile, "A Good Appetite," 204.
[66] Haile, "A Good Appetite," 202.
[67] Haile, "A Good Appetite," 253.

by means of which the individual is enabled to think or act in a specified way."[68] Porter adds that virtuous action consists not only in knowledge of what is good, but in appetites that have been aligned with a knowledge of the good.[69] In other words, one's virtuous habits incline one to not only act in a particular manner but also influence what one desires.[70]

Understanding virtue as a habit is central to Aquinas's unity thesis as is his conception of the relationship between the virtues. The cardinal virtues, "considered as distinct virtues, are connected." As Porter explains, the cardinal virtues

> are interlocked, in such a way that no one of them can function properly without the others. Prudence, considered as the capacity to discern and choose in accordance with one's overall desires for what is good, noble, and just, could not develop in someone who did not have these desires at all, or experienced them only fitfully or intermittently.[71]

Prudence plays a central role in Aquinas's understanding of the virtues, imparting the capacity to discern what action will bring about a good desire. Aquinas refers to prudence as "the principal virtue of the intellect considered as practical reason" which guides the development of the other virtues in his ethic.[72]

Aquinas's unity thesis argues for the interconnected development of all the virtues. Andrew Kim explains the unity thesis as referring "to the view that a single virtue cannot be possessed in isolation from the other virtues."[73] Aquinas's theory appears to invite critique born of both philosophical reasoning and common sense: if the unity of virtues is true, how is it possible for anyone to be virtuous? Kim argues that Thomas's version of the unity thesis avoids the aforementioned flaw, and supports his claim by comparing the concept of virtue that undergirds Aquinas's unity thesis with that of the Stoics and St. Augustine. The Stoics understood virtue as something one either fully possessed or totally lacked. In the Stoic understanding, if one has a modicum of courage, or has achieved a decent amount of courage, one still lacks courage. Therefore, one is not courageous at all. The Stoic Cicero explained the possession of virtue via an illustration of a man

---

[68] Jean Porter, "Virtue and Sin: The Connection of the Virtues and the Case of the Flawed Saint," *Journal of Religion* 75, no. 4 (1995): 524.

[69] Porter, "The Unity of the Virtues," 145.

[70] Haile, "A Good Appetite," 150.

[71] Porter, "Virtue and Sin," 524–525.

[72] Porter, "Virtue and Sin," 525. Porter's translation of Aquinas, I-II 58.4.

[73] Andrew Kim, "Progress in the Good: A Defense of the Thomistic Unity Thesis," *Journal of Moral Theology* 3, no. 1 (2014): 147.

drowning. Whether a man is lying face down in a puddle and drowning, or is flailing in the middle of an ocean without another human in sight, in both cases the man is still drowning.[74] In other words, "Anyone who has room left to morally progress lacks virtue completely.... [F]or the early Stoics, to be virtuous is to be beyond improvement, to be morally perfect."[75] The possession of virtue exists on an either-or scale for the Stoics. Either one possesses perfect virtue and cannot progress further in it because one already has it so cannot have more of it, or one lacks it totally.

Kim invokes Augustine's conception of virtue to critique the Stoic view. Augustine understands the Stoic presentation of virtue to be problematic because no one can actually become virtuous; the standard is impossible to reach.[76] Odon Rigaud points out that the Stoic approach is totalizing; in contrast to the Stoics' view, Augustine initiates "a tradition of challenging the totalizing claims associated with the Stoic definition of virtue."[77] Kim, summarizing Rigaud's view, states that "[T]he problem is that, given the Stoic definition of virtue only consisting in 'the highest state,' the Stoic version of the unity thesis is an outgrowth of the impossible standard set by the Stoic linking of virtue exclusively with the highest state."[78] Rigaud identifies the Stoics' three totalizing claims as: (a) virtue is an absolute; (b) it is the highest state which permits no room for gradation, nor degrees of possession; and (c) it consists of a pendulum-swing from a lack to complete possession.[79] Because of its totalization of virtue as an absolute state, Kim argues that the Stoic view does not function in real life.[80] Ultimately, "The Stoic view leads to the discounting of virtue as it manifests in the lives of actual people and entails either implausible descriptions of moral progress or eliminates the possibility of it altogether."[81] Kim agrees with Augustine's critique of the Stoic totalization of virtue and its subsequent lack of applicability in daily life.

Aquinas, contradicting the Stoics, presents virtue as existing in degrees and developing in three stages. Kim establishes this claim based on Aquinas's *De virtutibus in communi*, which says:

> The character of virtue does not consist in being the best of its kind in itself, but with reference to its object. For it is through virtue that someone is ordered towards the upper limit of his capacity, that is, towards doing things well. That is why Aristotle says that virtue is the

---

[74] Kim, "Progress in the Good," 149.
[75] Kim, "Progress in the Good," 150.
[76] Kim, "Progress in the Good," 151.
[77] Kim, "Progress in the Good," 151.
[78] Kim, "Progress in the Good," 153.
[79] Kim, "Progress in the Good," 153.
[80] Kim, "Progress in the Good," 155.
[81] Kim, "Progress in the Good," 155.

tendency of something complete towards what is best. However, someone can be more disposed or less disposed towards what is best; accordingly, he has virtue to a greater or lesser degree.[82]

Aquinas's definition contradicts the Stoics' totalized idea of virtue, by which one either fully possesses or lacks virtue. One can be "more disposed or less disposed towards what is best," which is reflected in an increase or decrease in one's possession of virtue. In Kim's words, "One becomes virtuous when the whole soul is brought into harmonious alignment with truthful vision of the way things are; this occurs by degrees in stages of time."[83] Aquinas presents the development of virtue in three stages (*triplex gradus virtutum*) in *De virtutibus cardinalibus*.[84] The first level consists of "natural dispositions to virtue which are wholly imperfect (*virtutes omnino imperfectae*), because they exist without prudence and so do not achieve right reason." Virtue's second stage of development "achieves right reason but does not reach God because they are not combined with charity. These virtues are complete in relation to the human good (*perfectae per comparationem ad bonum humanum*) but not perfect simply. They are true but imperfect virtues." Finally, the third level of virtue consists of virtue combined with charity (*simul cum caritate*), which Aquinas describes as simply perfect (*virtutum simpliciter perfectarum*). Thus, while the first stage of virtue is made up of "fragmented and unstable dispositions capable of actualizing the rational soul only in a wholly imperfect way," these dispositions represent the start of a journey through which one can reach simply perfect virtue.[85] If one never attempts to live virtuously, which will certainly result in pitfalls and failures at the beginning of and throughout one's quest toward perfect virtue, how can anyone become virtuous?

Aquinas, like Augustine, indicates that absolutely perfect virtue is unattainable in this life. For Aquinas, "Virtue unfolds in 'stages of time' and our virtue can be complete relative to that."[86] Thus, every life has the potential for continued moral improvement, based on Aquinas's aforementioned three stages of virtue development. Kim writes,

> Perfect virtue is distinguished from imperfect virtue, then, on the basis of attainment of the supernatural end, but also on the basis of the unity thesis. The *triplex gradus* resolves the apparent conflict between the first and second articles. Clearly there is no such thing, in Aquinas's

---

[82] Kim, "Progress in the Good," 154.
[83] Kim, "Progress in the Good," 162.
[84] Kim, "Progress in the Good," 162–163. The following articulation of the three gradations of virtue comes from Kim's reading of Aquinas's *De virtutibus cardinalibus*.
[85] Kim, "Progress in the Good," 164.
[86] Kim, "Progress in the Good," 170.

view, as disconnected virtues ordered to separated ends. In the second article, Aquinas is distinguishing supernatural, infused virtue (level 3) from acquired and connected virtue (level 2).[87]

In this way, the second level of virtue is perfect, insofar as the virtues in their varied, developmental stages are connected by prudence. Yet these same virtues are also imperfect when compared to the third level of virtue because they are not in perfect harmony with charity. Jean Porter explains that "perfected virtues will always give rise to morally good actions; in contrast, the imperfect virtues, which also qualify the desiderative faculties, typically result in actions which are good only in some limited respect (I-II 65.1). Aquinas thus accepts Augustine's definition of a moral virtue, not as any habit, but as a habit which is productive of good actions."[88] The extent to which one possesses perfected virtue is evaluated by the actions one produces. No one can be perfectly good all the time, but progress in choosing the good and becoming more virtuous is both possible and necessary in living the Christian life.

Aquinas understands virtue to develop proportionately, which is why he can uphold a unity thesis. Kim describes Aquinas's understanding of the growth of virtue as equated "to the manner in which a hand grows. As the whole hand grows, the fingers grow 'at a proportional rate.' Thus, with respect to acquired virtue, as prudence (the hand) grows so too the fingers (the moral virtues) at a proportional rate."[89] Subsequently, if a virtuous action or decision is to help one acquire virtue, it has to be aligned with right reason, for all virtues come to be possessed with and through prudence.[90] For Aquinas, "Becoming virtuous entails the unification of the virtues through prudence."[91] Yet, even if virtue always has room to grow in this life, Aquinas's theory of how to attain virtue reflects Aristotle's, who implores one seeking to become virtuous to do what a virtuous person would do: to act virtuously.[92] "Even though it is not possible to have the moral virtues without prudence or to have prudence without the moral virtues, it is possible to act virtuously without yet having acquired virtuous habits. Otherwise, the acquisition of any virtue (fragmented or otherwise) would indeed be impossible."[93] To attain virtue, one begins by enacting virtue, even if it has not yet been acquired as a habit—for it is by repeated action and choice in the context of grace that one begins to assume the habit of virtue.

---

[87] Kim, "Progress in the Good," 165.
[88] Porter, "The Unity of the Virtues," 144.
[89] Kim, "Progress in the Good," 168.
[90] Kim, "Progress in the Good," 168.
[91] Kim, "Progress in the Good," 165–166.
[92] Kim, "Progress in the Good," 167.
[93] Kim, "Progress in the Good," 167.

Both Porter and Kim, in their discussion of Aquinas's unity thesis, emphasize grace's role in the moral life and virtue development. Porter writes that because of the infinite chasm between God and creature, "It is not enough to act out of the dynamisms of one's created nature in order to attain God. The human person must receive a new and qualitatively different set of capacities, in order to attain an end which altogether transcends the natural *telos* of any created nature, namely, direct personal union with God."[94] Grace is necessary to transform the soul, and to help it acquire the infused virtues: faith, hope, and charity. Charity is accompanied by other virtues that transform a whole person.[95] It also works to transform the affective level of the person, making one connatural with divine things. Grace is not "something which works against a person's nature, but rather with (*cum*) her nature, perfecting her appetites and capacities and directing them ultimately towards their ultimate goal."[96] Natural human desires are perfected and oriented to their true goal through grace: perfect charity and union with God.

Understanding Aquinas's unity thesis is imperative to comprehending its usefulness as a response to the challenges presented by the contemporary thin-ideal and the challenges men and women experience with eating disorders. As the virtues grow together, they develop through practice and unfold over time with grace's aid. Grace is integral to virtue formation, perfecting our nature so that we come to be more fully in line with and oriented to the goal of unity with God. Aquinas's unity thesis and the influence of grace offer a new response to the challenges presented by the thin-ideal and its role in the formation of eating disorders.

THE UNITY THESIS AND EATING DISORDERS IN CONTEMPORARY MEDIA-DRIVEN TIMES

What does one do when one cannot avoid viewing thin-ideal images, images that studies show influence one's body image negatively and increase one's likelihood to engage in eating disorder behaviors? Haile's suggestion that women avoid fashion magazines and other sources of thin-ideal images, while helpful for an era in which internet and social media use was not a regular component of daily life, is almost impossible to implement for most women and young girls in the United States. While women may strive to limit their interaction with thin-ideal images by not following social media accounts that contain edited images, promote dieting or eating disorder behaviors (like pro-ana or thinspiration communities), or feature unnaturally thin women, women cannot stop advertisements from popping up that showcase

---

[94] Porter, "Virtue and Sin," 534.
[95] Porter, "Virtue and Sin," 535. Porter is referencing ST I-II 63.4.
[96] Haile, "A Good Appetite," 199.

new diet programs, the latest fashions modeled by extremely thin women, or suggest undergarments to slim their figure (guided by the societal assumption that their figure inherently needs slenderizing because thinner is always better). Completely removing oneself from social media platforms is possible but would realistically be very difficult, especially for young women for whom social media is a central mode of communication and connection. In addition, women who work or study are often required to spend extended period of times on the internet. They are highly likely, if not certain, to be exposed to advertisements and edited images promoting the thin-ideal. To abstain from all internet use is nearly impossible, especially for women enrolled in school or using a computer in their job.

Aquinas's unity thesis can be responsive to the question that Haile's dissertation, when shifted to the context of contemporary times, leaves unresolved: what to do when women cannot avoid being exposed to thin-ideal images which studies indicate increase their likelihood to engage in eating disorder behaviors and be dissatisfied with their bodies. Aquinas's unity thesis posits that the virtues grow together, guided by right reason or prudence, in the context of a grace-infused life. As prudence increases, it guides the growth and development of the other virtues. So, perhaps an alternate suggestion to abstaining from all thin-ideal images (and therefore the internet where they might appear) is to focus on the development of prudence and other virtues which, according to the unity thesis, will facilitate the growth of all virtues. An example will aid the elucidation of this concept as it applies to women struggling with eating disorders, but we must first turn to an analysis of temperance.

Many, if not all, women struggling with an eating disorder are also challenged by temperance. Haile describes temperance as developing "a bridge between the natural appetite—the first nature—and the acquired appetite or 'second nature' that follows from habit."[97] While struggles with temperance are usually associated with over-indulgence (enjoying a pint, not a serving of ice cream or watching an entire series of television shows in one sitting, not just an episode), for those struggling with eating disorders, temperance can be developed in either extreme direction. Those who struggle with bulimia binge and often purge; those struggling with anorexia do not eat enough to meet their body's caloric needs for normal daily activities.[98] Both bulimia and anorexia miss the mark of temperance whether by excess or defect. One who is temperate is able to discern not only what is too much but

---

[97] Haile, "A Good Appetite," 169.

[98] For a helpful foray into the complexities of regarding temperance as disposition, acquired virtue, and infused virtue, but beyond the scope of the current essay, see William C. Mattison, "Can Christians Possess the Acquired Cardinal Virtues?" *Theological Studies* 72, no. 3 (2011): 558–585, doi.org/10.1177/004056391107200304.

what is too little and has oriented their appetite to desire the right amount of food.

In order to build on Haile's work with Aquinas's unity thesis, it is important to examine Haile's treatment of temperance. Haile turns to the work of Nicholas Austin, SJ, to highlight temperance's liberative nature. Austin understands temperance to function in two ways, arguing "that temperance has two modes—restraint and what might be called 'enjoyment' or 'proper use': One can be too restrained, but one cannot be too temperate; temperance therefore, is not restraint alone....The appropriate response to human hungers and appetites can often be joyful fulfillment, in grateful recognition of the gifts of God."[99] Austin reminds us that temperance goes beyond a false image of brute strength forcing the passions into submission, or a spreadsheet calculation of what is "just right." Instead, when employed rightly with grace's aid, temperance is a "grateful recognition of the gifts of God" which results in the joyful fulfillment of our human appetites and desires. As Kim and Haile emphasize, the perfection of temperance (and all of the virtues) depends on training and habituation.[100] Temperance's habituation helps train the desires with and through the intellect, serving as a liberative virtue that "frees us from the pursuit of false desires and allows us to identify and satisfy those desires which are authentically ours."[101] Temperance allows us to orient our desires not toward what is immediately satisfying—like achieving a thin-ideal, no matter the cost to one's physical and mental health—but to our human *telos*, our flourishing that leads us toward communion with God.

Let us take, for example, a woman who is struggling to moderate her eating, or to exercise temperance in her food consumption. While she is, as of yet, unable to discontinue limiting her food to an unhealthy amount, she finds she is able to go to a therapist weekly. The habit of attending therapy that she is forming (in addition to the aid therapy itself provides) enables the habituation of other virtues like courage and fortitude.[102] According to Aquinas's unity thesis, in the context of and through grace's aid, developing courage and fortitude will help temperance grow as well. Both courage and fortitude will help this woman combat the thin-ideal's pressures and other factors that have contributed to the development of her eating disorder. It also

---

[99] Haile, "A Good Appetite," 173. Austin is cited in footnote 36.
[100] Haile, "A Good Appetite," 179.
[101] Haile, "A Good Appetite," 196.
[102] Jessica Coblentz presents a fascinating and related idea on 564–568 of her article "The Possibilities of Grace amid Persistent Depression," *Theological Studies* 80, no. 3 (September 2019): 554–71, doi.org/10.1177/0040563919857184, entitled "small agency" and details the flourishing it can bring about in the context of persistent depression.

appears reasonable that if, in other settings, she is able to practice temperance, her practice could strengthen her ability to be temperate, one day, in the context of her eating.

Re-habituating temperance—which is part of what my application of Aquinas's unity thesis to body image concerns and eating disorders necessitates—also requires exercising prudence, or right reason. Prudence brings one's action into alignment with reason "which sets the standard of goodness in any particular action."[103] Prudence's task is "to see the truth beyond the thin-ideal, and to recognize that excessive thinness as promoted in the thin-idealized media images is not an effective means of achieving the end of temperance—the pleasures afforded by this life."[104] Prudence can both remind and guide the intellect of and toward what is true, which helps re-habituate desire. Returning to our example, if the woman struggling to practice temperance in her eating is able to be temperate in other areas of her life, with prudence's guide, this can help ready her to become more temperate in her eating. Women who have practiced restrictive eating often apply their habituated rigid restraint to other areas of their lives, operating on strict regimens in regard to their time or other "indulgences" like watching television or engaging in hobbies that detract from study or work. Thus, if prudence helps an individual arrive at the conclusion that she can, indeed, watch not only one but two episodes of her favorite show to relax, her practice of prudence can help re-habituate temperance on a general level. One day, she may be able to permit herself a small dessert after dinner, or a second serving of a particularly delectable dish. These small steps, guided by prudence and enacted through the slow re-habituation of temperance accompanied by fortitude and courage, can help one struggling with an eating disorder to develop temperance, the virtue that helps one align their goal of human fulfillment with God's dream for them. Alignment is a liberative act, permitting the enjoyment of life's pleasures by fulfilling one's desire not with the false idol of the thin-ideal, but with the bounty of delight which God desires for us—beginning in life here and preparing us for fulfillment (in and through perfect virtue) in the next life.[105]

Developing the virtues both necessitates and mediates grace in the context of women's challenges with body image concerns and eating disorders. "Grace habituates the appetite to take pleasure in things

---

[103] Haile, "A Good Appetite," 181.

[104] Haile, "A Good Appetite," 193.

[105] Another paper could easily be written on the goods of friendship and community, and how they aid the recovery of those with eating disorders through support and growth in virtue. Space does not permit the elucidation of this idea here, but especially in communion with the Church and ritual worship, community and friendship can play an important role in the re-habituation of desire and can help develop both prudence and temperance through support, modeling, and the grace of both prayer and the sacraments.

which are ultimately conducive to happiness not through commands and rational precepts, but rather, through the sort of holy delight that comes from connaturality with the ultimate end."[106] Grace, working with and guiding prudence, can help one avoid becoming connatural to thin-ideal images by helping form women's desire to become connatural to their *telos*—a life of fulfillment with God, not a daily life in which one is enslaved to a calorie count, how much one exercises, or the amount that one weighs. Haile describes grace-inspired knowledge as "not a rational knowledge in the form of commands and precepts, but a deeper kind of knowing, inexpressible in words and concepts, of what is good and true and how to act in order to achieve happiness."[107] Grace not only deepens one's knowledge and helps rightly orient the desires but imparts strength and comfort to those striving to grow in virtue. Christ's grace "can go where others cannot. He can enter into the cemetery of the...soul in a way no one else can and encounter the inward man afflicted, crying out...and there not only comfort him but also heal his mind and return him to his family to tell of all the Lord has done for him."[108] Christ can, and does, heal our afflictions. The mystery of this healing is complex and raises difficult questions: why are some healed, and others pray fervently for healing but continue to struggle? This question's answer is frankly inexplicable, as it hinges on the working of a God who is completely "other," but as one invites Christ into one's struggle, healing can (and does) occur through Christ's accompaniment.

The hope that grace brings, whether for the possibility of complete healing or for support for the next step on a journey to recovery, is imperative for those struggling with the thin-ideal and its consequences in a social media age. While the consequences and pervasiveness of a thin-idealized society can fill one with despair, Christ's grace and the gift of the virtues offer hope. As the virtues grow together, under the influence and harmony of the intellect and the desires guided by prudence, they both mediate and aid our reliance on grace. The words of Jean Porter remind those struggling to live a virtuous life that grace is not moral ramen; it is not instant. She writes, "Yet it does not follow that all those who are justified by God's grace are paragons of moral virtue either. The infused cardinal virtues may be potentially present in an individual, who nonetheless finds it difficult to exercise them because of the effects of past habits or some other similar cause."[109] Thus, all those who struggle with body dissatisfaction, eating disorder behaviors, and other practices that are not in line with the

---

[106] Haile, "A Good Appetite," 224.
[107] Haile, "A Good Appetite," 221.
[108] Andrew Kim, "Newness of Life and Grace Enabled Recovery from the Sin of Addiction," *Journal of Moral Theology* 10, Special Issue no. 1 (2021): 124–142.
[109] Porter, "Virtue and Sin," 529–530. Porter is referencing (ST I-II 65.3 *ad* 2).

telos for which God made us are called to not only seek the virtues' development in unity, but to rely on Christ's generous gift of grace poured out in love. Coupled with the effort we exert in combating the sin around us and in our own lives, grace enables and aids the transformation of our hearts, selves, and society.[110] Grace is the essential ingredient in the pursuit of virtue, especially as one seeks to develop a good appetite in a thin-idealized, social-media driven society.[111] M

Megan Heeder is currently completing her PhD in Theology at Marquette University. Her research interests include the development of a theological approach to eating disorders informed by virtue ethics as well as theological aesthetics' capacity to redeem contemporary ideals of beauty. Her vocation as a theologian is inspired by a desire to translate the wisdom of the Catholic intellectual tradition into a medium capable of being responsive to modern challenges and impacting both the intellects and hearts of her students and those who engage with her scholarship.

---

[110] While this article approaches the issue of virtue and eating disorders from an interpersonal lens, the author is aware of the need to engage a social ethic/community-oriented hermeneutic in order to adequately address the topic of body image and eating disorders. The author will engage a socially-oriented lens to treat this issue in a separate essay.

[111] I am exceedingly grateful for the mentorship, insights, and generosity of Dr. Andrew Kim, whose work inspired my interest in the unity thesis, and all those who have been a part of my theological journey. Many thanks are also owed to the peer reviewers of this article; your suggestions have improved the essay immensely.

Journal of Moral Theology, Vol. 11, No. 1 (2022): 131–153

Revolution of Faith in *Les Misérables*: The Journey from Misery to Mercy in the Secular Age

Jean-Pierre Fortin

"La mort, c'est la même chose que la grâce."
-Victor Hugo

S HIS EPIGRAPHIC REMARKS SHOW, WITH *Les Misérables* Victor Hugo intended to provide a remedy for human igno-rance and misery.[1] Recasting the Christian way of life in terms of conscience, history, and progress, *Les Misérables* proposes a unique transposition of moral theology into the context of secular nineteenth century France. The Christian vision has yet to re-define European values and society for the better (1.5.11, 158). Hugo wishes to reform society, religion, and humanity to foster a communal harmony embracing diversity and transcending political, cultural, and religious conflicts.[2] Reflecting its exiled author's processing of the collapse of the second Republic, *Les Misérables* takes account of the serious obstacles to moral, spiritual, and social progress that are igno-rance (lack of access to education), poverty (human induced economic and spiritual misery), and criminality (habitual evil). Hugo struggles to keep his vision of a democratic society alive. At stake is the possi-bility of social-political and moral-spiritual reform empowering the people to take charge of its destiny. Hugo comes to terms with the fact that revolutions do not effect lasting positive social change, rather the opposite.[3]

Of the main characters, only Mgr. Myriel and Jean Valjean succeed at completing the journey from vice to virtue. With the exception of Myriel's influence on Valjean, both however strikingly fail at altering

---

[1] "Death is the same (thing) as grace" (translation, mine). Victor Hugo, *Les Misé-rables*, tr. Julie Rose (New York: Modern Library, 2009), 1. Hereafter cited by part, book, chapter and page numbers between brackets.

[2] See Victor Hugo, *Correspondance II: Années 1849–1866*, Œuvres complètes, Vol. 42 (Paris: Albin Michel, 1950), 400.

[3] See Daniel Sipe, "'Les horizons du rêve': Hugo's Utopianism," in *Approaches to Teaching Hugo's* Les Misérables, ed. Michal P. Ginsburg and Bradley Stephens (New York: MLA, 2018), 128.

the character of individuals with whom they interact and the structures of communities to whom they belong in lasting fashion. Some characters are forced by poverty and social exclusion to engage in self-destructive behavior (Fantine). Some remain entrenched in evil or an abstract sense of duty and intentionally attempt to thwart Valjean's moral development (Thénardier, Javert). Others persevere in the good throughout but lose their lives in defense of a lost cause (Gavroche, Éponine, Enjolras, Mabeuf). As for Valjean himself, he undergoes complete transformation of character and way of life, facing a series of moral dilemmas and crises whose outcome deepen his option for the good. Valjean's life, however, ends in at least apparent failure, for he is never recognized as citizen and his self-giving way of life is not embraced by others, not even by his adoptive daughter and son-in-law who are set to enjoy a privileged (*Bourgeois*) existence deprived of any reference to the transcendent.[4] Like the story of the passion it emulates, the self-sacrificial quest and ministry of vicarious representation of Jean Valjean, the "proletarian Christ,"[5] seems to involve only his own definitive moral-spiritual transformation.

Acknowledging, alongside Samuel L. Goldberg, that "imaginative literature has traditionally been, and still is, a distinctive and irreplaceable form of moral thinking,"[6] in what follows, I theologize in the medium of literature by taking a systematic look at the life of Jean Valjean, the lead character of Victor Hugo's *Les Misérables*, on the path that led him from criminality to self-sacrifice. With Frédérique Leichter-Flack, I argue that in the wake of failed revolutions, Hugo moved the quest and task of human transformation from the social and political realms into the moral and spiritual. The existence of a single instance of authentic conversion of a hardened criminal translating into the lifelong practice of virtue confirms the potential of all human beings to experience redemption.[7] Hugo provides an exemplary life designed to help readers recognize this truth and submit themselves to transformative self-examination. Exploring the morally possible enables the determination of a given individual's personal vocation, which becomes a standard against which "the subject's fidelity to this unique destiny"[8] can be measured. Moral life can then be understood

---

[4] See Philippe Moisan, "*Les Misérables* and the Nineteenth-Century French Novel," in *Approaches to Teaching Hugo's* Les Misérables, 78.

[5] Pierre-Étienne Cudmore, "Jean Valjean et les avatars du poète éponyme," *French Review* 61, no. 2 (1987): 171.

[6] Samuel L. Goldberg, *Agents and Lives: Moral Thinking in Literature* (Cambridge, Cambridge University Press, 1993), 63.

[7] See Frédérique Leichter-Flack, "Encore un mal que le roman nous fait? Morale du dilemme, de Hugo à Dostoïevski," *Romantisme* 142, no. 4 (2008): 73 and 80.

[8] Jose Ortega y Gasset, "In Search of Goethe from Within," in *The Dehumanization of Art and Other Essays on Art, Culture, and Literature* (Princeton, NJ: Princeton University Press, 1969), 144.

as "a set of potentialities that thrust and grow themselves into being, that necessarily strive to actualize or realize themselves in time, and in the course of this perhaps become subject to consciousness and so to voluntary evaluation and deliberate choice."[9]

Engagement with the humanity of another, even that of a fictional other, nurtures renewed relationship with one's own humanity. God reveals Godself (as Christ) to humans by revealing humans to themselves and one another. In this context, Victor Hugo's depiction of Jean Valjean's story can be understood as the author's attempt to enjoin his readers to experience vicariously the "revolutionary grace"[10] effecting the complete inner transformation of the lead character of *Les Misérables*. Hence, following Lisa Gasbarrone, I consider Valjean's life story to be "an apprenticeship of the sacred"[11] involving the "exploration of the meaning and practice of faith."[12] Through his embodiment of holiness, Valjean shows how the Christian ideal can be assumed and made incarnate by the miserable. The transformation of the human condition from sin to virtue and grace is a long walk and work in the dark, a journey to and in faith, whose ultimate outcome is not achieved or experienced in the present life. Valjean's story gives narrative articulation to Hugo's hope for humanity, grounded in the faith that all human beings are called to be mediators of the transcendent. Partaking in Valjean's experience of inner reform induced and guided by Myriel's embodiment of gratuitous love, the readers of *Les Misérables* may be led to recognize the humanity of others and their own, and join the struggle for the formation of a free people.[13]

---

[9] Goldberg, *Agents and Lives*, 73.

[10] André Brochu, *Hugo: amour, crime, révolution. Essai sur Les Misérables* (Montreal: Presses de l'Université de Montréal, 1974), 235.

[11] Lisa Gasbarrone, "Restoring the Sacred in *Les Misérables*," *Religion & Literature* 40, no. 2 (2008): 23.

[12] Gasbarrone, "Restoring the Sacred," 17.

[13] Surprisingly few studies consider the import and implications of Hugo's masterpiece for moral and spiritual theology. Jerry H. Gill discerns "patterns of grace" setting Valjean on a new life path and powerfully summoning him to remain true to the ideal and mission set and entrusted by Mgr. Myriel throughout his life. For Gill, Valjean embodies the transformative agency of "unconditioned goodwill" received and offered gratuitously, effecting positive change even in those who resist it, such as Javert ("Patterns of Grace in *Les Misérables*," *Encounters* 74, no. 1 [2013]: 29–40). In "Providence, Duty, Love: The Regeneration of Jean Valjean in Victor Hugo's *Les Misérables*" (*Heythrop Journal* 59 [2018]: 24–33), Gordon Leah similarly argues that Hugo upholds the existence and efficacy of divine providence, operating and speaking through the conscience of individuals transformed and commissioned by gratuitous forgiveness. Mgr. Myriel's compassion induced Valjean's regeneration, which itself led the latter to embrace a self-sacrificial way of existence. Mary Christian and Jean-François Chiron consider the economics of redemption; the gift of the silverware attests that the regeneration of the miserable requires not only moral or spiritual resources, but also material ones (in "Bought with Silver: Victor Hugo, George Bernard Shaw, and the Economics of Salvation," *Religion & Literature* 47, no. 2 [2015]: 1–22

SETTING THE STANDARD

The fact that the novel opens with an entire book dedicated to Mgr. Myriel, bishop of Digne, is not indifferent. Myriel embodies the religious ideal whose secular transposition the narrative operates in Jean Valjean, the lead character. Myriel teaches Jesus Christ using words and deeds that speak to everyone (1.1.4, 11–13). He never theorized but always spoke from the heart and through action (1.1.14, 48–49). To the salvation of others, he fully dedicated himself, never hesitating to put his life at risk to serve this purpose (1.1.7, 24). Myriel was materially poor but spiritually rich; with an economy of words and a multitude of deeds, he reaches out and brings God's merciful grace to those who, like him, are living in misery. His faith is rooted in the personal experience of God in the midst of destitution. Estranging himself from ecclesial politics, abstract teachings, and discriminatory practices, the bishop of Digne relates to the poor as one of them (1.1.11, 41).

In the same way that in his misery he encountered God and was saved, Myriel works at channeling grace to others. So claims the narrator of *Les Misérables*: "There are men who work hard, digging for gold; he worked hard, digging for pity. The misery of the world was his mine. Pain everywhere was an occasion for goodness always. *Love one another*: He declared this to be complete, desired nothing more; it was the sum total of his doctrine" (1.1.14, 49). Myriel's faith finds expression in absolute love, given especially to those who suffer and are lost. Henri Scepi notes that in *Les Misérables*, Myriel functions as the embodiment of Hugo's idea and ideal of charity; a life according to Christ, lived in simplicity and profusion of mercy.[14] Myriel indwells human misery as the moon inhabits the night. Through his words and

---

and "Ce que des chandeliers peuvent exprimer. Symbole et rédemption dans *Les Misérables*," *Theophilyon* 24, no. 2 [2019]: 459–91). Fatma Dore's analysis of Valjean's self-denunciation to spare the innocent Champmathieu from a sure conviction through the lens of consequential utilitarian ethics concludes, against the narrative and Hugo, that Valjean should not have followed his conscience ("Jean Valjean's Dilemma and Utilitarian Ethics," *Folklor/Edebiyat* 90 [2017]: 147–61). Dore claims that the impact of this decision on the people of Montreuil-sur-mer and the surrounding region was such as to justify allowing Champmathieu to be condemned for a crime he did not commit. While these studies do contribute to laying foundations for a contemporary theological interpretation of *Les Misérables*—not the least by providing ample justification for avoiding any easy Christian eisegesis of the text—they also share a basic deficiency: they do not take sufficiently (if at all) into account the nature and effects of misery on the physical, psychological, moral, and spiritual development and identity of the (main) characters. The present article attempts to demonstrate that this omission makes all the difference, for misery operates in the novel as milieu and mediation for particular manifestations of divine grace and human transformation in (conformity to) Christ.

[14] See Henri Scepi, "*Les Misérables*, 'Un livre de charité'?" *Romantisme* 180, no. 2 (2018): 49.

deeds, this servant of God acts as an instrument for divine grace effecting the conversion of other persons. In him, the magnificence of divine grace resides and shows through:

> His whole face was luminous with a vague expression of contentment, hope, and bliss. It was more than a smile, almost a radiance.... A reflection of this heaven lay over the bishop. It was at the same time a luminous transparency, for this heaven was inside him. This heaven was the internal light of his conscience. (1.2.11, 86)

Hugo's portrayal of holiness in the figure of Myriel is not unilaterally dithyrambic, for it also evokes darker shades and undertones. Myriel's charity does not alter unjust social structures; it limits itself to bringing solace to the latter's undeserving victims. Mary Christian aptly observes that "Hugo makes clear that the bishop, though eager to relieve individual suffering, has little or nothing to say about institutional injustices, being 'anything but a political animal.' ... The bishop does not question the political status quo or suggest that it may play a role in causing the poverty he lightens."[15] While Myriel's charity is not explicitly intended to be the figment of a social revolution, it does embody alternative relational dynamics and way of life. Based on the life and deeds of a real bishop (Mgr. de Miollis), the figure of Myriel is but a rare instance of authentic Christian identity.[16]

If faith is to play a significant role in the transformation of French society, Christianity and the church have yet to bring this potential to fruition. Hugo gives voice to the need for profound transformation of religious institutions and practices. Scepi convincingly argues that Hugo transfers the notion and reality of charity from the realm of sacred doctrine and theology into that of secular practice and philosophy. In this latter realm, charity translates into the right to receive forgiveness and redemption (no one is excluded from experiencing and contributing actively to moral and social progress).[17] Acknowledging the church's failure to act as an agent of social reform, Myriel operates from the margins of the church, inaugurating the secularization of grace by triggering the inner transformation of the miserable, even former inmates.

The move of Christian life and values outside the Church will be brought to completion with Valjean's heartfelt belief, prayer, and discipleship exempt of participation in formal rituals.[18] Myriel (and later Valjean) embodies Hugo's attempt to redefine the Christian understanding and practice of charity in secular social and political terms.

---

[15] Christian, "Bought with Silver," 8.
[16] See Christian, "Bought with Silver," 4.
[17] See Scepi, "*Les Misérables*," 50.
[18] See David Bellos, *The Novel of the Century: The Extraordinary Adventure of* Les Misérables (New York: Farrar, Straus & Giroux, 2017), 162.

This reconceived concept of charity focuses on the inclusive and invincible love for humanity and the clear affirmation of moral perfectibility.[19] Charity supersedes law to administer a superior kind of justice, taking the form of infinite mercy. Henri Scepi astutely remarks that by promoting such a conception of charity, Hugo is led to rethink the nature and effects of sin and redemption. Hugo advocates for a "right to expiate" one's faults. God's infinite mercy never gives up on human beings, granting them ever-renewed opportunities to repent and experience conversion. Infinite mercy creates a possible future for fallen humanity, including the miserable.[20] Thus reconceived, charity becomes the cornerstone of Hugo's post-revolutionary social-political vision, for it enables and sustains authentic compassion for every human being, independently from their intrinsic qualities or external circumstances. Compassion entails the experience and manifestation of a shared humanity, itself the foundation of and condition for a democratic society.[21] Pity, not judgment, is the beginning and guiding principle of morality.[22]

After nineteen years in prison, Jean Valjean experiences both human and divine clemency in and through the person and actions of the Bishop of Digne. Rejected on account of his criminal record, he walks from one village to another unable to get food or find a place to stay. Noticing him lying on a bench, a lady urges him to knock at the bishop's door. In a scene whose Eucharistic overtones bring to mind the disciples on the road to Emmaus, Myriel welcomes Valjean, shares a meal with him and provides him with a room without asking anything from him, not even his name. This latter fact is most significant, for it bespeaks of the main challenge to which Valjean is confronted: (re)building his (moral and social) identity and reputation. As Pierre-Étienne Cudmore notes, "*Les Misérables* is, at a fundamental level, the story of a man who loses, recovers, redeems and, lastly, relinquishes his name."[23] During the night, Valjean's traumatized and hardened heart yields to the temptation of stealing the bishop's silverware and the ex-convict flees away. Arrested the next morning, he is confronted by the bishop. To his amazement, the bishop informs the officers that the silverware was a gift to which assorted chandeliers are to be added. As he is handing the latter over to Valjean, the bishop spells out the true meaning of his generous gesture:

> Don't forget, don't ever forget, that you promised me to use this silver to make an honest man of yourself.... Jean Valjean, my brother, you

---

[19] See Scepi, "*Les Misérables*," 55.

[20] See Scepi, "*Les Misérables*," 50.

[21] See Claude Millet, "'Commençons donc par l'immense pitié' (Victor Hugo)," *Romantisme* 142, no. 4 (2008): 14.

[22] See Millet, "Commençons donc par l'immense pitié," 10–11.

[23] Cudmore, "Jean Valjean et les avatars du poète éponyme," 171 (translation, mine).

no longer belong to evil but to good. It is your soul that I am buying for you; I am taking it away from black thoughts and from the spirit of perdition, and I am giving it to God. (1.2.12, 90)

Myriel's charity is realistic, for the bishop saves Valjean with undeserved mercy *and* expensive silverware. Spiritual transformation supposes basic material needs are met. As Christian observes, "The bishop confers new spiritual value on the silver utensils even while reaffirming their function as an economic resource. It is the economic value of the silver, as well as the kindness with which it is given, that allows it to be the instrument for Jean Valjean's salvation."[24] Valjean is to be judged by his future actions and character, as well as the use he makes of the gifted silverware. This fact leads Christian to further claim that "the story of Jean Valjean, like that of Judas Iscariot, insists that how one gets or spends one's silver may have far-reaching consequences for one's soul."[25] This "spiritual economics," whereby individuals are led to display their moral quality in daily commerce, is challenged by the unfair administration of justice in society. Valjean is sent to jail for a loaf of bread he stole to feed starving nephews and nieces for whose needs his limited outcome does not enable him to provide. His sentence is lengthened on account of his repeated attempts to escape from jail. For these reasons, Jacques Dubois believes that Valjean's plight establishes *Les Misérables* as the "narrative of punishment without [proportionate] crime."[26] *Les Misérables* would thus be the story of the struggle of the undeservedly reprobate to find purpose and achieve moral-spiritual maturity in and through human misery. Many characters share in this plight; the names of Fantine, Cosette, Éponine, Gavroche and Mabeuf naturally come to mind. These characters are subjected to undeserved poverty and hardship and seek to remain faithful to themselves and to the good.

Only once Valjean has committed a further crime—the robbery of Petit-Gervais, a poor wandering orphan—does the demand placed on him by Myriel's figure and gesture come to bear weight. Valjean falls "in a trance, caught in a limbo between his past life of survival through theft and his present and future life as a reformed man under the influence of the previous night's experience."[27] He realizes what the bishop has done to him. The bishop of Digne's completely undeserved forgiveness is summoning him to undergo spiritual transformation. Myriel's mercy forces Valjean to revive and listen to his long buried

---

[24] Christian, "Bought with Silver," 5.
[25] Christian, "Bought with Silver," 20.
[26] Jacques Dubois, "Le crime de Valjean et le châtiment de Javert," in *Crime et châtiment dans le roman populaire de langue française du XIXe siècle*, ed. Ellen Constans and Jean-Claude Vareille (Limoges: Presses universitaires de Limoges, 2013), 325.
[27] Gordon Leah, "Providence, Duty, Love," 25.

conscience. He must now take a stand for or against undeserved goodness.

> He felt indistinctly that the old priest's forgiveness was the greatest assault and the most deadly attack he had ever been rocked by; that if he could resist such clemency his heart would be hardened once and for all; that if he gave in to it, he would have to give up the hate that the actions of other men had filled his heart with for so many years and which he relished; that this time, he had to conquer or be conquered and that the struggle, a colossal and decisive struggle, was now on between his own rottenness and the goodness of that man. (1.2.13, 94–95)

THE PANGS OF CONVERSION

Valjean then goes into terrible pain, for the pure love displayed by Myriel strikingly reveals his need for conversion. This new awareness results from his already begun inner transformation. Kathryn M. Grossman explains: "In divesting himself of his silver, Myriel invests in Valjean. All he demands of the recipient is that he prove worthy of the promise that he could not have made in his prison of sin, but that he will have made following his liberation."[28] It is by experiencing self-revealing transformative misery that human beings come to learn and responsibly assume the truth about their moral condition.

> One thing was certain,...he was no longer the same man, already everything about him had changed, and it was no longer in his power to act as though the bishop had not spoken to him, had not touched him to the quick.... The very moment he shouted "I am a miserable bastard!" he saw himself for what he was, and he was already so dissociated from himself that he felt he was now no more than a ghost. (1.2.13, 95–96)

Within Valjean's conscience, the bishop of Digne now shines brightly as *the* ethical and spiritual ideal to pursue. Valjean desires to dwell in divine mercy, nothing else. Directly gazing at the ideal of holiness, he then reinterprets his existence in its light and measures the depth of his sinfulness (1.2.13, 97).

Myriel's intervention opens a new future for Jean Valjean, a life dedicated to growing in virtue (2.4.3, 363). Valjean's road to holiness will lead him to mature appropriation of his sinful self. The misery he must endure will turn him into a prism diffusive of divine mercy. To become a virtuous citizen, Valjean chooses to hide his criminal past. The preservation of his reputation depends on the quality of his behavior and ability to conceal his status of ex-convict. The converted

---

[28] Kathryn M. Grossman, *Figuring Transcendence in* Les Misérables*: Hugo's Romantic Sublime* (Carbondale: Southern Illinois University Press, 1994), 128.

Valjean thus applies himself to fulfilling Myriel's demanding vision: truly to become a holy man (1.7.3, 185). Using his wits and the money obtained from the sale of the silverware,[29] Valjean—now going by the name of Madeleine—manages to establish himself as a successful entrepreneur whose visionary leadership and moral integrity sustain the prosperity of an entire region (1.5.2, 136–37). Moving the focus of his attention away from himself, Valjean dedicates his time and energy to creating conditions where others can prosper and flourish. The name Valjean chooses to go by—Madeleine—suggests significant connections. "Madeleine" is the French rendering of "Magdalene," the patronym of a biblical character. Mary Madgalene is a "fallen" woman in social disrepute thanks to actions and/or status unfairly attributed to her, to whom Jesus grants the ability to "redeem herself." Valjean is a new Magdalene insofar as he has been granted by Mgr. Myriel with the ability to become an honest man, and promised to complete the mission of a "fallen" woman (Fantine): be a parental figure to Cosette. As will become clear later, Valjean—again like Magdalene—is invited to stand and live at the foot of Jesus's cross partaking in a privileged way in his passion.

But holiness demands more than the successful dissimulation of one's troubled past under bounteous philanthropy. Madeleine's generosity shows limitations similar to Myriel's charity: the thriving economy of Montreuil-sur-mer does not prevent people like Fantine from falling into undeserved misery which in turn leads her to moral deprivation and an untimely death. Madeleine's "insisting and faultless"[30] presence and ministry nurture in the villagers moral and spiritual dependence upon his benevolence. Such "virtue" does not withstand the test of time. The virtue of the villagers reflects that of Valjean himself, who can only be generous under the cover of a false identity. Holiness entails complete spiritual translucence, that is, transparency to divine grace and mercy. Measured by the ideal set by Myriel, the demands of Valjean's conscience, therefore, cannot be satisfied with his self-dedication to others, if the latter is not grounded in the complete acceptance of all he is and has done. Valjean is summoned to find holiness in his own misery, to transform this misery into an abode for the transcendent.

A convicted and interned criminal, Valjean is aware that his existence in society is forfeit. Madeleine's remarkable success, affable personality, and reserve (with more than a touch of aloofness) set him apart. He is a benefactor who expresses a generosity no aristocrat

---

[29] Jean-François Chiron rightly observes that Valjean only sells the dinnerware, faithfully keeping the chandeliers to the end of his life. The chandeliers remind him—especially in times of moral crisis—of Mgr. Myriel's merciful gesture, offer, and symbol of salvation ("Ce que des chandeliers peuvent exprimer," 461).

[30] Dubois, "Le crime de Valjean," 321–22.

could display. His nobility exceeds nobility conferred by birth. His moral integrity is, however, tainted by his inability to acknowledge his origins, at once humble and unknown. Valjean's "virtue is not entirely pure.… His radical 'transfiguration' from sinner to saint, a conversion that he must renew daily, requires the continual stripping away of the subtle layers of hypocrisy and egotism that so often warp one's judgment."[31] Valjean's conversion is not instantaneous, but rather takes the form of a lifelong journey of transformation marked by evermore unsettling challenges. Isabel Roche explains: "Valjean's trajectory is built upon successive moments of crisis, increasingly internalized and self-imposed, and each capable of fully undoing his moral progress."[32] To change his bitter self-centered heart of stone into a loving other-oriented heart of flesh Valjean must die many deaths and come to life again under as many distinct identities. This transformative process will bring him to suffer his own humanity in a redeeming way. Estranged from God and outlawed by human society, the dislocated Valjean exists outside the human world.

Converted and blessed by God through the instrumental agency of Myriel, Valjean is summoned to follow the dictates of his conscience, the locus where God reveals and expresses Godself personally. Hugo finds in conscience a manifestation of the divine within the human.[33] The converted Valjean's mission is to enter human society and redeem himself by working at the salvation of others. He must live according to principles not of this world, and thereby condemn himself in the eyes of others and his own. When Champmathieu, a fellow ex-convict, is about to be condemned for his crimes, Valjean, in the person of Madeleine, the respected mayor of Montreuil-sur-mer, is led to denounce himself. Losing everything, he faces the prospect of a life in prison (1.7.3, 190).

Michael Hoffheimer rightly emphasizes the bearings of the Champmathieu affair on Valjean's life and social standing:

> The Champmathieu affair radically alters Jean Valjean's legal status. When he escapes for the second time, he does not just face the burden of prejudice visited on former convicts as he had at the outset. For the rest of the novel, as an escaped prisoner serving a life sentence, he

---

[31] Kathryn M. Grossman, "Hugo's Romantic Sublime: Beyond Chaos and Convention in *Les Misérables*," *Philological Quarterly* 60, no. 4 (1981): 474–75.

[32] Isabel K. Roche, "On (the Usefulness of Hunger and) Beauty," in *Les Misérables and Its Afterlives—Between Page, Stage, and Screen*, ed. Kathryn M. Grossman and Bradley Stephens (Farnham: Ashgate, 2015), 21.

[33] See Yves Gohin, "L'étrange existence de Jean Valjean," in *From Baudelaire to Lorca: Approaches to Literary Modernism*, ed. José Manuel Losada Goya and Alfredo Rodriguez Lopez-Vazquez (Kassel: Reichenberger, 1996), 90.

faces the prospect of life imprisonment, possibly even death, if his identity is discovered.[34]

Valjean knows that in this process of self-humiliation, he is being led by a greater power.

> He turned away from all delusion, detached himself more and more from earthly things and sought consolation and strength elsewhere. He told himself he had to do his duty.... He told himself that it was essential, that this was his fate, that it was not for him to disturb the way things were arranged up above, that in any case he had to choose: either virtue without an abomination within or holiness within and disgrace on show without. (1.7.3, 192)

Mayor Madeleine dies for the prisoner Valjean to rise again. The conflict then raging in his heart attests of his enduring temptation to fall away from grace and virtue and his corollary need for further spiritual maturing. Valjean is by no means perfectly righteous; at least in three critical situations—during the Champmathieu affair, Marius's rescue, and the final surrender of Cosette—his moral integrity is on the brink of collapse and giving free rein to selfish possessive desires.

Before being led to prison, Madeleine-Valjean makes a promise to the dying Fantine: he will care for her orphaned daughter Cosette. He will nurture humanity in the person of Cosette, the suffering innocent (4.15.1, 948). For Cosette to become his adoptive daughter, though, Valjean must find a way to extricate himself from the hold of legal authorities. This, he accomplishes by disappearing into the sea while saving the life of a sailor. Valjean then releases Cosette from the custody of the Thénardiers, who grievously mistreated her, and takes her to Paris. Constable Javert, who suspects Valjean is still alive, finds and chases him in the streets of the city. Climbing a wall to save his and Cosette's life, Valjean finds himself in a convent of recluse nuns where he decides to stay for a time. To free himself from the relentless pursuit of blind human (in)justice embodied in Javert,[35] and to be able to fulfill his promise, Valjean can only live in a place which, while being located in the center of the city, is not strictly speaking part of it (2.8.1, 433–34). To live peacefully with Cosette in the cloister, he must leave its precincts without being discovered by both the nuns and the police and be admitted in "legitimate" manner. Valjean, as illegal intruder, must suffer death to rise again, this time as Ultime Fauche-

---

[34] Michael H. Hoffheimer, "Jean Valjean's Nightmare: Rehabilitation and Redemption in *Les Misérables*," *McGeorge Law Review* 43 (2012): 171.

[35] See Géraldine Crahay, "*Serenity*'s Operative and *Les Misérables*' Inspector Javert: The Masculinity of Scrupulous Civil Servants," *Slayage* 15, no. 1 (2017): 9.

levent, the brother of the cloister's gardener. Thus death and resurrection will involve, for Valjean, burial in a cemetery in place of a deceased nun and an interview with the prioress.

THE IDEAL AND THE TEST OF REALITY

These requirements met, a long period of formation begins for Valjean and Cosette. Converted by a bishop, Valjean continues his spiritual transformation in the cloister, taking care of the gardens and Cosette. In the cloister, Valjean practices gardening in external and internal gardens. Physical and spiritual gardening are interwoven: Valjean is both gardener and garden.[36] The orphaned daughter of a miserable woman, Cosette incarnates human innocence preserved in and despite undeserved suffering. Under the guidance of Valjean and the nuns, the sparkle of Cosette's childhood purity will grow into the radiance of adult virginity.[37] Hugo makes it clear that Cosette is not holy in or by herself, but rather is made holy through Valjean's (and the cloister nuns') agency (5.7.2, 1152).

André Brochu notes that *Les Misérables* contains no example of biological fathers expressing healthy love for and providing proper care to their daughters. Similarly, *Les Misérables* presents no instance of biological mothers showing healthy love to and taking good care of their sons. There are, however, instances of biological mothers showing effusive love and care for their daughters (e.g., Fantine toward Cosette).[38] Brochu further observes that the novel only allows for fatherly display of love toward a daughter when the latter is an adopted child. Valjean did not receive love from his parents, was forced to provide for his older sister's children and never had the opportunity to experience romantic love. Love starved, Valjean is a romantic wanderer who then promises to care for a child to whom he can relate as adoptive grandfather, father, mother and husband.[39] Overcoming the temptation to assume all these roles proves to be quite a challenge for Valjean, as the following parts of the narrative reveal.

Valjean's sufferings were not intended to end in the Petit-Picpus convent. For once he had successfully raised Cosette's untainted humanity to maturity, he felt compelled to introduce her to human society. The irony is that by taking Cosette out of the convent, Valjean curtails her freedom. In nineteenth-century France, as Bellos explains, convents are "'ideal communit[ies]' offering women an escape from

---

[36] See Mauri Cruz Previde, "A Vereda de João Traços de *Bildungsroman* em *Les Misérables* de Victor Hugo," *Lettres Françaises* 6 (2005): 96.

[37] See Isabel K. Roche, "Type Transformed: Character and Characterization in *Les Misérables*," in *Approaches to Teaching Hugo's* Les Misérables, 197.

[38] See Brochu, *Hugo: amour, crime, révolution*, 212.

[39] See Brochu, *Hugo: amour, crime, révolution*, 216.

the contradictions of civilian life" and this because they form "autonomous, self-governing communities of women."[40] When he brings Cosette into secular society, he at the same time ensures that she will not assert herself and will remain completely dependent on him, unless another man challenges his authority over her. Marius precisely levels such a challenge on the grounds of romantic love. Valjean must let go of his almost obsessive need for Cosette's presence. In the same way he preserved and nurtured her innocence and purity, he will save Marius from certain death at the hands of the French army (whose soldiers are busy quenching the civil uprising in which Marius is involved), by carrying him through the city's sewer system, bringing him back to his family and facilitating his union to Cosette. This journey into the entrails of the city will put him to the test and bring his extraordinary dedication, endurance, and humanity to the limit.

The journey into the sewer system is imbued with significant symbolism. The sewer forms the most elementary discriminatory system of the city; in it, the rejected meet and blend, standing equal in their marginalization and/or exclusion from society. This leveling down effect leads Maxwell to speak of the "ultimate democracy of the sewer."[41] More importantly, the sections of the narrative on the history of Paris' sewer system and Valjean's flight through it embody Hugo's critique of Parisian/French society's blindness to its own exclusionary practices. "The long sewer digression," argues Lewis, "can be read as a call for the reintegration of society's outcasts along with its waste water."[42] Justice is so administered that the rehabilitation of the socially excluded is not possible. In this context, the police becomes the instrument used by the city to monitor closely the boundary between society and its underworld and ensure that while reputed citizens enjoy status and privilege, disreputable individuals are never allowed to (re)gain any. Hugo wishes to change that. Valjean's story shows one can live in misery through no significant fault of one's own and grow out of it, into social-spiritual maturity. Out of the mud of the sewer (the contemporary analogue to the biblical dirt and dust) a renewed human condition may thus be forged. The elevation of the miserable is effected by means of free self-humiliation (kenosis).[43]

Carrying the grievously wounded Marius on his back, Valjean— risking his life—does not hesitate to enter fetid waters. When all hope is lost and he finds himself about to drown, his foot hits a stone on which he can stand and begin to make his way out (5.3.7, 1062). This

[40] Bellos, *The Novel of the Century*, 185.

[41] Richard Maxwell, "Mystery and Revelation in *Les Misérables*," *Romantic Review* 73, no. 3 (1982): 314.

[42] Briana Lewis, "The Sewer and the Prostitute in *Les Misérables*: From Regulation to Redemption," *Nineteenth-Century French Studies* 44, nos. 3–4 (2016): 274.

[43] See Maxime Goergen, "Fonctions de la lutte des classes dans *Les Misérables*," *Nineteenth-Century French Studies* 45, nos. 1–2 (2016–17): 44.

physical test prefigures and leads to a spiritual one. Reaching the outer limit of the sewer, Valjean walks into a locked gate. There he meets with Thénardier, a hardened criminal who wishes to profit from Valjean's need of a way out. Thénardier (alongside the other members of Patron-Minette) bears witness to Hugo's recognition that there is such a thing as irreformable persistence in evil. As Bellos observes, in *Les Misérables*, "the destructive potential of hate," taking "the form of resentment and greed," remains "an unsolved problem," for Thénardier is not moved by Valjean's example, abandons his wife and children, and ultimately sails to the Americas to own slaves.[44] Entering the sewer to flee from the police and assuming Valjean has killed the man he carries, Thénardier offers to open the gate in exchange for monetary compensation. Forced to accept the offer, Valjean exits the underground and re-enters human society only to fall into the hands of Javert. Offering no resistance to his arrest, Valjean begs Javert to allow him to leave the injured Marius with his grandfather.

Recognizing in Marius's savior his own, Javert faces his greatest moral challenge. Precisely when, mechanically applying the law, he is about to fulfill his duty and put this relapsing criminal behind bars, Javert's conscience compels him to set Valjean free.

> To owe your life to a malefactor, to accept his debt and pay it back, to be, in spite of yourself, on a par with a fugitive from justice and to pay him back for a good deed done by another good deed; to let him say to you, "Off you go" and to say to him in turn, "You're free," to sacrifice duty, that all-encompassing obligation, to personal motives, and to feel in those personal motives something that was also all-encompassing and, perhaps, superior; to betray society in order to remain true to your conscience—that all these absurd things should happen and should come and heap themselves upon him, absolutely floored him.... One thing had amazed him and that was that Jean Valjean had spared him; and one thing had petrified him, and that was that he, Javert, had spared Jean Valjean. (5.4.1, 1080)

To foresee the depth of Javert's internal conflict, one must consider how much Javert attempts to deny and transcend his own origins. The son of an inmate and a prostitute, Javert is a miserable and, in this regard, no different from Valjean. His status and role of police inspector scrupulously imposing the rule of law enable him to elevate himself over and beyond his own condition. Javert completely projects himself into a constructed identity and life based on the rigorous distinction between just and criminal. His status of judge standing at the frontier of civilized society and its unlawful fringes depends on his

---

[44] Bellos, *The Novel of the Century*, 206. See also Leichter-Flack, "Encore un mal que le roman nous fait?" 73.

ability to play his part rigorously (admitting no mistakes). As Fiona Cox spells out:

> In his despair at his exile from society Javert forges an identity of ab-
> solute integrity for himself which enters into direct conflict with the
> identity that is his birthright. He is an actor playing a part which he
> has scripted for himself.... It is only by turning himself into a carica-
> ture that Javert is able to bear the ordeal of existing.... To become an
> actor in one's life is symptomatic of the loss of the self, as it points to
> either a sense of emptiness, or the sense of being the wrong person
> born into the wrong background.[45]

The constructed character of Javert's identity as dutiful servant of the law is rendered all the more obvious by the fact that he persists in his role while and as he is forced to swear allegiance to diverse politi-cal systems and rulers. For, as Crahay explains, "The inspector lives in troubled times and has experienced many changes of regimes, in-cluding absolute as well as constitutional monarchies, a revolution, a republic, and an empire. In spite of all the historical, political, and so-cial changes of his times, Javert remains true in serving law and order, regardless of their coming from an emperor, an absolute king, or a constitutional king."[46] None of these significant social and political upheavals and redefinitions lead Javert to question or alter his con-structed identity and administration of justice.

When he decides to obey his conscience and let Valjean go, how-ever, Javert completely redefines his moral identity, breaking "char-acter," freeing himself from his self-made role and subjecting his eth-ics of duty to a higher principle allowing for evil to be turned into good and sinfulness to be morphed into sanctity. Javert recognizes the pos-sibility and need for moral discernment; "He discovers with anxiety the constraint of thinking by himself."[47] Javert must reckon with the reality of moral and spiritual growth. Human justice must be subjected to divine mercy. During the civil uprising of 1832, Valjean had dis-played gratuitous mercy by setting him free instead of rightfully taking his life. He thereby protected, reasserted, and fulfilled human law through the expression of charity. Javert perceives this supernatural truth and is summoned by his conscience to emulate Valjean's behav-ior.

> A whole order of unexpected acts surged up and subjugated him. A
> whole new world appeared to his soul: kindness accepted and re-

---

[45] Fiona Cox, "'The Dawn of a Hope so Horrible': Javert and the Absurd," in *Victor Hugo: Romancier de l'abîme*, ed. James A. Hiddleston (Oxford: Legenda, 2002), 81.
[46] Crahay, *"Serenity's* Operative," 4–5.
[47] Crahay, *"Serenity's* Operative," 7.

turned, devotion, miséricorde, leniency, the havoc wreaked on auster-
ity by pity, acceptance of other people, no more definitive condemnation, no more damnation, the possibility of a tear pearling in the eye
of the law, some indefinable sense of justice according to God's rules
that was the reverse of justice according to man. He saw in the darkness the terrifying sun of an unknown morality dawning. (5.4.1, 1082)

Javert finds himself in a situation analogous to that of Pontius Pilate having to decide the fate of Jesus.

This man is forever a prisoner of the law; the law will do with him
what it likes. What could be more just? Javert had told himself all that;
he had tried to carry on regardless, to act, to apprehend the man, and,
then as now, he had not been able to; and every time his hand had shot
up convulsively toward Jean Valjean's collar, his hand had dropped
again, as though under an enormous weight, and in the back of his
mind, a voice, a strange voice, cried out to him: "Go on, then. Hand
over your savior. Then have them bring you Pontius Pilate's washba-
sin and wash your claws." (5.4.1, 1082)

Javert foresees that Valjean's radical spiritual transformation and
free self-sacrifice reveal God. While he manages to muster enough
courage to release Valjean, he—and in him human law and justice—
cannot accept to subject himself to the supernatural justice of God—
the law of love—and commits suicide. The recognition of Valjean's
humanity and his own shows to be too much for Javert to handle. The
narrator explains that after his conversion, Valjean can no longer use
violence against himself or others. The aggressive use of force implies
the denial of the divine purpose and human dignity embodied in one's
person and that of others. Suicide bears eternal consequences (5.3.11,
1073).

CONFESSING THE TRUTH

The narrator of *Les Misérables* claims that the purpose served by
the novel resides in the provision of a figure that can lead humanity to
take "a step from bad to good, from the unjust to the just, from the
false to the true, from night to day, from appetite to awareness, from
rottenness to life; from bestiality to duty, from hell to heaven, from
nothingness to God" (5.1.20, 1018). The person and moral-spiritual
journey of Jean Valjean embody this figure. Following his conscience
led Valjean to allow his personal identity to be absorbed in God's, for
"God is not only his guide, but is controlling his entire character."[48]
Valjean's self-sacrifice for others turns him into "another Christ."[49]

---

[48] Leah, "Providence, Duty, Love," 31.
[49] Jean Malavié, "Victor Hugo et la prière: sa présence dans *Les Misérables*," in ADI-
REL, *Travaux de littérature* (Paris: Klincksieck, 1993), 253.

On his deathbed, Valjean confesses the name of the one in whose footsteps he was summoned to follow: the crucified Christ (5.9.5, 1190-91). Converted by Myriel's clemency, Valjean was called to sacrifice and suffer everything to obey his conscience, serving God by demonstrating altruistic love. Throughout his life,

> He had been subjected to horrific trials and tribulations; not a single assault and battery of an ill-starred life had ever been spared him; the ferocity of fate, armed with every act of vengeance and every kind of social scorn, had taken him up and hounded him relentlessly. He had not backed down or flinched before any of it. He had accepted, when he had to, every violent blow; he had sacrificed his inviolability as a man redeemed, surrendered his freedom, risked his neck, lost everything, been to hell and back, and had remained disinterested and stoical, to the point where at times you might have thought him dissociated from himself in the manner of a martyr. (4.15.1, 947)

Valjean dedicates everything he is and does to the salvation of others (Cosette and Marius, especially). His vocation is one of perpetual devotion (5.6.4, 1134). Humanity now stands under divine judgment. Hugo has the narrator unambiguously assert: "The earth is not unlike a jail. Who knows if man is not an ex-convict of divine justice? Look closely at life. It is so made that you can sense punishment everywhere" (4.7.1, 810). Humanity's primary access to truth resides in suffering, for "whoever does not weep, does not see" (5.1.16, 1001). Misery is therefore the crucible into which the moral identity of each person is forged for good or ill. Confronting those subjected to it with absolute humiliation, misery excludes neutrality and half-measures. The miserable wholly commit themselves to God (Valjean) or reject him completely (Thénardier) (3.5.1, 560). Removing that which, in the human soul, is materially superfluous, misery fosters spiritual contemplation (3.5.3, 565–66).

Not all experiences of suffering and misery, however, induce spiritual growth. As Porter notes, for Hugo "suffering is a necessary but insufficient precondition for spiritual progress. It must be understood and transformed through a connection to God—through conscience (God's voice speaking to humans) and prayer (humans speaking to God)."[50] Valjean's ethical-spiritual dilemmas and struggles deepen and intensify as he grows in faith and holiness. In Mary O'Neil's apt words, "Jean Valjean's transformation from a brutish criminal without a moral conscience into an honest father and citizen requires vigilance and commitment.... Hugo insists upon the anguish suffered by his protagonist, who most often contemplates alternatives alone in a darkness

---

[50] Laurence M. Porter, "The Grotesque and Beyond in *Les Misérables*: Material Privation and Spiritual Transfiguration," in *Les Misérables and its Afterlives*, 50.

that suggests his doubts. Choice becomes more difficult rather than easier."[51]

Misfortune can thus lead to an encounter with God, when God wishes to disclose Godself and pour out grace into miserable humanity. "The pupil dilates in the night and ends up finding a kind of daylight there, just as the soul dilates in misery and ends up finding God" (5.3.1, 1047). Judged and condemned by human justice and society, God invites Valjean, through the mediation of Myriel, Fantine, and Cosette, to suffer the punishment unjustly imposed upon him. After having over-expiated his own crimes in prison, Valjean enters the Petit-Picpus convent to learn how to take upon himself human sinfulness on behalf of others. Valjean comes to understand that

> The most divine form of human generosity [is] atonement for others.... the sublime summit of self-abnegation, the highest peak of virtue possible—that innocence that forgives men for their sins and atones in their stead; servitude endured, torture accepted, torment sought out by souls who have not sinned in order to exempt from such torment souls that have faltered; the love of humanity losing itself in the love of God, yet remaining there, distinct and imploring; gentle weak creatures taking on the misery of those who are punished. (2.8.9, 472)

Like the cloistered nuns, Valjean lives by faith, identifying with "those humble and august souls who dare to live on the very brink of mystery...aspiring to the void and the unknown, their eye fixed on the unmoving darkness, on their knees, overcome, stunned, shivering, half lifted up at certain moments by the deep breaths of eternity" (2.7.8, 432). Out of his entire person a living and open prayer is made.[52] Valjean's humanity becomes a privileged locus for the manifestation of the divine in this world. In Valjean's suffering, endured out of love, humanity is perfected and meets with God, for "to put the infinite below in touch with the infinite above, in thought—this is what we call prayer" (2.7.5, 428).

FOR A TRULY EMPOWERING RELIGIOSITY

While the previous considerations demonstrate that the author of *Les Misérables* upholds modern society's need for the Christian faith, in this work Victor Hugo also expresses views highly critical of the way of life adopted by a majority of Christians in his day. The problem is that, in most cases, intense religious devotion leads to disengagement from real life and world, leaving the faithful unaffected by historical events and changes. Truly devout Christians do not take enough

---

[51] Mary A. O'Neil, "Pascalian Reflections in *Les Misérables*," *Philological Quarterly* 78, no. 3 (1999): 343–44.

[52] For a detailed treatment of Hugo's relationship to and practice of prayer, see Malavié, "Victor Hugo et la prière," 225–61.

of an active part in the transformation of society. Their asceticism leaves them trapped in an emotional and moral standstill. See, for instance, how Hugo's narrator characterizes the spiritual life of Marius's aunt, as she reacts to the many changes affecting her existence:

> Aunt Gillenormand studied all this with her unflappable placidity. She had had a certain dose of emotion in the space of five or six months.... Then she reverted to her usual indifference, the lack of interest of a first communicant. She regularly went to church services, said her rosary, read her prayer book, which she called a *Euchologion*, whispered *Aves* in one corner of the house while they were whispering *I love you*s in the other, looked on Marius and Cosette as two shadows. She was the shadow. There is a certain state of inert asceticism in which the soul, neutralized by torpor, foreign to what might be called the business of living, does not pick up any human impressions, whether pleasant or painful—with the exception of earthquakes and other disasters. (5.5.6, 1108)

Hugo wants nothing to do with a religious practice which "cannot smell anything of life"; he is looking for a religiosity that permeates the whole person, empowering her to engage history in a transformative way. God reveals and accomplishes his will in history. Those who do not interpret and engage history have no access to the supernatural aspect of human existence (4.1.4, 688). God is the goal of history, the aim and purpose of human action, life, and society. Progress is the means and way that leads from the current human predicament—that is, misery—to the ideal that is God (5.1.20, 1013). God is not an abstract truth, but a practical absolute, an ideal that leads to and empowers for righteous action. Hugo's God speaks to human beings from within their hearts, as the binding voice of conscience.[53] For Hugo, the true power of Christianity resides in its ability to enter and indwell misery, to effect the conversion of the human soul by sharing in the condition of the destitute and to bring authentic consolation by humbly embodying the divine in the midst of poverty. To this mission, Mgr. Myriel and Jean Valjean after him devote their whole persons and lives (2.7.6, 430). Valjean experienced the resuscitation of his conscience by Mgr. Myriel. As Bellos notes, "possession, emulation, duty, conscience and the divine are all wrapped up"[54] to form a cohesive process of moral (trans)formation. The encounter with Mgr. Myriel and the undeserved expression of mercy received make such an impression on Valjean that they lastingly take hold of him and become a standard he feels summoned to imitate.

From then on, Valjean recognizes the sacredness of human existence and refuses to commit any act denying the dignity or preventing

---

[53] See Bellos, *The Novel of the Century*, 258.
[54] Bellos, *The Novel of the Century*, 258.

the moral-spiritual progress and flourishing of any human person. Valjean finds in his conscience a transcendent norm for action. In the fateful encounter between Myriel and Valjean, Victor Hugo is offering no less than "a reversal of Mephistopheles's pact with Dr. Faust" which has "Myriel purchase the ex-prisoner's soul with an unsolicited and almost inconceivable gift."[55] Divine mercy, expressed through the mediation of a righteous person, and not knowledge or power, redeems humankind. Valjean takes this process one step further by including his own life in the gift. He repeatedly puts his life on the line to protect the lives of those he loves. He ultimately overcomes his own selfish desires and chooses to give his life to expiate for others. He learned this from the Petit-Picpus recluse nuns. Having lost his biological family through crime, Valjean binds himself to all human beings in mercy. Altruistic love and service demand the surrender of self to receive others.[56] Valjean is not only officiating as priest, but also as offering presented to God. The Eucharistic and Christlike overtones of the final scenes of the narrative cannot be missed or denied.

Hugo's *Les Misérables* serves an overarching purpose: affirm "the possibility of transformation and transcendence, on economic, social, moral and spiritual planes."[57] To achieve this goal, the narrative demonstrates that education and language can be "a vector of human diversity and of the human potential for change."[58] Progress occurs through the expression of an excess of trust and love going far beyond the legitimate demands of human justice. Myriel and Valjean believe and love humanity in an unfathomable way. They believe and love humanity to the point of giving their life to redeem it. Faith and love move history forward by empowering people to embody the transcendent ideal in unprecedented ways. As Laurence Porter remarks, Victor Hugo invokes the Christian concept of the communion of saints, which he sets as both the means and goal of social activism and transformation: "A person who has benefitted from a generous act by another is inspired to 'pay it forward' by selflessly helping someone else."[59] Under the sure guidance of divine providence, history will ultimately bring about the emergence and "consecration of a classless, egalitarian, democratic republic."[60] As Mgr. Myriel's encounter with the former revolutionary illustrates—by having the bishop recognize that though their respective ways of enacting it differ significantly, they do share a common vision of truth—Hugo's premise and conclusion is, as Julia Viglione argues, that "redemption must extend to all

---

[55] Bellos, *The Novel of the Century*, 254.
[56] See Kathryn M. Grossman, "Homelessness, Wastelands, and Barricades: Transforming Dystopian Spaces in *Les Misérables*," *Utopian Studies* 4 (1991): 32.
[57] David Bellos, "Sounding Out *Les Misérables*," *Dix-Neuf* 20, nos. 3–4 (2016): 249.
[58] Bellos, "Sounding Out *Les Misérables*," 249.
[59] Porter, "Teaching Social Class," 63.
[60] Porter, "Teaching Social Class," 63.

humanity, not just the exceptional Christian."[61] Hugo uses Christian values (charity, mercy, altruistic service, and sacrifice) to assess the shortcomings of and respond to the challenges confronting society in his time. Hugo invokes these values to critique both secular society and the Church (institutional religion) and proposes to fulfill the first and complete the mission of the second by realizing the democratic ideal.[62] Hugo advocates for a new Church in the world, as transformed world. Hugo's secular ecclesiology does not envision a world Church, but rather a church World.

In the end *Les Misérables* certainly does not offer easy recipes for quick and comprehensive social transformation, for as André Brochu observes, "The only successful revolution in the book is Valjean's, thanks to which Cosette and Marius will be able to live their love in full."[63] Valjean's moral, social, and spiritual revolution is personal, that is, fully accomplished only in his own person and this at the cost of great sacrifices. The completion of Valjean's salvation occurs in and through death, which means he could not definitively overcome the conflict between sinner and saint raging in his heart in this life. Final resolution and true holiness are granted only after and beyond the current existence. Luther's *simul justus et peccator* finds emphatic reaffirmation in Hugo's famous narrative. Valjean never becomes a respectable citizen; he can only provide for Cosette who will become one through marital alliance. "Valjean's true identity," argues Isabel Roche, "is and remains undesirable throughout. It is, in fact, his decision to reveal his true name, first to Javert and then to Marius, that brings about Valjean's subsequent and ultimate dispossession of self."[64] The prevailing capitalist social order is not affected by Valjean's personal transformation and salvation, which only results in the emergence of new Bourgeois consumers.[65] The decline of the prosperity of Montreuil-sur-mer after the demise of Mr. Madeleine only confirms such an assessment. Motivated in part by romantic grief (over the supposed move of Cosette to England), Marius's involvement in revolutionary activism dies with his marriage. Cosette does not promise to become more than a submissive housewife.[66] The deaths of other inherently "good" or "just" characters such as Fantine,

---

[61] Julia Douthwaite Viglione, "*Les Misérables* and the French Revolution: How to Keep That 'Unfamiliar Light' Aflame," in *Approaches to Teaching Hugo's* Les Misérables, 132.

[62] See José Rafael Arce Gamboa, "La justicia y la misericordia en *Los Miserables*," *Revista de Lenguas Modernas* 19 (2013): 718.

[63] Brochu, *Hugo: amour, crime, révolution*, 242 (translation mine).

[64] See Roche, "Type Transformed," 195.

[65] See Viglione, "*Les Misérables* and the French Revolution," 135.

[66] See Laurence M. Porter, "Teaching Social Class and the Dynamics of History in Hugo's *Les Misérables*," in *Approaches to Teaching Hugo's* Les Misérables, 58.

Éponine, Gavroche, Enjolras, and Mabeuf further demonstrate that personal redemption does not coincide with social transformation.[67]

With the main narrative not altering prevailing social conditions and structures, with so many character arcs reaching an inconclusive ending, readers feel entitled to enquire as to what Hugo wished to accomplish with *Les Misérables*. By disrupting the natural flow of the narrative, the author forces readers to take critical distance from their interpretive expectations.[68] Self-questioning precisely is that with which Hugo himself was confronted in the wake of the failed revolution of 1851, as he spent more than a decade in exile and revised the manuscript that would be released in 1862 as *Les Misérables*. Hugo then still believes in the ideal and motto set forth by the French revolution—Liberty, Equality, Fraternity—but he holds these values higher than national identity and pride. To him, these values are universal and respond to global ills—ignorance, poverty, and criminality (resulting from destitution and despair).[69]

The failure of revolution does not lead Hugo the social reformer to give up on his faith in the possibility of creating a "classless, egalitarian, democratic republic."[70] To sustain this belief, he retrieves from the Christian tradition the theological virtue of charity, which he understands as the principle and expression of infinite compassion providing healing, purpose, and a future to those in need, especially the miserable (guilty and innocent). Hugo foresees and professes that successful revolutions involve conversion, that is, complete inner transformation. Valjean's story is at once the proposal and enactment of a "programme of social action."[71] The accomplishment of this revolutionary programme is made possible by the free decision of individuals who, listening to their conscience, take a leap of faith and express gratuitous mercy, even and as no objective external confirmation or inner consolation ensue. Mgr. Myriel and Jean Valjean teach us to acknowledge and transform our condition of miserable by receiving and offering in our own turn the gratuitous mercy giving life and hope. Despite and against all odds, shattered dreams, and unfulfilled expectations, these characters are empowered to reinvent themselves to give form to a different way of being human. Through them, Hugo invites his readers to elect the way of boundless love, the way of God, the way to God, the true human way. ▣

---

[67] See Roche, "Type Transformed," 198.
[68] See Timothy Raser, "No Expectations: An Aspect of Misery in *Les Misérables*," in *Approaches to Teaching Hugo's* Les Misérables, 186.
[69] See Victor Hugo, *Letter of 18 October 1862 to Gino Daëlli*, cited in Bellos, *The Novel of the Century*, 237.
[70] Porter, "Teaching Social Class," 63.
[71] See Bellos, *The Novel of the Century*, 202–03.

Jean-Pierre Fortin is Associate Professor of Practical Theology at the Faculty of Theology of the University of St. Michael's College (Toronto, Canada). He is currently working on his third book, *Evolving Grace: Spiritual History of a Christian Doctrine*, to be released by Fortress Press. His teaching and research focus on the spiritual formation of the human person through the processing of traumatic experiences.

Journal of Moral Theology, Vol. 11, No. 1 (2022): 154–166

"All Creatures Moving Forward": Reconsidering the Ethics of Xenotransplantation in Light of *Laudato Si'*

Skya Abbate

The ultimate destiny of the universe is in the fullness of God, which has already been attained by the risen Christ, the measure of the maturity of all things. Here, we can add yet another argument for rejecting every tyrannical and irresponsible domination of human beings over other creatures. The ultimate purpose of other creatures is not to be found in us. Rather, all creatures are moving forward with us and through us towards a common point of arrival, which is God, in that transcendent fullness where the risen Christ embraces and illumines all things. Human beings, endowed with intelligence and love, and drawn by the fullness of Christ, are called to lead all creatures back to their Creator. – *Laudato Si'*, no. 83.

T HE SCIENTIFIC AND MEDICAL INTERVENTION of xenotransplantation involves the transfer of non-human tissues or organs into human recipients.[1] As a scientific option designed to augment the shortage of living organ donors and deceased organ donation, which aim to prolong and improve the quality of life of people with life-threatening illnesses or proximate death, xenotransplantation encounters scientific hurdles and poses ethical problems. The ethical issues that lie at the center of this process include the use of non-human animals for experimentation and organ donation, the sacredness of the human genome and human procreation, and the ethics of zoological responsibility according to the Catholic tradition. For all people and the global community, the safety of the process remains a concern.

While xenotransplantation is not mentioned in the papal encyclical *Laudato Si'*, addressed to all people, Pope Francis expounds on the ethics of xenotransplantation by offering a broad philosophical framework for bioethical decision-making through his discussion of the en-

---

[1] Tushar Samdani, "Xenotransplantation," *Medscape*, November 13, 2018, emedicine.medscape.com/article/1432418-overview#a3.

vironment, planetary justice, and the natural relationship between humans and non-human animals. Grounded in the Catholic tradition and building upon Sacred Scripture and Catholic social teaching (CST), *Laudato Si'* constitutes the most mature and promising, albeit incomplete, articulation of human and non-human animal relationships seen within the integral wholeness of all creation. The ethical permissibility of xenotransplantation in the Catholic community requires further discussion and reconsideration in light of *Laudato Si'* to meet the ethical obligations of safety, respect, and dignity owed to humans and living creatures.

XENOTRANSPLANTATION: HARMS AND BENEFITS

Xenotransplantation has evolved as a response and a potential solution to the worldwide shortage of human organs for human transplantation, known as allotransplantation, which is the transfer of an organ or tissue from one organism to another within the same species.[2] The major source of organs for transplantation derives from the voluntary informed consent of donors prior to brain death.[3] Other avenues of organ procurement exist, such as living organ donation through voluntary informed consent or deceased organ donation through presumed consent practiced to varying degrees in Europe in countries such as Spain and Austria.[4] The increasing incidence of vital organ failure and an inadequate supply of organs, especially through deceased organ donation, creates a wide gap between organ supply and demand, resulting in long waiting lists for transplants and increasing numbers of deaths.[5] As of February 21, 2021, over 107,000 Americans remained on organ transplant waiting lists.[6]

To meet the demand for organ shortages, pigs have been identified as the most genetically compatible potential donors to humans. Until recently, questions remained on the safety of porcine endogenous ret-

---

[2] G. M. Abouna, "Ethical Issues in Organ Transplantation," *Medical Principles and Practice* 12 (2003): 54, www.karger.com/Article/Abstract/68158.

[3] Rafael Beyar, "Challenges in Organ Transplantation," *Rambam Maimonides Medical Journal* 2, no. 2 (2011): e0049, doi.10.5041/RMMJ.10049 RMMJ/, www.rmmj.org.il.

[4] Amber Rithalia, Catriona McDaid, Sara Suekarran, Lindsey Meyers, and Amanda Sowden, "Impact of Presumed Consent for Organ Donation on Donation Rates: A Systematic Review," *British Medical Journal* 338, no. 7689 (2009): 338a.3162, doi:10.1136/bmj.a.3162.

[5] *Health Resources & Service Administration*, www.organdonor.gov/statistics-stories/statistics.html.

[6] *Health Resources & Service Administration*.

roviruses and their spread to future patients and the general population.[7] However, there is no evidence to suggest their virulence.[8] Nevertheless, the impact of xenotransplantation on the discovery of numerous new viruses identified from the study of the porcine virome remains uncertain.[9] More than a decade's worth of experience with the HIV pandemic illustrates the delayed expression of animal-to-human infection.[10] The possibility of latent, occult disease may not manifest for years.[11] Consequently, safety issues concerning zoonotic infection, which is infection from non-human animals to humans, persist as unknown harms.

The use of non-human animals for experimentation and organ donation is the foundation of xenotransplantation. The ethical arguments regarding animal experimentation form the infrastructure of xenotransplantation and run the spectrum from the permissibility of experimentation to limited use with less-complex organisms (such as bacteria and cells) to complete prohibition.[12] Xenotransplantation advocates justify experimentation by distinguishing the perceived difference between animal and human equivalency.[13] A utilitarian perspective leads some to conclude that the adverse effects of transgenic pig donors do not outweigh the potential benefits to human recipients.[14] For many researchers, the permissibility of xenotransplantation hinges on observing the principles of biomedical ethics and the respect they believe should be accorded to animals.[15] It is noteworthy that the implementation of xenotransplantation necessitates largescale breeding and killing of animals.[16] Such actions compound the existing largescale killing of animals for food in industrial breeding settings.

---

[7] Joachim Denner, "The Porcine Virome and Xenotransplantation," *Virology Journal* 14, no. 1 (2017): 171, doi.10.1186/s2985-017-0836-z.

[8] C. Smetanka and D. K. Cooper, "The Ethics Debate in Relation to Xenotransplantation," *Review of Scientific Technology* 24, no. 11 (2005): 335.

[9] Denner, "The Porcine Virome."

[10] NCBI, Institute of Medicine (US) Committee on Xenograft Transplantation, *Xenotransplantation: Science, Ethics, and Public Policy* (Washington, D.C.: National Academies Press, 1996).

[11] NCBI, *Xenotransplantation*, 11.

[12] D. Sachs and M. Sykes, "A Tolerance Approach to Xenotransplantation," *National Institutes of Health*, www.grantome.com/grant/NIH/P01-A1045897-15.

[13] *HOPES, Huntington's Outreach Project for Education at Stanford*, hopes.stanford.edu/animal-research/.

[14] *HOPES*, 4.42.

[15] Paul B. Thompson, "Animal Biotechnology: How to Presume," *American Journal of Bioethics* 6 (2008): 49.

[16] Nuffield Council on Bioethics, *Animal-to-Human Transplants: The Ethics of Xenotransplantation* (London: Nuffield Council, 1996), 4.1.

THE CATHOLIC POSITION INFORMS THE ETHICS OF XENOTRANS-PLANTATION

The Catholic tradition, embedded within Sacred Scripture and CST, offers guidance on the Catholic moral assessment of xenotransplantation. Furthermore, *Laudato Si'* builds upon these teachings and papal promulgations on the relationship between humans and non-human animals, which is the foundational premise of xenotransplantation. These teachings and their historical timeline require examination to evaluate the consistency of Catholic moral thought on xenotransplantation and to appreciate *Laudato Si'* as a paradigm that could transform CST and the future of this ethical issue.

Prior to Pope Pius XII's first papal articulation on transplants, Thomas Aquinas began this conversation on the nature and treatment of non-human animals in his *Summa Theologiae*. In his writing, while always maintaining the superiority of human beings as the summit of rationality, he acknowledges that non-human animals have a natural end to grow to a state of maturity characteristic of its species. Aquinas is somewhat conflicted by placing human beings in this hierarchy, but his writings show that he is not anthropocentric since he perceives that each creature has a role in the perfection of creation. While Aquinas could surely not have predicted xenotranplantation, his broad range theology establishes the premise that non-human animals have a value independent of their usefulness to human beings as unique manifestations of a triune God (ST I q.47, a. 2). This philosophy can be seen in later magisterial thought.

On May 14, 1956, in an allocution to the Italian Association of Cornea Donors, Clinical Oculists, and Legal Medical Practitioners, Pope Pius XII outlined Catholic views of acceptable conditions for allotransplantation and xenotransplantation.[17] He noted the following in his address: 1) the transplanted organ cannot impair the integrity of the genetic or psychological identity of the recipient; 2) the transplant must have a proven biological record of possible success; and 3) the transplant cannot involve inordinate risk for the recipient.

The reasonable safety of the human recipient comprised the common denominator of these conditions in the voluntary donation of vital organs. Counteracting the existing utilitarian attitude of subordination of the individual to the common good characteristic of his time, Pius XII insisted that doctors should seek to protect and restore health and bodily integrity for "in humanity each individual is a value in himself, although related to others."[18] Donation was construed as an act of charity. Pius XII declared,

---

[17] John Paul II, "Address to the 35th Assembly of the World Medical Association," October 29, 1983, *L'Osservatore Romano*, English edition, December 5, 1986, 11.

[18] Gerald Kelly, "Pope Pius XII and the Principle of Totality," *Theological Studies* 16, no. 3 (1955): 373–396.

One cannot say that every kind of transplantation of tissue that is biologically possible between individuals of different species is to be
morally condemned, but it is still less true to say that no kind of het-
erogeneous transplant biologically possible could be prohibited or
could give rise to any objections. One must distinguish according to
the case and see which tissue or which organ it is a question of trans-
planting. The transplantation of sexual glands of animals into humans
is to be rejected as immoral; but on the other hand, the transplantation
of the cornea of a non-human organism into a human organism does
not pose any moral difficulties if it is biologically possible and medi-
cally indicated.[19]

Over 30 years later, in December 1987, Pope John Paul II wrote in
Sollicitudo Rei Socialis that moral demands impose a limit on the use
of the natural world. The dominion granted to humans by the Creator
is not an absolute power or a freedom to use, misuse, or dispose of
things as one pleases (no. 34). His thoughts assist in defining the concept of dominion found in Genesis as "power that has limitations."
While not addressing xenotransplantation, this epistemology of the
use of the natural world might give rise to xenotransplant objections.

Later, on January 1, 1990, when John Paul II spoke of the integrity
of creation in his *Message on the Celebration of the World Day of
Peace*, he continued to define dominion as power circumscribed by
the relationship between human activity and the whole of creation (no.
5). In this proclamation, John Paul II underscored the nobility of the
human vocation to participate responsibly in God's creative action in
the world by emphasizing respect for life and, above all, the dignity of
the human person as the ultimate guiding norms for any sound economic, industrial, or scientific progress (no. 7). The pope encouraged
fraternity with living things that Almighty God has created and humanity's serious obligation to respect and watch over them with care.
Again, while not specific to xenotransplantation, these overarching
themes of relationship in the created order presaged later Catholic
thought on the solidarity between human and non-human animal species found in the *Catechism of the Catholic Church* and the *Compendium on the Social Doctrine of the Church*.

Renewing the Earth, a November 1991 pastoral statement by the
United States Conference of Catholic Bishops, continued the development of CST to be later expanded upon by Pope Francis in *Laudato
Si'*. *Renewing the Earth* devoted itself to the biblical values of stewardship and how people must live in harmony with creation through
their social structures. The goodness of creation (Genesis 1:32) and
the mandate to cultivate and care for it (Genesis 2:15) serve as the

---

[19] Pius XII, "Address to Eye Specialists," May 14, 1956.

basis for the interpretation of stewardship.[20] Stewardship places upon humans the responsibility for the care of all of God's creatures, who are not to be seen as a means of human fulfillment.

The 1994 version of the *Catechism of the Catholic Church* examines the relationship between humans and non-human animals. This relationship allows non-human animals to be used for food, clothing, and labor. Human dominion over non-human animals was not conceived of as absolute but within "reasonable limits" as long as "needless suffering" was averted. The *Catechism* qualifies that human power has its limits and that it is contrary to human dignity to cause animals to suffer or die needlessly for every act of cruelty towards any creature is contrary to human dignity (no. 2418). The *Catechism* teaches that experimentation on animals is moral only if it remains within reasonable limits and contributes to saving human lives and the necessities of human life (no. 2417). All such uses and experimentation require religious respect for the integrity of creation (no. 2415). While acknowledging the inherent worth of non-human animals and the necessities of human life, such as food, tension persists in applying these concepts to the Catholic moral assessment of xenotransplantation. The lack of definitions on reasonable limits, needless suffering, and the necessities of human life and the failure to mention xenotransplantation contributes to these problems.

On August 29, 2000, in the conclusion of his "Address of the Holy Father John Paul II to the 18th International Congress of the Transplantation Society," Pope John Paul II broached the topic of xenotransplantation. He commented that xenotransplantation remains in the experimental stages and that it was not his intent to explore in detail the problem of its legitimacy as raised by Pius XII. Nevertheless, John Paul II affirmed that the principles outlined by Pius XII on the safety required for humans remain unclear (no. 7). He went on to encourage allotransplantation when he spoke: "There is still a need to instill in people's hearts, especially in the hearts of the young, a genuine and deep appreciation of the need of brotherly love, a love that can find expression in the decision to become an organ donor" (no. 8).

Shortly thereafter in 2001 the Pontifical Academy for Life issued their work, *Prospects for Xenotransplantation: Scientific Aspects and Ethical Considerations.* Here, they upheld Pius XII's original position that, from the standpoint of moral theology, the ethical conditions required for every other kind of transplant apply to xenotransplantation. For instance, no organs such as the brain or gonads that ensure procreative identity and embody the characteristic uniqueness of a person's

---

[20] United States Conference of Catholic Bishops, *Renewing the Earth: An Invitation to Reflection and Action on the Environment in the Light of Catholic Social Teaching* (Washington, DC: United States Catholic Conference, 1991), 5, www.usccb.org/sdwp/ejp/bishopsstatement.

identity can be used (no. 20). While the Pontifical Academy and the *Catechism* pay attention to the human problems of suffering and disease, the Pontifical Academy cautioned that risks, scientific uncertainties, and moral quandaries remain with xenotransplantation. The Academy acknowledged that, if an important benefit could be derived for humans, even when it involved experiments on non-human animals or genetically modifying them, xenotransplantation could be justified if needless animal suffering could be prevented.

Although these criteria were established as acceptable, the Academy still failed to adequately address additional moral issues that arise in the process of inserting human DNA into a pig, which is required to ensure the biocompatibility needed for successful transplantation from a donor pig into a human recipient. It is important to address these neglected moral issues that follow from transgenesis, the process of introducing a gene from one organism into another. First, xenotransplantation crosses the medical and moral boundaries between what is human and what is animal. Second, the sacredness of human procreation by which humans cooperate with God is violated when transgenesis is the method of procreation. This may lead to confusion of the identity and status of the host. Third, the question of humanness becomes one of degrees. At what point is the pig less pig and more human? On the scale of the whole pig genome, in which there may be as many as thirty-five thousand endogenous genes, for the pig these genetic changes are not particularly significant in altering the fundamental nature of the transgenic pig. The pig will not appear to be a different species, although it is not strictly a pig genonomically. Its human characteristics would be at the biological level and would not produce changes that raise questions about whether it has gained moral agency.[21] What remains unanswered is at what point might these boundaries become blurred if more genes are introduced into the host animal? Human-animal transgenesis represents the failure to respect the sacredness of the human genome and the sacredness of human generation.[22] It also fails to respect the nature of the pig species.

Years later, *The Compendium of the Social Doctrine of the Church* posited that the Church is not opposed to technology for humanity's use (no. 457). However, it qualified that a central point of reference for every scientific and technological application is respect for men and women, which must be accompanied by a necessary attitude of respect for other living creatures (no. 459). *The Compendium* noted that the creatures that surround humans are gifts to be nurtured and safeguarded (no. 464).

---

[21] Nicholas Tonti-Filippini, John I. Fleming, Gregory K. Pike and Ray Campbell, "Ethics and Human-Animal Transgenesis," *The National Catholic Bioethics Quarterly* 6, no. 4 (2006): 689–704, doi 10.5840/ncbq2006648.

[22] Tonti-Filippini, et al. "Ethics and Human-Animal Transgenesis."

In 2015, Pope Francis amplified the principles of CST—care for creation and the dignity of human life—in his encyclical *Laudato Si'*. *Laudato Si'* advances an environmental ethic of care for all creation. Here, Francis proffers a paradigm of Catholic thought on the interconnectedness of all life and the authentic relationship between humans and non-human animals that is at the heart of xenotransplantation. While not devoted to xenotransplantation or any sustained treatise on the treatment of non-human animals, inferences can be drawn regarding Francis's position on care of our common home not only as an environmental ethic but also as it pertains to non-human animals and humans and their unique place in creation, which can inform the overall purpose or end of humans and other animals. We can apply Francis's metaethics to the ethical issue of xenotransplantation.

Francis expands upon *Renewing the Earth's* plea to theologians, scripture scholars, and ethicists to help explore, deepen, and advance the insights of the Catholic tradition, especially the dignity of the person and the responsibility to care for all of God's creation. He professes in *Evangelii Gaudium*, "We humans are not only beneficiaries but also stewards of other creatures" (no. 215). In *Laudato Si'*, he writes that often, "dominion" and "stewardship" are pitted against each other as opposing biblical worldviews. Dominion over the universe must be understood more properly in the sense of responsible stewardship (no. 116):

> If we approach nature and the environment with this openness to awe and wonder, if we no longer speak the language of fraternity and beauty in our relationships with the world, our attitude will be that of masters, consumers, ruthless exploiters, unable to set limits on their immediate needs. By contrast, if we feel intimately united with all that exists, then sobriety and care will well up spontaneously. The poverty and austerity of Saint Francis were no mere veneer of asceticism, but something much more radical: a refusal to turn reality into an object simply to be used and controlled (no. 11).

Francis's central argument of what he terms "integral ecology" calls people to feel intimately connected with all that exists.[23] Francis clarifies that our insistence that each human being is made in the image of God should not make us overlook the fact that each creature has its own purpose (no. 84). Made in the image and likeness of God and sharing in the son's divinity and humanity, humans are the penultimate creature, destined to be perfect as the Father is perfect. Thus, the encyclical goes further with concern toward non-human animals and

---

[23] Eli McCarthy, "Breaking Out: The Expansiveness of Restorative Justice in *Laudato Si'*," *Journal of Moral Theology* 5, no. 2 (2016): 66–80.

provides direction on how animals should be treated as fellow inhab-
itants.[24] Francis recalls the *Catechism's* teaching that human intervention on plants and animals is permissible when it pertains to the necessities of human life and that experimentation on animals is morally
acceptable only if it remains within reasonable limits and contributes
to saving human lives (no. 106). He writes, "All such use and experimentation require a religious respect for the integrity of creation" (no.
107). Francis believes that it is not enough to think of different species
as potential resources to be exploited while overlooking the fact that
they have intrinsic value (no. 33). Non-human animals have more than
instrumental value. Francis expands upon the notion of respect for the
integrity of creation, giving people pause about altering and manipu-
lating God's creatures.

Francis understands non-human animals in a uniquely Trinitarian
way by offering a theology of non-human animals. He sees every creature as the object of the Father's tenderness, who gives it its place in
the world. He writes that even the fleeting life of the least of these
beings is the object of his love, and, in its few seconds of existence,
God enfolds it with his affection (no. 77). Francis, borrowing from his
namesake St. Francis of Assisi and referring to St. Bonaventure's
teachings, echoes that each creature bears a specifically Trinitarian
structure so real that it could be readily contemplated if only the human gaze were not so partial, dark, and fragile (no. 239). Surely, the
profundity of this theology can only be contemplated, but it suggests
that the triune God, in God's fullness, animates all life in a mystery of
relationship. Francis maintains that any legitimate intervention will act
on nature only to favor its development in its own line, that of creation
as intended by God (no. 112).

> The ultimate destiny of the universe is in the fullness of God, which
> has already been attained by the risen Christ, the measure of the ma-
> turity of all things. Here, we can add yet another argument for reject-
> ing every tyrannical and irresponsible domination of human beings
> over other creatures. The ultimate purpose of other creatures is not to
> be found in us. Rather, all creatures are moving forward with us and
> through us towards a common point of arrival, which is God, in that
> transcendent fullness where the risen Christ embraces and illumines
> all things. Human beings, endowed with intelligence and love, and
> drawn by the fullness of Christ, are called to lead all creatures back to
> their Creator (*Laudato Si'*, no. 83).

Francis makes his case that there is a difference between tyrannical
anthropomorphism that serves the perceived primacy of humans and

---

[24] Anatoly Aseneta R. Angelo, "*Laudato Si'* on Non-Human Animals," *Journal of
Moral Theology* 6, no. 2 (2017): 230–245.

using non-human animals consistently with their end purposes. He explains,

> In our time, the Church does not simply state that other creatures are completely subordinated to the good of human beings, as if they have no worth in themselves and can be treated as we wish. The German bishops have taught that, where other creatures are concerned, "we can speak of the priority of being over that of being useful." The Catechism clearly and forcefully criticizes a distorted anthropomorphism: Each creature possesses its own particular goodness and perfection.... Each of the creatures, willed in its own being, reflects a ray of God's infinite wisdom and goodness. Man must therefore respect the particular goodness of every creature to avoid any distorted use of things (no. 51).

Xenotransplantation, as an intervention, takes root in what is technologically possible—what could be called the technocratic paradigm. Nature no longer acts as the normative limit of human intervention but rather constitutes the material scientists use for an infinite number of interventions.[25] The problem of the technocratic paradigm, Francis writes, is the way humanity has taken up technology and its development according to an undifferentiated and one-dimensional paradigm, a paradigm that exalts the concept of a subject who, using logical and rational procedures, progressively approaches and gains control over an external object (no. 106). He maintains that the technological paradigm has become so dominant that it would be difficult to do without its resources and even more difficult to utilize them without being dominated by their internal logic (no. 108). Xenotransplantation, which assists in organ availability, at its root stems from a paradigm of technological dominion over a theological view of creation.

Theologies of animality continue to favor humans in a hierarchical ontology. However, this historical review of Catholic thought demonstrates the evolving concern and respect for creation and its integral wholeness begun by Aquinas, who laid the groundwork for a broader lens of inclusion of non-human animals, into an ethic of relationship with humans culminating with Francis. Catholic thought must continually be reinterpreted and renewed against modern-day circumstances where biological facts change along with an interpretation of creation and an understanding of the nature of humans and non-human animals. Each creature has its own end and a role in creation, a manifestation of divinity, and a relationship with humans, which is towards the good. Humans have an obligation towards non-human animals that includes

---

[25] Hille Haker, "Beyond *the Anticipatory Corpse*—Future Perspectives for Bioethics." *Journal of Medicine and Philosophy: A Forum for Bioethics and Philosophy of Medicine* 41, no. 6 (December 2016): 597–620, doi-org.archer.org/10.1093 /jmp/jhw025.

responsible care of the non-human world, not only for the sake of the animals but for the betterment of humanity.

SOLUTIONS AND ALTERNATIVES TO XENOTRANSPLANTATION

The ethics of xenotransplantation can only be answered against the backdrop of a broader paradigm of where humans fit in the universe, what is the purpose of other creatures, and their interrelationship. We do not seem to have these answers. Despite the technological leaps that persist to this day, no successful animal-to-human whole organ transplants have been performed.[26] Additionally, the lack of evidence-based data to rule out the potential of zoonotic illnesses incurred by interspecies contact, problems with gene editing, organ rejection, the necessity for a lifetime of anti-rejection drugs, and a short time frame wherein another transplant may be needed illustrate flaws in the technocratic paradigm. While these problems might be resolved through future technology, this is not at the heart of the Catholic moral view on the issue. The goal of saving humans through non-human animal donation in the face of a limited donor pool, the reality of disease and suffering, and the finiteness of human life do not outweigh respect as the end point of all creatures' lives.

As an alternative, the Pontifical Academy maintains that adult stem cell research offers a therapeutic option for xenotransplantation.[27] Adult stem cell biology holds the potential to replace failing organs, reduce immunological intolerance, and minimize or dispense with the current use of immunosuppressive drugs required for transplantation, which often cause toxicity and life-threatening infections.[28] Three-dimensional bioprinting, also known as rapid or additive prototyping, presents some promise for overcoming the shortage of human organs.[29] While not without its challenges, 3D-printed organs, which use a computer-aided transfer process, could customize biological materials and living cells.[30] In both cases, the use of non-human animals could be supplanted.

To increase public awareness of human organ donation, religious leaders can encourage eligible donors to consent to human organ donation.[31] Healthcare providers, public health officials, and individuals

---

[26] Bryan Mitton, "Xenotransplantation in Pediatrics: Overview, Xenograft Rejection and Prevention of Rejection, Xenograft Function," *Medscape*, emedicine.medscape.com/article/1014080-overview#a3.

[27] Pontifical Academy for Life, *Prospects for Xenotransplantation*.

[28] Abouna, "Ethical Issues."

[29] Zengmin Xia, Jin Sha, and Ye Kaiming, "Tissue and Organ 3D Bioprinting," *SLAS Technology* 23, no. 4 (2018): 301.

[30] Brian Derby, "Printing and Prototyping of Tissues and Scaffolds," *Science* 338, no. 6109 (2012): 921-926, doi.10.1126/science.1226340.

[31] Beyar, "Challenges in Organ Transplantation."

can advocate for allotransplantation. Allotransplantation endures as a vital part of modern medical practice and stewardship. Without it,

> [w]e would progressively lose what is perhaps the deepest and highest symbolic moral and existential significance of organ transplantation, its gift dimension...that the living parts of persons are offered in life and death to known or unknown others, to our strangers and our enemies as well as to our kin, in the form of a gift beyond duty and claim, beyond reckoning and rule.[32]

MOVING FORWARD

From its first articulation by Pius XII to today, as summarized in the *New Charter of Health Care Workers* (no. 118), the Catholic Church does not prohibit xenotransplantation, assuming the transplant is safe for human recipients, has a chance of success, will not impair the psychological identity of the recipient, and does not involve an organ that confers identity. Questions on the safety, success, and psychological identity remain unknown. Likewise, the issue of "needless animal suffering" addressed in the *Catechism* and by the Pontifical Academy for Life has not been sufficiently explored and is difficult to define.

Clearly, *Laudato Si'* is not about xenotransplantation. However, *Laudato Si's* general approach to planetary care and social justice fills the ethical gap in thinking about the use of non-human animals for human life extension. Through his theology of creation, good stewardship is contrasted with "tyranny" and "irresponsible domination" of animals. Just as Pope John XXIII threw open the windows of the Church to let in the fresh air of the Spirit in the summons of Vatican II, the light of *Laudato Si'* illuminates the path to restore justice in the created world.

Xenotransplantation requires society to confront its fundamental cultural, ethical, and spiritual beliefs about what it means to be human, about relationships with other species, and about how factors such as compassion and human need influence biotechnology.[33] It asks what type of world people choose to imagine and create. While the safety issues keenly perceived by Pius XII endure, *Laudato Si'* adds the new pivotal dimension of the sacredness of all life.

The Catholic tradition supports the advancement of science and human creativity to solve the world's problems, including end-organ failure and debilitating disease, but xenotransplantation is not a moral answer. A consideration of the most significant Church teachings on

---

[32] Institute of Medicine (US) Committee on Xenograft Transplantation, *Xenotransplantation: Science, Ethics and Public Policy* (Washington DC: National Academies Press, 1996), quoting Renée Fox.

[33] Toi te Taiao: The Bioethics Council, *The Cultural, Ethical, and Spiritual Aspects of Animal-to-Human Transplantation*, www.bioethics.org.nz.

human-animal relationships leads to the conclusion that xenotransplantation violates responsible stewardship toward non-human animals and creation, the sacredness of the human genome, the sacredness of human procreation, and zoological responsibility. *Laudato Si'* serves as a springboard for a more robust ethic of care for our common home that extends into medicine and technology to achieve beneficence towards humans and non-human animals. Issues of life and death require reflection and interpretation with the repository of Scripture, tradition, and the magisterium. The answers are already present in Francis's condemnation of the preeminence of the technocratic paradigm and the worth of creation as manifestations of divinity.

Catholic thought itself makes clear that: all beings have intrinsic value, they have their own natural ends and goods, we should only use them in accordance with their own ends, and we are spurred to value the non-human world as God's creation and our common home. The encyclical *Laudato Si'* and its ethic of communion and justice widens and focuses the theological lens and assists in clarifying the ethics of xenotransplantation. It is incumbent upon the Catholic community to engage in further discussion and reconsideration of xenotransplantation in light of *Laudato Si'* before the technocratic paradigm replaces the ethical obligations of safety, respect, and dignity owed to humans and all living creatures moving forward and back to their Creator together. ◼

Skya Abbate, DBe, DOM is a graduate of Loyola University, Chicago (2020), where she earned her Master's and doctoral degrees with a specialization in Catholic bioethics. She also holds a Master's degree in Pastoral Studies (Loyola University New Orleans, 2012) and a Master's degree in Sociology (University of RI, 1978). She is the Executive Director of Southwest Acupuncture College, Santa Fe, NM, where she teaches as a licensed doctor of Oriental Medicine.

Journal of Moral Theology, Vol. 11, No. 1 (2022): 167–192

Resurrecting Justice

Daniel Philpott

UCH TURNS ON HOW WE CONCEIVE OF justice. Justice defines what we may expect from one another in our families, workplaces, economic dealings, religious communities, civic associations, and, most quintessentially, political communities. Thinkers as diverse as Thomas Aquinas and John Rawls have held that justice is the first virtue of political institutions.

In today's constitutional liberal democracies, great prestige is enjoyed by a manner of conceiving of justice that is rooted in Roman law and developed through medieval, enlightenment, and modern liberal thought. It is expressed classically as the constant will to render another his due and today in terms of rights, equity, fairness, equality, and retribution. Justice in this conception is what people are owed, entitled to, deserve, or indebted to pay or perform. Debtors pay their bills, achievers garner rightful honors, workers receive fair compensation, convicted criminals render their debt to society, parties to a contract collect what they agreed to, nobody suffers wrongful discrimination, the poor receive a rightful distribution of goods, and everyone, everywhere enjoys human rights. Such justice contrasts with other kinds of behavior that are admirable, commendable, and perhaps lofty but are not due to anyone: generosity, mercy, gift, friendship, forgiveness, and love. Justice is outward behavior, not inner virtue or the ordering of the soul. It is known entirely through reason.

So thoroughly pervasive is this conception of justice that many western Christians never pause to ask: Is it ours? Is it the same justice as that found in the Bible, their divinely inspired founding story? I argue that the Bible's justice is markedly, although not entirely, different. Found in the Old Testament and New Testament, used to describe the actions of God and to prescribe the actions of kings, prophets, priests, merchants, judges, obedient Jews, and faithful followers of Jesus, justice carries an overarching meaning of comprehensive right relationship, consisting of right conduct in all spheres of life. Biblical justice includes obligations to render others their due but also obligations that extend beyond what is due. It describes inner virtue, the right ordering of the soul, as well as actions directed towards other people, towards the entire creation, and towards God. It is known both through reason and through faith in God's revelation. The justice that humans are to practice is shaped by the justice that God practices towards humans.

The aim of this essay is to propose, defend, and explicate comprehensive right relationship as the Bible's conception of justice. It elaborates this conception through a typology that arrays the Bible's many expressions of justice into four categories: divine primary justice, divine rectifying justice, human primary justice, and human rectifying justice. Evidence for this conception of justice and its four dimensions is found in the Hebrew and Greek words that are most plausibly and commonly translated as justice, the meaning of which arises from their closely surrounding context as well as the larger narrative of salvation that they describe. The four dimensions help to depict this larger narrative as one of God's justice unfolding through God's interaction with humanity. The climax of this narrative is the death and resurrection of Jesus Christ, events that the scriptures describe as justice and that express this justice in its fullest sense. The meaning of this justice, as well as the endeavor of retrieving and plumbing it, then, is resurrecting justice. The aim of resurrecting justice is to offer Christians a better understanding of their own justice in a world where justice is defined differently.

DEFINITIONS AND LANGUAGE

Words that may express justice appear in the Bible hundreds of times, situated in manifold settings. Does any overarching meaning enfold them? Yes, I contend: comprehensive right relationship.[1] The acts that constitute right relationship are elaborated and distinguished through four dimensions, arrayed in the table below. The two rows are the two sides of a distinction, pivoting on agency, between divine justice, which God enacts, and human justice, which human beings perform. The two columns set forth a distinction, borrowed from philosopher Nicholas Wolterstorff, between primary justice, which defines what it means to live in right relationship, and rectifying justice, which

---

[1] Other scholars who see biblical justice as right relationship include James D.G. Dunn, "The Justice of God: A Renewed Perspective on Justification by Faith," *Journal of Theological Studies*, 43, no. 1 (1992): 16; A. Katherine Grieb, "'So That in Him We Might Become the Righteousness of God' (2 Cor 5:21): Some Theological Reflections on the Church Becoming Justice," *Ex Auditu* 22 (2007): 59; Elizabeth Achtemeier, "Righteousness in the OT," in *The Interpreter's Dictionary of the Bible*, ed. G.A. Buttrick, vol. 4 (Nashville, TN: Abingdon, 1962), 80–85 at 80; Gerhard von Rad, *Old Testament Theology*, trans. D.M.G. Stalker, vols. I and II, (Peabody, MA: Prince Press, 2005), 371–372; John R. Donahue, SJ, "Biblical Perspectives on Justice," in *The Faith that Does Justice*, ed. John C. Haughey (New York: Paulist Press, 1977), 69; Scot McKnight, *A Community Called Atonement* (Nashville, TN; Abingdon Press, 2007), 126; and Douglas Harink, *Resurrecting Justice: Reading Romans for the Life of the World* (Downers Grove, IL: InterVarsity Press, 2020), 1–18.

addresses past wrongs.[2] What emerges is a fourfold typology that begins with divine primary justice, the moral order that God establishes and upholds. Second comes divine rectifying justice, God's restoration of right relationship in response to sin. Third is human primary justice, the acts through which people enact right relationship with God and with other people and cultivate virtue within their soul. Fourth is human rectifying justice, through which people seek to restore right relationship with others and with God after they have broken right relationship. These dimensions of justice are necessary, distinct, and related. An account of Biblical justice missing one of them would be incomplete; one failing to separate them would be confused; and one omitting connections between them would be ill suited to describe the unfolding story of God's relationship with humanity.

[2] Nicholas Wolterstorff, *Justice: Rights and Wrongs* (Princeton, NJ: Princeton University Press, 2008), ix–x.

Four Dimensions of Justice

	Primary Justice	Rectifying Justice
God (divine justice)	God performs justice by establishing right relationship in the world through his original creation and through his covenants with humanity, which set forth the norms that make up human justice. God orders the world out of his character, which is marked by justice.	God enacts justice by responding to the sin of humanity through punishment, forgiveness, vindication of the cause of the poor, and other measures that bring about the restoration of right relationship in God's covenant. God's saving justice is manifested most fully in the death and resurrection of Jesus. It is equivalent to justification and reconciliation.
Human beings (human justice)	Humans enact right relationship towards one another, with respect to the natural environment, towards God, and by cultivating virtue in their souls so as to be disposed to right action towards others and God. The norms that define right relationship include the moral, judicial, and ceremonial precepts of the Old Testament and the New Law that Jesus taught and manifested most fully in his death and resurrection.	Humans respond to the wrongs of others, including in judicial contexts, according to norms set forth by God (examples include the *lex talionis* and Jesus's teaching against retaliation and in favor of forgiveness). This response involves the restoration of right relationship between humans.

This argument, that justice in the Bible means right relationship in the senses that this typology sets forth, rests upon the claim that the

English word justice properly translates words in the Bible that denote comprehensive right relationship in its original languages, Hebrew and Greek. This claim in turn comprises two assertions, corresponding to two sides of the translation task – first, determining the meaning of terms in the origin language, and second, finding the best words to express these terms in the destination language.

The first of these assertions is that certain terms in the original languages of the Bible denote comprehensive right relationship. The most important of these terms are the Hebrew noun *sedeq*, whose feminine form is *sedeqah*, in the Old Testament, and the Greek noun *dikaiosune* in the New Testament. *Sedeq* and *sedeqah* densely populate the Old Testament. Words with the root *sdq-* occur 523 times, *sedeq* 119 times, and *sedeqah* 157 times, with more than two-thirds of all *sdq-* words concentrated in Isaiah, Ezekiel, Psalms, and Proverbs.[3] *Sedeq(ah)* contains a wide variety of meanings, but I follow the renowned Old Testament scholar Gerhard Von Rad who, along with other scholars, holds that these terms carry an overarching meaning and that they denote both divine and human agency.[4] As I detail below, *sedeq(ah)* is God's establishment of an order of right relationship, God's restoration of his people to right relationship following their sin, and the right relationship that humans are to practice towards one another as prescribed by God's covenants, most importantly, the Torah given to Moses.

In composing the Septuagint, the third century BCE Greek translation of the Hebrew Bible, translators used *dik-* words to translate 90 percent of instances of *sedeq(ah)* and commonly translated both *sedeq(ah)* and *mishpat* through *dikaiosune*.[5] *Dikaiosune* then appears 92 times in the New Testament, more frequently than any other *dik-* term, and echoes the meaning of *sedeq(ah)*.[6] As with *sedeq* and *sedeqah*, *dikaiosune* in the New Testament involves both divine and human agency, connoting the saving action through which God restores the world to right relationship through the death and resurrection of Jesus Christ as well as the entire meaning of right relationship

---

[3] K. Koch, "*sdq*," in *Theological Lexicon of the Old Testament*, vol. 2, ed. Ernst Jenni and Claus Westermann, trans. Mark E. Biddle (Peabody, MA: Hendrickson Publishers, 1997), 1048–1049.

[4] Von Rad, *Old Testament Theology,* 370. Similar statements on the sweeping importance of *sedeq*, understanding it to be related to justice, can be found in Rolf Knierim, *The Task of Old Testament Theology: Method and Cases* (Grand Rapids, MI: Eerdmans, 1995), 87–88; Donahue, "Biblical Perspectives on Justice," 68; and McKnight, *A Community Called Atonement*, 127. Arguing for the overarching character of justice in the Old Testament is Walter Brueggemann, *Old Testament: Testimony, Dispute, Advocacy* (Minneapolis, MN: 1997), 421–425.

[5] Christopher D. Marshall, *Beyond Retribution: A New Testament Vision for Justice, Crime, and Punishment* (Grand Rapids, MI; Eerdmans, 2001), 47.

[6] John Reumann "Righteousness (NT)," in *The Anchor Bible Dictionary*, ed. D. N. Freedman (New York, NY: Doubleday, 1992), 747.

that Jesus teaches humans to enact, towards both other humans and God.

Two other terms, *saddiq* and *dikaios*, the adjectives that correspond to *sedeq* and *dikaiosune*, denote virtue, the character of one who acts consistently with right relationship. In some instances in the Bible, this agent is God; in others, it is a human person such as Noah (Genesis 6:9) or Joseph, the guardian of Jesus (Matthew 1:19).[7] *Saddiq* appears 206 times in the Old Testament, in Psalms and Proverbs far more than any other book, while *dikaios* shows up 79 times in the New Testament, concentrated most in the Gospels of Matthew and Luke.[8]

A final term, *mishpat*, can also mean comprehensive right relationship. Like *sedeq(ah)*, it pervades the Old Testament, appearing 422 times. Often, it means more narrowly the standards that govern the courtroom or economic dealings: fairness, equity, right procedure. At other times, though, it means general right behavior, enacted by God or by humans: the entirety of God's law, deeds that God loves, and deliverance. In numerous instances, *mishpat* appears with *sedeq* or *sedeqah* as a hendiadys, or pairing of words, that means right behavior in the social and political realm, often pertaining to a king.[9]

The second assertion is that the English word justice soundly translates the terms that connote comprehensive right relationship in Hebrew and Greek. Translators of the Bible into English have turned to the words justice and righteousness, and more generally to the family of words with the root just- (justice, justify, justification) and to the family of words with the word right- (righteous, righteousness) in order to translate the Bible's families of words that have the *sdq-* root and the *dik-* root. It is uniquely English that contains both the just-family, which carries a Latin lineage, and the right- family, which carries an Anglo-Saxon one.[10]

Some translators of the Bible into English, including some of the earliest translators in the sixteenth and seventeenth centuries, adopt the term righteousness to refer to personal piety or to God's atonement for people's sins, and justice to refer to juridical social norms that are

---

[7] Unless otherwise indicated, Bible verses in this article are drawn from the New American Bible. In places, I add the term justice to righteousness so as to read righteousness/justice in order to convey the argument of the paper.

[8] Koch, "*sdq*," 1049; Reumann, "Righteousness (NT)," 747.

[9] Barbara Johnson, "Mishpat," in *Theological Dictionary of the Old Testament*, ed. G. Johannes Botterweck, Helmer Ringgren, and Heinz-Josef Fabry, trans. David E. Green, IX (Grand Rapids, MI: Eerdmans, 1998), 89; on the hendiadys and its social connotations, see Moshe Weinfeld, *Social Justice in Ancient Israel and in the Ancient Near East* (Minneapolis, MN: Fortress Press, 1995), 7–56.

[10] John Reumann, "Justification and Justice in the New Testament," *Horizons in Biblical Theology* 21 (1999): 28–29.

germane to government, courtrooms, and commerce and involve equity, fairness, or just deserts.[11] Such a scheme of translation, though, reflects—and has surely done much to lodge into the English language—a dichotomy that is not found in the Hebrew and Greek terms that connote comprehensive right relationship. It is exactly this dichotomy that I wish to challenge—one that confines the meaning of justice to what is due, public, and involving external conduct.

In fact, both of the English words justice and righteousness are far more semantically elastic and enjoy usages that convey holism, encompassing both personal, pious uprightness as well as adherence to public, juridical norms. English speakers may understand each term more narrowly, depending on when, where, and among whom they live, but the English language also offers wider meanings. The Oxford English Dictionary, for instance, defines righteousness as "[t]he state or quality of being righteous or just; conformity to the precepts of divine law or accepted standards of morality; uprightness, rectitude; virtue, integrity," a definition that includes the word "just" and that could apply to behavior that is private or public, inward or outward, and practiced in any sphere.[12]

Likewise, the term justice also finds holistic meanings in English, as five instances of supporting evidence show. First, certain philosophers and theorists writing in English put forth a concept of justice that means something much like comprehensive right relationship. Contemporary examples include theorists of restorative justice and "care feminists."[13]

Second, English translators of Greek literature long have employed justice to translate *dikaiosune* in instances where the word carries a holistic meaning. They do so, for instance, in Plato's *Republic*, where justice is right order in the soul and, by analogy, in the city, where each person performs his duty to others according to his station, and in Aristotle's *Nicomachean Ethics*, where general justice governs the entirety of one's relationships to others.[14]

---

[11] Reumann, "Righteousness (NT)," 746; Michael J. Gorman, *Becoming the Gospel: Paul, Participation and Mission* (Grand Rapids, MI: Eerdmans, 2015), 222–223.

[12] "Righteousness," *Oxford English Dictionary*, oed.com.

[13] On restorative justice, see John Braithwaite, *Crime, Shame, and Reintegration* (Cambridge, UK: Cambridge University Press, 1989); and Howard Zehr, *Changing Lenses: A New Focus for Crime and Justice* (Scottdale, PA: Herald Press, 1990). On care feminism, see Elizabeth R. Schiltz, "West, MacIntyre, and Wojtyla: Pope John Paul II's Contribution to the Development of a Dependency-Based Theory of Justice," *Journal of Catholic Legal Studies* 45 (2006): 369–414.

[14] Plato, *The Republic*, trans. Allan Bloom (New York: Basic Books, 1968), Bk. 4; and Aristotle, *Nicomachean Ethics*, trans. Robert C. Bartlett and Susan D. Collins (Chicago: University of Chicago Press, 2011), Bk 5.

The third instance of supporting evidence is found in the translation of the Bible itself. Various translations of the Bible into English embody varying choices about whether to use justice or righteousness (and their respective cousins) to translate the same terms in the original Hebrew or Greek. This suggests a fluidity, some scholars even would say an interchangeability, between these English words such that justice can include the range of meanings attributed to righteousness and vice-versa. At least one translation, the Douay-Rheims Bible, consistently uses just- words to translate *sdq-* and *dik-* words.[15]

Fourth, the Vulgate, dating back to the fourth century, translates *sdq-* and *dik-* words, with all of their holistic connotations, into Latin words such as *justus* or *justitia*, which in turn translate readily into English just- words.[16] Because Latin lacks the competing family of right- terms, translators face no dilemma in readily employing just-terms. So, in encountering translations of the Bible from Latin, as well as translations of classic theological works written in Latin that quote the Bible, English speakers will read justice where they may be accustomed to reading righteousness. The reason why the Douay-Rheims Bible uses just- terms is that it is translated from the Vulgate. So, too, English speakers will read in Gregory of Nyssa's sermons on the beatitudes "blessed are they who hunger and thirst after *justice*"; in Aquinas's *Commentary on the Gospel of Matthew,* "seek first the kingdom of God and his *justice*"; and in Aquinas's commentary on Romans, "the *justice* of God is made manifest."[17] They will find in the works of Augustine usages of justice that embody the holistic meaning of *sedeq* and *dikaiosune* and are even equated to the love of God and neighbor.[18] Likewise, words closely resembling the English justice are used in translations of the Bible into Romance languages such as French, Spanish, and Italian (*justice, justicia, guistizia*).

---

[15] On this fluidity, James D.G. Dunn and Alan M. Suggate, *The Justice of God: A Fresh Look at the Old Doctrine of Justification by Faith* (Grand Rapids, MI: Eerdmans, 1993), 32–37; Marshall, *Beyond Retribution*, 35–37; Enrique Nardoni, *Rise Up, O Judge: A Study of Justice in the Biblical World*, trans. Seán Charles Martin (Grand Rapids, MI: Baker Academic, 2004), 217, 267; John C. Haughey, "Jesus as the Justice of God," in *The Faith That Does Justice: Examining the Christian Sources for Social Change*, ed. John C. Haughey (Eugene, OR: Wipf and Stock Publishers, 1977), 276–288; and William C. Mattison III, *The Sermon on the Mount and Moral Theology: A Virtue Perspective* (Cambridge: Cambridge University Press, 2017), 32, 49–50; Wolterstorff, *Justice*, 110–113.

[16] Von Rad, *Old Testament Theology*, 370; Koch, *"sdq,"* 1049.

[17] St. Gregory of Nyssa, *The Lord's Prayer, The Beatitudes*, trans. Hilda C. Graef (New York: Newman Press, 1954), 117; Saint Thomas Aquinas, *Commentary on the Gospel of Matthew Chapters 1–12*, trans. Jeremy Holmes and Beth Mortensen (Green Bay, WI: Aquinas Institute, 2018), 230; Saint Thomas Aquinas, *Commentary on the Letter of Saint Paul to the Romans*, trans. Fr. Fabian R. Larcher, OP (Green Bay, WI: Aquinas Institute, 2018), 98, italics added.

[18] See Robert Dodaro, *Christ and the Just Society in the Thought of Augustine* (Cambridge, UK: Cambridge University Press, 2004), 10–12, 72–114.

Finally, certain contemporary scholars, including Pope Benedict XVI, follow suit in deploying justice widely in their translations of the Bible and in interpreting it holistically.[19]

If righteousness and justice each enjoy holistic usages in English, then no definitive case exists for adopting one or the other word to translate biblical terms that mean comprehensive right relationship. What I am arguing for is not the necessity but rather the merited possibility of using justice (and related *just-* terms) for this translation, a possibility that is warranted if justice is understood in a wide, holistic sense. If, in turn, justice translates the Bible's Hebrew and Greek terms for comprehensive right relationship, then it will describe a remarkably wide range of actions that God performs and calls upon humans to perform. What will emerge is a distinctively Christian notion of justice.

DIVINE JUSTICE IN THE BIBLE: GOD'S ESTABLISHMENT AND RESTORATION OF RIGHT RELATIONSHIP

Divine Primary Justice

Out of God's just character, God proclaims commandments that govern the entirety of human beings' relationships to one another and to God; fashions human beings so that they flourish through following these commandments; attaches blessings and curses for following or failing to follow these commandments; and constantly sustains all of these realities, which together make up God's right order. This is nothing other than the justice of comprehensive right relationship. Insofar as God establishes and upholds this justice according to his character, it is divine justice. Because this divine justice sets forth right relationship and its orientation towards human fulfillment, it is primary justice. Divine primary justice is that of the upper left-hand quadrant in the table above.

Help in understanding this dimension of justice in the Bible comes from Thomas Aquinas, who argued that God first exercised mercy in creating the universe and then justice in giving right order to his creation. The "order of the universe...shows forth the justice of God," he wrote (ST I q. 21, a. 1, co.) With respect to humanity, God first created humans out of his goodness (or mercy), and then, out of justice, gave humans a rational soul that befitted their humanity, and then hands that

---

[19] See, for instance, Pope Benedict XVI, "The Justice of God Has Been Manifested Through Faith in Jesus Christ: Pope's Lenten Message for 2010," February 4, 2010, www.vatican.va/content/benedict-xvi/en/messages/lent/documents/hf_ben-xvi_mes_20091030_lent-2010.html; Michael J. Gorman, *Participating in Christ: Explorations in Paul's Theology and Spirituality* (Grand Rapids, MI: Baker Academic, 2019), 191–201; and Darrin W. Snyder Belousek, *Atonement, Justice, and Peace: The Message of the Cross and the Mission of the Church* (Grand Rapids, MI: Eerdmans, 2012), 369–380.

befitted their rational nature. God's will towards this right order is his justice, Aquinas holds (ST I q. 21, a. 1, co; ST I, q. 21, a. 4, co.).

The Bible expresses divine primary justice through justice words found mainly in Psalms and Isaiah. Psalm 11:7 conveys God's just character and its close link with God's laws, "[t]he Lord is just (*sedeq*) and loves just deeds; the upright shall see his face," while Psalm 119: 137–138 declares, "You are righteous/just (*saddiq*), Lord, and just are your edicts (*mishpat*). You have issued your decrees in justice (*sedeq*) and in surpassing faithfulness." Other verses speak to God upholding justice, including Psalm 36:7, "Your justice (*sedeqah*) is like the highest mountains; your judgments (*mishpat*), like the mighty deep; all living creatures you sustain, Lord"; Psalm 9:5, 8–9, "You upheld my right (*mishpat*) and my cause, seated on your throne, judging justly (*sedeq*).... The Lord rules forever, has set up a throne for judgment. It is God who governs the world with justice (*sedeq*), who judges the peoples with fairness"; and Isaiah 9:6, "His dominion is vast and forever peaceful,/ From David's throne, and over his kingdom, which he confirms and sustains/ By judgment (*mishpat*) and justice (*sedeqah*), both now and forever."[20]

Divine Rectifying Justice

The justice of the upper right-hand quadrant is divine rectifying justice, which describes the action through which God restores right relationship in response to sin. In the Old Testament, it is *sedeq(ah)* that communicates this justice most frequently. Synonymous with God's salvation and deliverance, it shows up multiple times in the Psalms, appears in Hosea, Micah, Amos, and Judges, but is most concentrated in its occurrence and rich in its meaning in Second Isaiah, Books 40–55.[21] The setting of Second Isaiah's drama is Israel's exile in Babylon, and the plot of the drama is Israel's return to its homeland. *Sedeq(ah)* is the justice of a God who is faithful to the covenant by which God freely and graciously promises to make Israel his people and to be their God (Isaiah 55:3). Isaiah 46:13 is only one of many instances where *sedeq(ah)* means God's salvific action: "I am bringing

---

[20] For other verses that express primary divine justice, see Psalm 11:7; Psalm 35:28; Psalm 65:6; Psalm 71:17–19; Psalm 95:15; Psalm 97:1–6; Psalm 98:7–9; Psalm 99:4; Psalm 101:1; Psalm 111:7; Psalm 116:5; Psalm 119:159–160; Psalm 119:172; Isaiah 5:16; Isaiah 30:18; Isaiah 32:16; Isaiah 33:5; Isaiah 41:10; Isaiah 42:4; Isaiah 45:8; Isaiah 51:6–7; Jeremiah 9:23; and Zephaniah 3:5.

[21] J.J. Scullion, "Righteousness (OT)," in *Anchor Bible Dictionary*, ed. David Noel Freedman, vol. 5 (New York: Doubleday, 1992), 732–734. Scullion notes that *sedeqah* occurs 34 times in the Psalms, 9 of which refer to God's saving action. For examples of the term, see Psalm 7:10; Psalm 31:2; Psalm 35:24; Psalm 35:28; Psalm 40:10; Psalm 51:16; Psalm 71:2; Psalm 71:15; Psalm 71:16; Psalm 71:19; Psalm 99: 4; Psalm 103:6–7; Psalm 143:11; Judges 5:11; Amos 4:24.

on my justice (*sedeqah*), it is not far off, my salvation shall not tarry."[22]

God's restorative, salvific justice is both punitive and regenerative. In Isaiah 10:22, justice (*sedeqah*) "demands" the "destruction" of Israel, only a remnant of which is to remain. In Second Isaiah, God "poured out wrath upon," rebukes, displays anger, and speaks of vengeance towards Israel.[23] Exile is punishment for Israel's sins. Yet punishment is not permanent. Second Isaiah also makes it clear that Israel's "service is at an end" and that God will "restrain my anger," "not accuse forever," not remember the events of the past, and restore Israel.[24] Frequent is the language of payment. God has redeemed, ransomed, and secured recompense, expiation, and "service" from Israel.[25] God likewise promises to requite Israel's foes and take vengeance on Babylon.[26] All told, what emerges is a disciplining punishment through which God carries out his overarching plan of restoring right relationship with Israel according to his covenantal promises.[27]

Renewal is sung, too. Israel is to be restored to its land, with Jerusalem again its central city, as well as to right relationship within the community. "In justice (*sedeqah*) shall you be established," reads Isaiah 54:14. Second Isaiah, along with Third Isaiah's vision of Israel restored, returns repeatedly to the uplifting of the poor—the afflicted, needy, blind, hungry, thirsty, imprisoned, and dejected.[28] Conveying Isaiah's restorative vision are natural images, especially that of water bringing nourishment to dry land, often alluding to peace and prosperity.[29] God conducts his salvific action through the figure of a servant, whose mission is justice, with whom the New Testament identifies Jesus.[30] "I the Lord have called you for the victory of justice (*sedeq*)," reads Isaiah 42:6, shortly following verses in which God announces that the servant "shall bring forth justice (*mishpat*) to the nations" (42:1) and "[establish] justice (*mishpat*) on the earth" (42:4).

In the New Testament, divine rectifying justice is found first in the Gospel of Matthew (12:18–21), where Jesus quotes Isaiah 42 directly and identifies himself with the servant who brings justice to victory. Earlier in Matthew (3:15), Jesus also presents himself as justice in his

[22] Isaiah 45:8; 45:13; 45:19; 45:21; 46:12; 46:13; 49:8; 51:1–8; 54:14; 56:1; 59:17.

[23] Isaiah 42:25; 43:19; 47:3; 48:9; 52:20; 57:17; 59:17; 63:4; 65:1–7.

[24] Isaiah 40:2; 44:22; 48:9; 57:16; 62:4–12.

[25] Isaiah 40:10; 41:14; 43:1; 43:14; 44:22; 44:23; 47:3; 48:20; 49:4; 49:26; 50:1–2; 51:11; 59:20. On Israel's payment of debt in Second Isaiah, see Gary A. Anderson, *Sin: A History* (New Haven, CT: Yale University Press, 2009), 44–50.

[26] Isaiah 41:2–3; 41:10–11; 47:1–15; 49:26; 59:18.

[27] Marshall, *Beyond Retribution*, 51–53; Achtemeier, "Righteousness (OT)," 83.

[28] Isaiah 41:17; 42:7; 42:16; 43:8; 49:9–10; 55:1–2; 57:15; 58:6–10.

[29] Isaiah 41:17–19; 42:15; 43:19–28; 44:3–4; 48:18–21; 49:8–10; 51:3; 52:12.

[30] Several authors of the New Testament link Jesus to the Suffering Servant of Isaiah; see Matthew 8:1–7; Luke 22:37; John 12:38; Acts 8:32–33; 1 Peter 2:21–25.

reply to John the Baptist concerning his own baptism: "Allow it now, for thus it is fitting for us to fulfill all righteousness." Why does Jesus allow himself to be baptized? Fulfill means to bring to pass what was prophesied, prefigured, or foretold. The object of fulfill in this passage is *dikaiosune*, which, reflecting the pattern I have identified, is translated in most English Bibles as righteousness but is translated in the Douay-Rheims Bible as justice and in the Latin Vulgate as *justitiam*. So, what is the righteousness or justice that scripture prophesied and that Jesus is now fulfilling by being baptized? Arguably, justice here is the saving justice of God, denoted by *sedeq(ah)* in the Old Testament and translated by *dikaiosune* in the Septuagint. Although, as we shall see, Matthew uses *dikaiosune* elsewhere in his gospel to denote the human justice that Jesus commends to his followers, here, justice is performed by Jesus himself, the one whom John the Baptist has just identified as the mighty one who will baptize with the Holy Spirit and fire (3:11–12). It is divine rectifying justice, prefigured in Second Isaiah, brought to a climax in Jesus's death and resurrection, and launched here in his baptism. In baptism, Jesus identifies himself with the repentant sinner, whose cleansing he will bring about definitely through his sacrifice on Calvary. At the end of the baptism passage, in Matthew 3:17, God's voice from heaven says, "[t]his is my beloved Son, with whom I am well pleased," paralleling the words that God spoke in Isaiah to the servant who will bring about justice.[31]

It is in Paul's letters that we find the preponderance of references to the saving action of the cross and resurrection as justice. Much as the Psalms identify justice as a characteristic of God, so, too, Paul writes in his First Letter to the Corinthians (1:30) that "Christ Jesus… became for us…righteousness/justice," where righteousness is *dikaiosune*, the word that Paul uses for the saving justice of God. Out of his just character, Jesus Christ performs his saving justice on behalf of humanity.[32]

God's act of saving justice through Jesus Christ is the unifying theme of Paul's Letter to the Romans.[33] Pivotal is the term *dikaiosune*

---

[31] In this interpretation, I found helpful John P. Meier, *Matthew* (Collegeville, MN: Liturgical Press, 1980), 241–242; Reumann, "Righteousness (NT)," 755.

[32] On divine action emanating from divine character, see Thomas D. Stegman, SJ, "Paul's Use of *Dikaio-* Terminology: Moving Beyond N.T. Wright's Forensic Interpretation," *Theological Studies* 72 (2011): 502.

[33] Making this claim, among others, are Grieb, "So That in Him," 58–59; Reumann, "Righteousness (NT)," 759; Belousek, *Atonement, Justice, and Peace*, 369; Marshall, *Beyond Retribution*, 39; Colin Gunton, *The Actuality of Atonement: A Study of Metaphor, Rationality, and the Christian Tradition* (London, UK: T&T Clark, 1988), 102; and Gorman, *Participating in Christ*, 193–194. Gorman cites the similar claim of L.T. Johnson, *Reading Romans: A Literary and Theological Commentary* (Macon, GA: Smyth and Helwys, 2001), 13, 19–30, 47, 52–62.

theou, translated into English as the righteousness of God, or the justice of God. Paul writes in Romans 1:17, "[f]or in it [the gospel] the saving righteousness/justice of God (*dikaiosune theou*) is revealed"; in Romans 3:21–22, "[b]ut now, apart from the law, the saving righteousness/justice of God (*dikaiosune theou*) has been disclosed"; and in Romans 10:3, "the righteousness/justice that comes from God (*dikaiosune theou*)."[34] Although theologians long have disputed the meaning of *dikaiosune theou*, in recent years several have made a strong case that it denotes both a quality of God and an activity manifesting this quality.[35] Echoing Psalms and Isaiah, God's saving justice is closely related to God's faithfulness, expressed, according to some scholars, in the phrase *pistis Iēsou Christou*, which also refers to both the character and action of God, manifested in Jesus Christ (Romans 3:22; Galatians 2:16).[36]

The fruit of divine justice is human justice, the comprehensive right relationship that people enact towards other people and towards God. Human justice will be considered more thoroughly in the following section but is noted here as a manifestation of divine justice. This can be seen strikingly in the only instance where *dikaiosune theou* appears outside of Romans, which is in 2 Corinthians 5:21. Here, immediately following the phrase, "For us [or 'for our sake'] God made the one who did not know sin to be sin"—referring to Jesus taking on humanity's sin on the cross—comes the purpose that this act realizes: "so that in him we ourselves would become the justice of God (*dikaiosune theou*)."[37] God's saving justice is what the Christian actually becomes—one who lives as Jesus does.

Paralleling Isaiah and other Old Testament passages, these passages from Paul witness to God's restoration of humanity through Jesus's cross and resurrection, a restoration that takes place through a double movement of a negation of sin and a regeneration of humanity, as a wide range of metaphors in the New Testament (and not only in Paul's letters) express. In this justice, God is defeating sin through his loving sacrifice, restoring right relationship, and extending this restoration from Israel to all of humanity. Conveying the negation of sin are images that include acquittal, freedom from bondage and captivity,

---

[34] For Romans 1:17 and Romans 3:21–22, I draw from the translation offered by Gorman, *Participating in Christ*, 194.

[35] Stegman, "Paul's Use of *Dikaio-* Terminology," 502; Frank J. Matera, *God's Saving Grace: A Pauline Theology* (Grand Rapids, MI: Eerdmans, 2012), 107, 232–233; Dunn, "The Justice of God," 17.

[36] On this reading of the phrase *pistis Iēsou Christou*, see Stegman, "Paul's Use of *Dikaio-* Terminology," 508; Gorman, *Participating in Christ*, 123–129; and, for the fullest argument, see Richard B. Hays, *The Faith of Jesus Christ: The Narrative Substructure of Galatians 3:1–4:11* (Grand Rapids, MI: Eerdmans, 2002).

[37] Gorman, *Participating in Christ*, 197; Grieb, "So That in Him," 64–66. The translation here is Gorman's in *Participating in Christ*, 224.

forgiveness, liturgical sacrifice, payment of debt, ransom, and re-demption.[38] Conveying regeneration are Paul's references to life, peace, grace, the presence of the Spirit, and new creation.[39] Life in particular is a term that Paul repeats often in Romans to mean the condition of being made just—and thus being restored to right relationship, full of God's life—by God's saving justice. "Through one righteous/just act acquittal and life came to all," Paul writes in Romans 6:18, and elsewhere speaks of "walk in the newness of life," (6:4); "we shall also live with him" (6:8); "reign in life" (6:17); and "the law of the spirit of life in Christ" (8:2). Summing up concisely these negating and regenerating movements as well as the establishing of human justice through divine justice is 1 John 1:9: "If we acknowledge our sins, he is faithful and just (*dikaios*) and will forgive our sins and cleanse us from every wrongdoing."

Divine Rectifying Justice and the Justice of Rendering Due

God's rectifying justice in the Bible contains elements of, but is also wider than, the classical notion of justice, rendering another her due. In rectifying justice, due means deserving punishment, the core idea of retribution. The Old Testament is replete with episodes in which God requites, inflicts his wrath upon, or otherwise punishes Israel or Israel's enemies for their sins, as Isaiah exemplifies. In the New Testament, due is conveyed through terms and metaphors that describe the deserved punishment from which Jesus saves humanity: acquittal, debt for sin, expiation, and ransom. In Romans 1 and 2, Paul describes humanity as meriting God's wrath for its sins. Several passages speak of rewards and punishments in the afterlife and in the final judgment.[40]

God's rectifying justice, though, cannot be confined to rendering due. The Old Testament recounts many episodes in which God forgoes or withdraws punishment. Vivid is Psalm 103:8–10: "Merciful and gracious is the Lord, slow to anger, abounding in kindness. God does not always rebuke, nurses no lasting anger, [has] not dealt with us as our sins merit, nor requited us as our deeds deserve." Jesus's saving act of death and resurrection confounds retribution in several ways. It was not necessary: God, acting justly, either could have punished humanity or have waived the penalty. In paying humanity's debt for sin, Jesus thwarts retribution's requirement that the perpetrator of a deed be punished. Flouting retribution most of all, this act is, as Paul insists, a "gracious gift" that God bestowed "while we were still sinners," and

---

[38] Matthew 20:28; Mark 10:45; Mark 10:45; Romans 3:25; Romans 4:7; Romans 5:16; Romans 8:33; 1 Corinthians 6:20; 1 Corinthians 7:23; Galatians 3:13; Galatians 4:5; 1 Timothy 2:6; 1 Peter 1:18; and 2 Peter 2:1.
[39] Romans 5:1–2; Romans 8:6; Romans 8:10; 2 Corinthians 5:17.
[40] Matthew 5:12; Matthew 6:1; Matthew 25:41–43; Luke 6:23; Luke 14:13–14; Luke 16:19–31.

not on the condition that humanity pay up in advance (Romans 5:8; 5:15).

Divine Rectifying Justice in Relationship to Justification and Reconciliation

Two concepts in the Pauline letters—justification and reconciliation—extend the reach of God's divine justice in the scriptures in that they turn out to share the content of this justice. Justification, of course, has been a disputed concept, particularly since the Reformation. While I cannot fully argue the case here, I am persuaded by theologians who show that justification involves exactly the negation of sin and restoration of right relationship that God's saving justice does. The verb, justify, *dikaioō*, and the noun, justification, *dikaiōsis*, both belong to the *dik-* family and share in its meaning of right relationship. Theologian Michael Gorman, through a detailed analysis of the passages where justification appears, including Galatians 2:15–21 and Romans 3, 4, 5, 6, and 8, as well as 2 Corinthians 5:14–21, where the term does not appear but the concept resides, makes a strong case that justification involves not only acquittal and release from sin but also life, peace, the imparting of grace, the gift of the Holy Spirit, resurrection, and the presence of righteousness/justice as denoted by *dikaiosune*. This is none other than the restorative justice of the cross and resurrection. Through faith, people may participate in Christ's justification, dying to sin and becoming resurrected through him.[41]

The second concept is reconciliation, a term that appears fifteen times in the New Testament, thirteen of these in Paul's letters, including Romans, First and Second Corinthians, Ephesians and Colossians. Reconciliation is God's saving action through the cross and resurrection, bringing about a comprehensive restoration of right relationship between humans and God, between humans, within the soul, and, in light of certain verses, within the whole cosmos. The resulting restored relationship is a condition of being reconciled. Reconciliation, then, is essentially the same as God's saving justice and the same as justification.[42] This close relationship is apparent in Romans 5, where reconciliation is mingled with Paul's discussion of justification through the

---

[41] Gorman, *Participating in Christ*, 116–235. On justification as both liberating from sin and restorative, see Stegman, "Paul's Use of *Dikaio*-Terminology," 499. Others who argue that justification is closely linked with justice include Dunn and Suggate, *The Justice of God;* Perry Yoder, *Shalom: The Bible's Word for Salvation, Justice, and Peace* (Newton, KS: Faith and Life Press, 1987), 65; Marshall, *Beyond Retribution*, 53–59; Haughey, "Jesus as the Justice of God," 282–286; Belousek, *Atonement, Justice, and Peace,* 130; Douglas Harink, "Setting it Right," *Christian Century,* June 14, 2005, 25; and L. Cerfaux, *Christ in the Theology of St. Paul,* trans. Geoffrey Webb and Adrian Walker (New York: Herder and Herder, 1959), 138–142.

[42] Arguing that reconciliation and justification are exceedingly close in meaning are Gorman, *Participating in God,* 207; Ralph P. Martin, *Reconciliation: A Study of*

messiah's death and resurrection. In Romans 5:10, Paul describes reconciliation through the same double movement found in saving justice and justification: "[I]f, while we were enemies, we were reconciled to God through the death of his Son, how much more, once reconciled, will we be saved by his life." Reconciliation is also a strong theme in 2 Corinthians 5:14–21, where the word appears five times in this passage about the accomplishment of the cross and resurrection. The phrase, "[i]n Christ God was reconciling the world to himself, not counting their trespasses against them, and entrusting the message of reconciliation to us" (5:19), appears shortly before the verse that speaks of the resulting right relationship: "For us [or 'for our sake'] God made the one who did not know sin to be sin so that in him we ourselves would become the righteousness/justice of God" (5:21).[43] The comprehensiveness of reconciliation is expressed in Colossians, which reads, "[f]or in him the fullness was pleased to dwell, and through him to reconcile all things for him," shortly following a passage proclaiming that in Christ "all things were created in heaven and on earth" and that "in him all things hold together" (Colossians 1:16–20).

Reconciliation, like justification, is the same as the divine rectifying justice of Second Isaiah, which several scholars believe Paul had in mind in describing Jesus Christ's atoning action.[44] The servant with whom the gospels identify Jesus is one who performs saving, delivering justice on behalf of God and, in the Fourth Song, "gives his life as an offering for sin" and "[t]hrough his suffering…shall justify many, and their guilt he shall bear" (Isaiah 53:10–11). The rectifying justice of Jesus the Messiah is comprehensive, saving the entire world from its bondage to sin and inaugurating the total restoration of all things, in which humans are invited to join.

The Bible uses the language of justice to describe this total restoration following a Last Judgment in which God finally and definitively "makes all things new" (Isaiah 43:19; Revelation 21:5). An eschatological narrative in Second Isaiah (45:23) reads, "I have sworn by myself, the word is gone out of my mouth in righteousness/justice (*sedeqah*), and shall not return / That unto me every knee shall bow, every tongue shall swear"; while 2 Peter 3:13 declares, "We await new heavens and a new earth in which righteousness/justice (*dikaiosune*) dwells."[45] Likewise, the *Catechism*, commenting on the biblical nar-

---

Paul's Theology (Eugene, OR: Wipf and Stock, 1989), 37, 76, 80; Brevard S. Childs, *Biblical Theology of the Old and New* Testaments (Minneapolis, MN; Fortress Press, 2011), 485–486; and Matera, *God's Saving Grace*, 108–109.

[43] Again, the translation is Michael Gorman's in *Participating in Christ*, 6, 224.

[44] See, for instance, Stegman, "Paul's Use of *Dikaio* Terminology," 523–24.

[45] The translation of Isaiah is from the King James Version. Justice language also appears in eschatological contexts in Isaiah in Isaiah 9:7; 11:5; 26:2; 26:7; and 26:9.

rative, reads, "The Last Judgment will reveal that God's justice triumphs over all the injustices committed by his creatures and that God's love is stronger than death" (no. 1040).

HUMAN JUSTICE: RIGHT RELATIONSHIP RESTORED

If divine justice establishes and restores the human justice of comprehensive right relationship, what is the character of this human justice? It is revealed in the scores of instances of justice words—*sedeq(ah), mishpat, dikaiosune,* and their cousins—that describe how God summons human beings to live in conformity with right relationship and to restore right relationship after it has been broken. This is the justice of the bottom two quadrants, consisting of human primary justice, found in the lower left-hand quadrant, and human rectifying justice, found in the lower right-hand quadrant.

The Original Justice of the Garden of Eden and the Injustice of Sin

Resulting from God's original establishment of justice was the state of right relationship in which the first humans participated, the human justice of the Garden of Eden as described in Genesis. Reflecting on the Bible, major voices in the tradition, including Anselm, Aquinas (ST I-II, q. 85, a. 3, co), the Council of Trent, and today's *Catechism of the Catholic Church* (no. 375), have called this condition "original justice."[46] Sustained by grace, this justice was comprehensive in enfolding three dimensions of right relationship. First, the original humans lived in friendship with God, obeying and acknowledging him. Second, they lived in harmony with each other according to God's design (a harmony that was extended to all of creation). Third, there existed right relationship within the soul, where reason governed the lower parts, as Aquinas explains (ST I-II q. 85, a. 3, co.). Interior justice is the console from which the other two dimensions are enacted. A rightly ordered soul is disposed to act consistently with right relationship towards God and others.

That the Bible conceives of justice as right relationship, involving these three dimensions, is evident in its language for the action that severs this right relationship: sin. "The sinner rebels against the order of justice," writes theologian Matthew Levering in his interpretation of Aquinas's thought on the Bible.[47] On twenty-five occasions, New Testament writers denote sin with *adikia,* a word that attaches the prefix *a* to a *dik-* word, indicating the opposite of the justice that is right

---

The latter half of the quote from Isaiah 45:23 is used by Paul to describe Jesus in Philippians 2:10–11.

[46] The *Catechism* quotes the First Decree of Session V of the Council of Trent; find at www.thecounciloftrent.com/ch5.htm.

[47] Matthew Levering, "Creation and Atonement," in *Locating Atonement: Explorations in Constructive Dogmatics,* ed. Oliver D. Crisp and Fred Sanders (Grand Rapids, MI: Zondervan, 2015), 61.

relationship.[48] In the Septuagint, *adikia* frequently translates the Hebrew word, *'âvôn*, which means sin in the broad sense of both an offense and the wide destruction of persons and relationships. In Romans, Paul uses *adikia* to refer to the condition of sin to which cross and resurrection respond. In Romans 1:18, he uses *adikia* to mean sin or "wickedness" immediately following verse 17, where he writes of the righteousness/justice (*dikaiosune*) of God and of the righteous/just (*dikaios*) person who lives by faith. Then, in Romans 3:10, the phrase "there is no one just (*dikaios*)" begins a passage (3:10–18) that describes sin and is followed with the dramatic turn, "But now the righteousness/justice (*dikaiosune*) of God has been manifested apart from the law." Paul contrasts sin to the justice of right relationship.

Adikia and *'âvôn* are not the Bible's only words for sin, but through all of its references to sin, in all of their contexts, in both Old and New Testaments, the Bible depicts the breaking of right relationship in its threefold sense—with God, with others, and within the soul. Sin incurs humans' separation from God, a debt of punishment to God, a loss of God's glory and grace, and God's punishment, sometimes in the form of God's allowance of ill consequences, sometimes through measures that God wills directly. Sin ruptures relationships between persons, including in the sociopolitical realm, especially in the context of Old Testament kingship, as well as with respect to the natural world (Romans 8:20–22). Sin disintegrates the soul, too, illustrated by metaphors like burden and stain, culminating in death. What sin damages is the justice of comprehensive right relationship.

Human Justice in the Old Testament

The Old Testament conveys the comprehensiveness of human justice through numerous instances of *sedeq(ah)*, and sometimes *mishpat*, that imply generality—simply, all that God commands of his followers in every sphere of life—and through the adjective, *saddiq*, which describes a person who is faithful to these commands in a general sense.[49] Comprehensiveness is expressed in Psalm 119:172, "[m]ay my tongue sing of your promise, for all of your commandments are just (*sedeq*)," as it is in Deuteronomy 16:20, "Justice and justice alone shall be your aim," as well as in Deuteronomy 6:25, "Our justice (*sedeq*) before the Lord, our God, is to consist in carefully observing all these commandments he has enjoined on us." This last verse indicates that human justice is prescribed by God, most prominently through his covenants. The verse appears just after Moses reveals the Ten Commandments on Mount Sinai and introduces an exposition of God's law. This justice promotes well-being. The same verse is preceded by one reading, "Therefore, the Lord commanded us

---

[48] Reumann, "Righteousness (NT)," 747.
[49] On the comprehensiveness of *sedeq(ah)*, see footnote 4.

to observe all these statutes in fear of the Lord, our God, that we may always have as prosperous and happy a life as we have today," (Deuteronomy 6:24) while Psalm 106:3 offers the beatitude, "Happy those who do what is right (*sedeqah*), whose deeds are always just (*mishpat*)."

The content of this justice is the sum total of the Old Testament's commandments and the actions that they prescribe or proscribe. Again, Thomas Aquinas comes to our aid, this time by offering an enduring taxonomy of these commandments that begins with the Decalogue, which he calls the moral precepts, and teaches that they express justice, are revealed by God, and are also knowable through reason, belonging to the natural law (ST II-II q. 122, a. 1, co). The first three of the Ten Commandments express human obligations towards God and the final seven, obligations between persons. The hundreds of other precepts found in the Old Testament are derivative of the Ten Commandments, revealed by God, but not known through reason alone. What Aquinas calls the ceremonial precepts entail duties towards God and are derivative of the first three commandments, whereas what he calls the juridical precepts involve the duties of Israelites towards one another and outsiders and derive from the last seven commandments. Both sets of precepts are found in the Torah. Spread throughout the Old Testament are also verses that stress the interior origins of these commandments, often referring to the heart. The exposition of God's law in Deuteronomy, for instance, contains the Shema, part of which runs, "You shall love the Lord, your God, with all your heart" (Deuteronomy 6:4).

The Old Testament's invocations of justice extend to the social and political realm, especially in books written during the period of monarchy.[50] In all three parts of Isaiah (i.e., chaps. 1–39, 40–55, and 56–66), God's restoring justice brings about a just Israel or Jerusalem—a "city of justice (*sedeq*)," as Isaiah 1:26 puts it. Frequently, especially in the Psalms and Isaiah, *sedeq* is paired with *mishpat* in a hendiadys that connotes kingship and its attendant qualities. Sometimes, it is God's rule that is meant, but other times a human king's.[51] Isaiah 16:5, for instance, declares that "[a] throne shall be set up in mercy, and on it shall sit in fidelity [in David's tent]/ A judge upholding right (*mishpat*) and prompt to do justice (*sedeq*)." Justice is meant to be practiced by the king and by subjects in social and political affairs.

---

[50] Nardoni, *Rise Up, O Judge*, 95–121.
[51] God's rule is referenced in Psalms 9:9; Psalms 45:4; Psalms 89:15; Psalms 97:2; Psalms 98:9; Isaiah 9:6; Isaiah 16:5; Isaiah 33:5; and the king's rule in Psalms 72:1; Psalms 72:2; Psalms 99:4; Isaiah 16:5; Isaiah 32:1; and Jeremiah 22:3.

A prime characteristic of this justice is right treatment of the vulnerable, whom the Old Testament identifies as widows, orphans, resident aliens, and the poor.[52] The prophet Jeremiah (22:3) recounts that the Lord told him to tell the King of Judah: "Do what is right (*sedeqah*) and just (*mishpat*). Rescue the victim from the hand of his oppressor. Do not wrong or oppress the resident alien, the orphan, or the widow, and do not shed innocent blood in this place."

Human justice in the Old Testament also includes rectifying justice, that of the lower right-hand quadrant, which is found in the portion of the judicial precepts governing the redress of wrongs, most of which are found in the Torah's compendium of laws for the Israelite community. Many issues surround these precepts, including their stipulation of capital punishment, the meaning of the *lex talionis*, the place of restitution, and their underlying rationales.[53] What is important here is that they are included in the righteousness/justice that comprehends all criteria for action.

Human Justice in the New Testament

In the New Testament, too, justice words sometimes mean the comprehensive right relationship that God calls humans to enact, expressed by the noun *dikaiosune*, and the interior disposition toward this action, expressed by the adjective *dikaios*. In these instances, justice words refer not to a characteristic of God, God's establishment of justice, or the saving justice that God performs, as is true for the Bible's divine justice, but rather to the justice that persons enact towards other persons, towards God, and in cultivating their own character.

Though scattered throughout the New Testament, these terms are concentrated particularly in the Gospel of Matthew. Greek words with the root *dik-* appear there 26 times: *dikaios*, 17 times, the verb *dikaioo*, twice, and *dikaiosune*, seven times, five of which are found in the Sermon on the Mount.[54] In one instance, that of Jesus's words to John the Baptist at Jesus's baptism, *dikaiosune* means divine saving justice, as I argued above. The other instances arguably mean human justice. In the Sermon on the Mount, *dik-* words are "an umbrella concept that envisages what Jesus expects of his disciples so that they may enter the kingdom of heaven," argues Bible scholar Jonathan Pennington. Especially important is *dikaiosune*, which Pennington claims is one of

---

[52] Nardoni, *Rise Up, O Judge,* 80–81.
[53] An excellent treatment is that of Marshall, *Beyond Retribution,* 120–127, 201–241.
[54] Jonathan Pennington, *The Sermon on the Mount and Human Flourishing: A Theological Commentary* (Grand Rapids, MI: Baker Academic, 2017), 88.

the two main ideas in the Sermon on the Mount (along with the Kingdom of God) and argues that it means "whole-person behavior that accords with God's nature, will, and coming kingdom."[55]

In two instances in the Sermon on the Mount, *dikaiosune* opens a long passage in which Jesus expounds upon what it means to act rightly.[56] In Matthew 5:20, Jesus says, "unless your righteousness/justice (*dikaiosune*) surpasses that of the scribes and Pharisees, you will not enter into the kingdom of Heaven," and continues with six contrasts—"you have heard that it was said...but I tell you"—in which he deepens and renders more demanding the moral law of the Torah (Matthew 5:21–48). The passage ends with the injunction, "be perfect," implying the entirety of human behavior and interior disposition. Pennington holds that "this idea of *greater righteousness* [is] the meta-category that makes sense of the whole Sermon."[57] Then, in Matthew 6:1, Jesus says, "Take care not to perform righteous/just (*dikaios*) deeds in order that people may see them," and proceeds to enjoin his hearers to act with the motive of serving God the Father in giving alms, praying, and fasting, actions that people direct respectively towards other people, God, and the soul—the entirety of right relationship.[58]

Jesus also speaks of general right behavior when he exhorts, "seek first the Kingdom of God and his righteousness/justice (*dikaiosune*)" (Matthew 6:33).[59] *Dikaiosune* appears in Matthew 5:6, one of the beatitudes, as that for which the blessed hunger and thirst—that is, they desire to see right relationship realized in the world.[60] In Matthew

---

[55] Pennington, *The Sermon on the Mount*, 88–91. Italics removed from the latter quoted phrase. Pennington cites other scholars who share in his judgment about the importance and meaning of *dikaiosune* in the Sermon, including Ulrich Luz, *Matthew 1–7: A Commentary*, rev. ed., trans. James F. Crouch (Minneapolis, MN: Fortress, 2007), 177; Johan C. Thom, "Justice in the Sermon on the Mount: An Aristotelean Reading," *Novum Testamentum* 51 (2009): 315; and W.S. Davies and Dale C. Allison, Jr., *A Critical and Exegetical Commentary on The Gospel According to Saint Matthew*, vol. 1 (Edinburgh, UK: T&T Clark, 2004), 499. Sharing in this judgment is also Frank J. Matera, *The Sermon on the Mount: The Perfect Measure of the Christian Life* (Collegeville, MN: Liturgical Press, 2013), 31.

[56] Most translators of *dikaiosune* render the term as righteousness, but as I have been arguing all along, the term could equally well be justice. See footnote 15, especially the reference in Mattison, *The Sermon on the Mount and Moral Theology*, 31, 32, 49.

[57] Pennington, *The Sermon on the Mount and Human Flourishing*, 89; Matera, *The Sermon on the Mount*, 4.

[58] See Mattison, *The Sermon on the Mount and Moral Theology*, 157.

[59] For this interpretation, see Mattison, *The Sermon on the Mount and Moral Theology*, 181; Matera, *The Sermon on the Mount*, 96; and Pennington, *The Sermon on the Mount and Human Flourishing*, 250. Pennington also cites Luz, *Matthew 1–7*, 344.

[60] Mattison, *The Sermon on the Mount and Moral Theology*, 32; Matera, *The Sermon on the Mount*, 37.

5:10, *dikaiosune* identifies faithful behavior as that for which the blessed are persecuted.[61]

The Gospel of Matthew also features the adjective *dikaios*, which describes the person who lives in all of the ways that God has set forth. When Jesus teaches, for instance, that "your heavenly Father…causes rain to fall on the just (*dikaios*) and the unjust (*adikaios*)," he means by *dikaios* those who keep the law faithfully (Matthew 5:45). When Jesus speaks of the righteous or just (*dikaios*) at the last judgment, he means those who saw him in the hungry, the thirsty, the prisoner, the ill, and the stranger and acted accordingly (Matthew 25:37, 46).

These justice words, *dikaiosune* and *dikaios*, are found elsewhere in the New Testament, for instance, in the Letters of John, where they are situated in passages that exhort followers of Jesus to keep all of the commandments and to avoid sin, as well as in Paul's letters, in James, and in Hebrews, where they also mean living rightly in general or the qualities of a person who does so.[62]

Dikaiosune includes the entirety of the commandments that Jesus taught, ones that deepen and do not discard the justice of the Old Testament. The Sermon on the Mount summarizes this "new justice," as theologian Servais Pinckaers calls it, manifesting the new law, promulgated from a mountain by the new Moses.[63] Jesus calls for a more stringent and interior adherence to the moral law, avoiding not merely adultery but also all lust, not merely murder but also all hatred, and so on.[64] Like the law of the Old Testament, the new law charts the contours of human flourishing, doing so most explicitly through the beatitudes, which prescribe blessedness or happiness.

Human Justice and the Justice of Rendering Due

As was true for divine justice, human justice in the Bible both entails and exceeds the justice of rendering due. With respect to the lower left-hand quadrant, primary human justice, due implies rights, that is, entitlements that require the respect of others. While explicit mentions of rights mottle the Bible, rights arguably have a greater presence in the Bible by virtue of being entailed in obligations: what recipients of actions are entitled to assert mirrors what performers of

---

[61] Matera, *The Sermon on the Mount*, 37.

[62] 1 John 2:29; 1 John 3:7; 1 John 3:10; 1 John 3:12; Romans 14:17; 1 Corinthians 9:10; Philippians 1:11; 1 Thessalonians 2:10; 1 Timothy 1:8–9; 1 Timothy 6:11; 2 Timothy 3:16; Titus 2:12; Hebrew 12:11; James 3:18.

[63] Servais Pinckaers, *The Sources of Christian Ethics*, trans. Sr. Mary Thomas Noble, OP (Washington, DC: Catholic University of America, 1995), 143; Thomas Weinandy, *Jesus Becoming Jesus: A Theological Interpretation of the Synoptic Gospels* (Washington, DC: Catholic University of America Press, 2018), 146.

[64] See also Matthew 15:1–20.

actions are required to do. A right not to be killed, robbed, or cuck-olded is entailed in the commandments against murder, stealing, and adultery.[65]

Not all duties, though, entail corresponding rights. Some are wide duties, which require an end to be pursued but leave open how, when, where, and to what degree, and lack the specificity of those duties that are paired with a matching right. "Bear one another's burdens, and so you will fulfill the law of Christ," a norm that Paul teaches in Galatians (6:2), is unspecified and unlimited in its discharge, as are Jesus's com-mands to love one's neighbor and to take up one's cross and follow him (Luke 9:23). The Bible employs justice language to describe wide duties such as practicing generosity towards the poor. Ezekiel 18 in-cludes "[giving] food to the hungry and [clothing] the naked" in "[do-ing] what is right (*mishpat*) and just (*sedeqah*)." In Matthew 25, Jesus calls righteous/just (*dikaios*) the one who sees and serves him in the poor. In Paul's Second Letter to the Corinthians (9:9–15), he describes as justice (*dikaiosune*) giving generously to the poor and quotes Psalm 112:9, which makes the same link.[66] The Bible also associates justice with the open-ended commandment to give alms, as in the Book of Tobit (12:8) and in Jesus's articulation of giving alms as a right-eous/just deed in the Sermon on the Mount (Matthew 6:1).

Jesus departs from due more markedly with respect to justice in the lower right-hand quadrant, pertaining to what people may demand from one another in the aftermath of a wrong. In this dimension of justice, due means retribution, the repayment of wrongs with a penalty against the wrongdoer. Jesus zeroes in on retribution in the Sermon on the Mount in one of the six contrasts that reads, "You have heard that it was said, 'An eye for an eye and a tooth for a tooth.' But I say to you, offer no resistance to one who is evil" (Matthew 5:38–39). A long tradition of interpretation that includes Augustine and Aquinas holds that Jesus is teaching his hearers to reach beyond keeping their retri-bution proportionate and dispense with retribution altogether.[67] Paul echoes in his Letter to the Romans, "[d]o not repay anyone evil for evil" (Romans 12:17).

Jesus teaches similarly with respect to forgiveness. In the Lord's Prayer, also situated in a section of the Sermon on the Mount that is prefaced as one about justice, Jesus teaches his hearers to pray, "for-give us our debts, as we forgive our debtors," implying that the sinner owes payment both to God and to the person wronged and that the

---

[65] John Finnis, *Aquinas*, 134–136.

[66] Katherine Grieb, "So That in Him," 59.

[67] Aquinas, *Commentary on the Gospel of Matthew*, 180; Augustine of Hippo, "From Against Faustus, Book 19," in *From Irenaeus to Grotius: A Sourcebook in Christian Political Thought, 100–1625*, eds. Oliver O'Donovan and John Lockwood O'Do-novan (Grand Rapids, MI: Eerdmans, 1999), 115–117; see also Nicholas Wolterstorff, *Justice in Love* (Grand Rapids, MI: Eerdmans, 2011), 119–133.

person wronged ought to forgo this debt. Jesus amplifies the lesson in Matthew 18, where he enjoins Peter to forgive seventy times seven times and elaborates with the story of a king who forgave the debt of a servant who then refused to forgive the debt of a fellow servant and was thus harshly punished by the king: "So will my heavenly Father do to you, unless each of you forgives his brother from his heart" (18:35).

Human Justice as the Fruit of Cross and Resurrection and Reconciliation

Human justice, the new law, is defined, authorized, and empowered by Jesus's death and resurrection. As Gorman explains, "Righteousness...is not only *derived* from the Messiah's death but also *defined* by the Messiah's death."[68] This new definition of righteousness, or justice, involves a loving, sacrificial gift of self—"No one has greater love than this, to lay down one's life for one's friends" (John 15:13)—which bestows new meaning upon the beatitudes, which in turn deepen the meaning of the Ten Commandments. In this way, Jesus fulfills, and does not abolish, the law (Matthew 5:17).[69]

Paul employs *dikaiosune* to describe the ways of the person who is transformed and renewed by the cross and resurrection. He writes, "Freed from sin, you have become slaves of righteousness/justice (*dikaiosune*)" in Romans 6:18, and "through the obedience of one the many will be made righteous/just (*dikaios*)" in Romans 6:20.[70] It is through faith that a person comes to embody this justice, as Paul argues in Romans 1:17 when he writes, "The one who is righteous/just (*dikaios*) by faith will live," and as he expresses in Romans 10:6 through the phrase, "the righteousness/justice (*dikaiosune*) that comes from faith."[71]

This human justice is the fruit of reconciliation, the ways of one who has been reconciled. This person becomes an ambassador of reconciliation, a new creation, one who suffers for others, loves his enemies, and practices "righteousness/justice [*dikaiosune*], peace, and joy in the Holy Spirit" (Romans 14:17).[72] Cross and resurrection give the new law a divine imprimatur, the authority of the God who triumphed over death. They also enable people to live the new law through grace. The same Holy Spirit who empowered the resurrection empowers people to participate in the life that Jesus taught and exemplified, a life in

---

[68] Gorman, *Participating in God*, 141.

[69] On how cross and resurrection shape the beatitudes, see Weinandy, *Jesus Becoming Jesus*, 146–178.

[70] See also 1 Peter 2:24: "freed from sin, we might live for righteousness/justice (*dikaiosune*)."

[71] See also Philippians 3:9.

[72] Corneliu Constantineanu, *The Social Significance of Reconciliation in Paul's Theology* (London, UK: T&T Clark, 2010), 99–206.

communion with the Holy Trinity. The new justice is an infused justice.[73]

All told, human justice acts in intimate partnership with divine justice. God enacts divine justice in establishing human justice in creating the world and in promulgating his covenants, most definitively the new covenant in Jesus Christ. The people who received this justice both followed it and turned away from it, and after they turned away, God enacted divine justice anew by exiling his people, bringing them home from exile, and ultimately redeeming all of humanity by way of Jesus's cross and resurrection, through all of these actions restoring and redefining human justice. The human justice set forth by Jesus Christ is not merely a new form of wisdom but is also a participation in God's renewal of the world.

CONCLUSION

As biblical justice comes unveiled, its contrast with modern liberal justice becomes clearer. What is most distinct about biblical justice is the authorship of God, who establishes, sustains, and restores the right relationship that God calls humans to practice towards one another. Biblical justice enfolds but exceeds obligations to render others their due, including wide obligations such as service to the poor and living as a gift to others as well as forms of restoring right relationship that are not retributive. Biblical justice involves not merely external behavior but also rightly ordered souls that are disposed towards right action towards other persons and God. The full meaning of biblical justice, manifesting all of these qualities, defining right relationship most comprehensively, is the death and resurrection of Jesus Christ. Modern liberal justice, by contrast, is secular, known solely through reason, revolves around due, and is a matter of external behavior.

Other contrasts and implications warrant exploration. Theologians in the Christian tradition have conceived justice solely in terms of the natural law as well as almost completely apart from the natural law, whereas the present argument suggests that justice is a synthesis of the natural law, known through reason, and the divine law, which God reveals and that widens, deepens, and specifies the natural law. The contrast and the synthesis merit further analysis. So, too, does the relationship between the justice of comprehensive right relationship, an umbrella concept, and the narrower dimensions of justice that it arguably encompasses, for instance, distributive justice, commutative justice, restorative justice, and the justice embodied in the panoply of rights. Worth probing, too, is the meaning of comprehensive right relationship for areas of social life such as economic dealings, immigrants and refugees, humanity's relationship with the natural environment, and the family. Finally, the connection of this justice with other

---

[73] Mattison, *The Sermon on the Mount and Moral Theology*, 202–203.

virtues and fruits such as mercy, faith, and peace begs to be plumbed. The task at hand has been limited to establishing that biblical justice is comprehensive right relationship. That this justice summons these further tasks points to its power and its possibilities.[74] ▣

Daniel Philpott is Professor of Political Science at the University of Notre Dame. He is the author of *Just and Unjust Peace: An Ethic of Political Reconciliation* (Oxford, 2012) and is writing a Christian account of justice.

---

[74] For helpful comments on the piece, the author wishes to thank Gary Anderson, Michael J. Gorman, Brian Lee, William Mattison, Kevin Offner, and Jonathan Pennington.

Journal of Moral Theology, Vol. 11, No. 1 (2022): 193–206

Book Reviews

The Structures of Virtue and Vice. By Daniel J. Daly. Washington, DC: Georgetown University Press, 2021. x + 245 pages. $44.95.

Those of us who have appreciated Daniel J. Daly's work on social structures and Catholic ethics have been eager to receive his book-length treatment of this topic. *The Structures of Virtue and Vice* fulfills and exceeds these expectations, offering a satisfying elaboration of Daly's body of work in moral theology that has already influenced how the field understands virtue ethics, social structures, and agency. Daly aims both to update Catholic virtue theory and to develop the relationship between social structure and moral agency. These proximate goals support his ultimate goal of articulating moral concepts capable of ethically categorizing and scrutinizing social structures. The book contains a clear and logical progression, moving from a diagnostic analysis of social structures in Part I to an investigation of resources for developing the tradition in Part II. Finally, Part III synthesizes and applies Daly's constructive framework for the structures of virtue and vice.

Beginning with a case study of the collapse of Rana Plaza, the building in Bangladesh which housed a massive sweatshop and resulted in the deaths of 1,127 garment workers (12–13), Chapter 1 argues that manualist approaches to moral reasoning struggle to address contemporary problems that provoke new questions about the relationship between agents and structures. Chapter 2 expounds this problem through an investigation of the role of social structures in Catholic thought. Daly's analysis of magisterial teaching, liberation theologies, and recent Catholic moral theologies unveils the tradition's struggle to develop an understanding of social structure that undergirds its account of the relationship between personal and structural sin.

In Chapter 3, Daly turns to critical realism to elaborate the meaning of social structure in Catholic thought with special concern that this account reflects reality while also resonating with three Catholic "control beliefs": (1) that humans are relational, (2) that humans possess fundamental human dignity, and (3) that humans have agency (68–69). He argues that critical realism, which maintains that reality exists independent of human consciousness and can be known through reason, provides a social theory that comports with these beliefs. Chapter 4 then unveils three developments in the magisterial teachings of John Paul II, Benedict XVI, and Francis—first developed in the works of theologians—that are useful for constructing an ethical approach to social structures: (1) the rise of a theocentric vision, (2) the emergence of personalism, and (3) the return of virtue ethics.

Part III marshals these social and theological resources toward providing a constructive account of the structures of virtue and vice. After elaborating personalist virtue ethics in Chapter 5, which identifies virtue as enabling the agent to "love God and who and what God loves," (162), Daly's book reaches its apex in Chapter 6's discussion of structures of virtue and vice where he integrates critical realist social theory within a theocentric personalist virtue theory. This move allows Daly to demonstrate how structures contribute to or detract from the well-being of persons and communities. Chapter 7 offers analysis of the capacity of his framework to produce practical claims of virtuous action and structure.

In a particularly helpful turn, Daly persuasively demonstrates parallels between John Paul II, Benedict XVI, and Francis's articulation of the moral significance of social structures, providing a useful device for scholars and students to recognize the unhelpful opposition often attributed to their respective moral teachings. Daly's text thus presents itself as a useful teaching resource in both graduate and undergraduate settings where such dichotomies can thwart deeper understanding of magisterial teaching.

Daly has produced a rich and challenging work, calling upon his colleagues in Catholic moral theology to engage in a more disciplined consideration of both the relationship between agency and structures as well as our own underdeveloped conceptions of structures themselves. Daly is clear about the need for greater receptivity of sociological methods among Catholic ethicists even as he reaffirms the necessity for engaging this material in a distinctively Catholic manner. In this way, Daly's work is as much a proclamation of the Catholic faith as it is an astute analysis of Catholic thought. This is despite Daly's expression of wariness of Catholic social thought becoming "more inspirational than analytical" (2). Daly's own achievement shows that the dichotomy between rigorous analysis and inspiring sermon is a false one, one that potentially reinforces an undesirable relegation of that which is beautiful to the margins of that which is true and good. If moral theology is social analysis grounded in our faith, as Daly's work proclaims, then it must preach even as it analyzes.

NICHOLE M. FLORES
University of Virginia

A Creed for Today: Faith and Commitment for Our New Earth Awareness. By Donal Dorr. Maryknoll, New York: Orbis Books, 2021. 256 pages. $26.00.

As statements of Christian faith, creeds serve to both summarize the precepts of the faith and unite Christians in that faith. In his work *A Creed for Today: Faith and Commitment for Our New Earth Awareness,* Irish theologian Donal Dorr re-imagines the traditional creed with an emphasis on deeper understandings of the Trinity; the universe and our place in it; what Incarnation means; and how creation itself reveals God's nature and being. In this re-conception, he produces a nuanced, deeply theological, and poetic creed that ties theology, spirituality, and ecology together in a prophetic and profound witness to both the mystery of God and the concrete reality of the created world.

This work was prompted not just by the current ecological crisis facing humanity but also in response to what Dorr sees as a fourth major development in spirituality after Vatican II, the first three being humanistic psychology, feminist theology, and theologies of liberation. None of these are adjunct to the central understandings of Christian faith but rather serve to deepen our understanding of God and human life and the relationships in which all people are embedded. In the same way, ecological perceptions and actions are not simply supplemental to our knowledge of the relationship between human beings and God but are central to that understanding. Stewardship of creation and care for all beings is thus an imperative, not merely a good action.

The essays which make up the bulk of the book are focused mainly on bringing together ecological ethics and spirituality with fundamental Christian beliefs, primarily centered on the Trinity, adding greater depth to traditional Christian theological understandings of these foundational Christian precepts. The major strength of the work is this reframing and deeper explication of these familiar concepts in light of an ecological spirituality. The section on Jesus, titled "Integral Incarnation," is especially original in its approach to the embodied human life of Jesus of Nazareth. For example, Dorr points out that Jesus exists not just as a human being in a certain point in history but is also the result (as we are) of evolutionary processes that existed before his birth and that the "matter" which made up his body is with us still, recycled into our own world as material from all human bodies eventually will be (63–64). The section on the Holy Spirit, which follows the insights of Christ as savior and transformer not just of humanity but all of the created world, is similarly original, expanding traditional understandings of the work of the Spirit in creation and in human lives and relationships.

Overall, this book provokes a depth of thought unlike most other works on ecology and ethics. Some may find his conclusions a bit over the top in their approach, or too poetic to be practical, but they are conclusions grounded in solid theological reasoning rooted in Scripture (which is liberally referred to throughout) and Christian history. This is married to science and current understandings of the ecological crises humanity currently faces, producing a "creed for today" that affirms authentic Christian belief while situating that belief in our current lived reality. This has the effect of both enhancing the mystery of the divine while also making this mystery more concrete and integral to human life.

This work would be suitable for advanced undergraduates in theology or ethics and is especially suitable for students of spirituality and ecological ethics. It is also a thought-provoking work for personal spiritual introspection and growth, especially for those who sometimes struggle to articulate the deep connections that exist between the created world and Christ.

MARI RAPELA HEIDT
Notre Dame of Maryland University

Thought Experiments in Ethics. By Gusztáv Kovács. Pécs, Hungary: Episcopal Theological College of Pécs, 2021. iii + 291 pages. $20.95.

Thought Experiments in Ethics is an attempt to provide a novel view of thought experiments from the perspective of the university professor who aims to go beyond theoretical education. Through Kovács's work, lecturers in Christian ethics and anthropology now have a chance to experience working with thought experiments in a way which goes beyond the limits of argumentation. The originality of the book is in its treatment of thought experiments: they are not simple illustrations, or elements of ethical lines of thought, but rather tools for education. The challenge they pose to the intuitive apparatus of students might not only lead to understanding, but to true ethical conversion.

Kovács works not only with the "classics" of thought experiments, such as the trolley problem, the violinist scenario, or the experience machine, but tries to broaden the scope by including stories from the Bible and literature. The most characteristic example comes from FerencSánta's *The Fifth Seal*, a novel centered around the story of Tomoceuszkakatiti and Gyugyu, an evil tyrant and a slave. Kovács confronts the reader with the necessity to choose between the fate of the two protagonists of the story and thus successfully demonstrates how thought experiments transcend the limits of argumentation. In being whirled by the dilemma, readers can have firsthand experience about how thought experiments work. They have a certain "existential force" due to their power to "reveal something hidden about ourselves" (7), they work with specific rules, such as "Tertia non datur!" (9) and are analogous with the reality of the readers (10). The key role of these three features is also demonstrated through the Parable of the Good

Samaritan, taking the reader back to its original setting and underlining once more the context bound character of thought experiments and helping preachers and teachers to understand why their audience might miss the point of biblical parables today. The use of the term "pragmatics" is also justified by the emphasis on the context, the pragmatic force and the effect on the hearer.

The book explicitly reaches back to the revolution of the teaching of ethics in 1960s America, when a "new generation of philosophers emerged who were less interested in the discourse on the philosophy of language and keen to explore questions of practical interest" (76). Kovács names Judith Jarvis Thomson, Michael Tooley, Philippa Foot, and James Rachels, most of whom published regularly in the journal *Philosophy & Public Affairs*. They coined many of the thought experiments which are now part of any standard curriculum of ethics. Kovács underlines the innovative character of thought experiments especially in the field of bioethics, where complex questions "could now be brought before the public using a simple story and a well-formulated question" (78). Despite his obvious enthusiasm for the use of thought experiments in the classroom, Kovács is also critical and aims to show the limits of teaching with the help of imaginary cases.

The second part of the book discusses particular thought experiments in detail, sparking the intuition of the readers in a careful fashion. The original and numerous alternate versions of Robert Nozick's Experience Machine, Richard Sylvan's Last Man Argument, Philippa Foot's Trolley Problem, and Judith Jarvis Thomson's Violinist Analogy, offer a playful and demanding introduction to these classics of thought experiments. They approach different questions of human life, such as the importance of reality, the value of nature, our "not-fitting-into-the-world" (210), and the delicacy of the bond between parents and children. At this stage Kovács turns the focus from ethics to anthropology as he stresses that thought experiments "entail a certain implicit anthropology," which manifests "in the clash between intuitive responses and moral expectations" (210).

Critics, especially moral theologians, might find one flaw in Kovács's book. One might feel disappointed by the lack of solutions to the numerous ethical puzzles in the book. Opposed to the tradition of casuistry, Kovács describes thought experiments as tools for challenging our intuitions, but it does not seem to be his goal to provide solutions for those facing an ethical dilemma. Nevertheless, the whole book appears to be a persuasive argument for professors of ethics and moral theology to make a better use of thought experiments in lecture halls.

PIOTR MORCINIEC
University of Opole

Justice and Charity: An Introduction to Aquinas's Moral, Economic, and Political Thought. By Michael P. Krom, Grand Rapids, MI: Baker Academic, 2020. xv +237 pages. $29.99.

Within a myriad of new books on St. Thomas Aquinas, we find occasionally a fresh approach that not only faithfully expresses the thought of the Angelic Doctor but also makes it accessible to a broader audience beyond the Thomistic bubble. Michael Krom's *Justice and Charity: An Introduction to Aquinas's Moral, Economic, and Political Thought* brings Aquinas's thought to bear on relevant, contemporary issues; issues, in fact, that are pressing for the future of society. Catholic social teaching is premised on the fact that universal moral issues, stemming from the natural law and clarified by divine revelation, can guide prudential decisions in society. St. Thomas remains an essential guide in the Church's public discourse, as Krom makes clear. In four sections, he addresses Aquinas's moral theory, its application in economic and political life, and finally its applicability today. In the first three sections, he presents a chapter devoted to the foundation of the natural law and another to its supernatural fulfillment. It is clear that the book flows forth from fruitful teaching, explaining St. Thomas's teaching in a clear manner while also applying it to life. Krom explains his approach: "I wrote this book out of the conviction that those who want to heed the Church's call to engage our culture need to look to the past; in particular, they should familiarize themselves with the writings of St. Thomas Aquinas, the Church's Angelic Doctor" (2–3). The book rightly roots the practical organization of society upon the right moral ordering of the human person.

Krom begins with Aquinas's articulation of the good life, understood as the proper use of freedom in the pursuit of happiness. While the cardinal virtues, and especially justice, lay the foundation, the second chapter looks at how the infused virtues and gifts perfect the acquired virtues and the natural desire for happiness. This desire for happiness, however, leads to the active pursuit of the good, both as a citizen and member of the Body of Christ, "and for this reason moral theology is completed by a study of how justice and charity are to be put in practice in economic and political life" (70).

In dealing with a Thomistic approach to economics in the second section, Krom focuses on the right use of goods to promote human happiness, both on the level of justice in society and charity in the Church. Even after turning from the topic of moral theology, he remains focused on the goal of human life, because "the use of material goods must be directed to the end of human happiness" (75). Virtue must guide the right use of things for one's own good, although also in subordination to the common good. In line with this, Krom engages in an important discussion of the value of goods from both a philosophical and theological perspective.

Politics also must be judged from the perspective of human flourishing, as "a government cannot be called 'good' unless it promotes
just moral and economic relationships between its citizens" (121).
This is precisely the purpose of government—to promote right order
and peace. In an age of problematic individualism and collectivism,
the common good must arise from the proper relation of the individual
good within the whole. The common good orients the moral life. Our
ultimate good, however, is God, not the political life. There are not
"two ends to human existence, the earthly and the heavenly .... [T]here is only one end, the beatific vision" (162).

To this end, *Justice and Charity* provides an important reflection
on thinking about human life in society from the perspective of that
one end, distinguishing between the goods of nature and supernatural
ones, while realizing that they must be integrated and ordered toward
our true end in God. Its clarity and thoughtfulness make it an important
overview of Aquinas's moral, economic, and political thought that can
provide an aid to teaching and an inspiration for broader discussion of
Catholic social thought.

R. JARED STAUDT
Augustine Institute, Graduate School of Theology

Jonah and the Human Condition: Life and Death in Yahweh's World.
By Stuart Lasine. London: T&T Clark, 2020. xv + 165 pages. $108
hardback, $39.95 paper.

This concise but erudite book is difficult to characterize in terms
of discipline and method. It is a contribution to the field of biblical
studies and an illuminating reading of the book of Jonah, but it is also
a philosophical reflection on the human condition that draws liberally
on insights from psychology. Moreover, Lasine brings the Hebrew Bible's meditations on life and death into conversation with ancient
Greek philosophical and literary perspectives on the human condition.

Part One (chapters 1 to 4) is a broad survey of answers to the question "what is the human being" in the Hebrew Bible, in conversation
with other ancient and modern perspectives on that question. Part Two
(chapters 5 to 7) is a more focused study of the book of Jonah, particularly as it has been understood by thinkers outside of biblical studies
who have treated Jonah as an "Everyman" character. While the first
part, not surprisingly, favors biblical texts such as Job and Qohel-
eth/Ecclesiastes that have traditionally been classified as "wisdom literature," biblical scholars do not often look to the book of Jonah for
insights about the human condition.

The introductory chapter concludes that the Hebrew Bible, like ancient Greek literature, bears witness to conflicting perspectives on
what it means to be human. The second chapter narrows the focus

somewhat, to the question of whether pessimism about the human condition is warranted, given the nature of the biblical God and of the world. On the one hand, Lasine is addressing a literary question about the death wishes of certain biblical characters (Moses, Elijah, Jonah and Jeremiah), but on the other hand, he is asking a philosophical question, following William James, about whether pessimism is a realistic stance in relation to the world.

Chapter 3 anticipates the analysis of the book of Jonah by examining examples of the metaphor "life is a sea voyage" elsewhere in the Hebrew Bible, in conversation with examples of this metaphor in other ancient and modern literature. Again, although the analysis is literary, the conclusion has philosophical (or theological) implications: nautical metaphors "convey a *realistic* portrait of human life in Yahweh's universe" (61, emphasis original). Chapter 4 extends Lasine's line of inquiry in a more practical direction, asking whether, given its dearth of reassurances about life after death, the Hebrew Bible offers a "safe space" within which readers can come to terms with their inevitable demise.

Chapters 5 and 6, on the character Jonah and the plot of the book of Jonah, respectively, offer critiques of others' psychological interpretations of the book of Jonah, particularly Jungian ones. Lasine presents numerous literary parallels to motifs in Jonah that he understands as symbolizing childhood fears and the "perils of adulthood." The concluding chapter brings the insights of Part One, especially about the biblical God, to bear on the interpretation of Jonah.

Perhaps unsurprisingly, but nevertheless unconventionally, the book ends with the author's meditation on his own death, in which he aligns himself with William James and distances himself from Freud, one of his primary interlocutors throughout the book.

The most striking thing about this book, however, is the sheer number and diversity of its interlocutors, which attests to the breadth of Lasine's reading and thought. It is unfortunate that the author Lasine cites most often is himself, because he genuinely engages with a much wider range of thinkers than most biblical scholars do. This book does have something of the feel of a retrospective of his scholarship, but it is a creative contribution, nevertheless.

KARINA MARTIN HOGAN
Fordham University

The Business of War: Theological and Ethical Reflections on the Military-Industrial Complex. Edited by James McCarty, Matthew Tapie, and Justin Bronson Barringer. Eugene, OR: Cascade Books, 2020. xx + 257 pages. $33.00.

The Business of War belongs to *The Business of Modern Life* series, which aims to evaluate the tendency for market systems to pervasively co-opt dimensions of contemporary human life. This goal takes an interesting form in application to modern military activity because, as the editors note in their Introduction, there are substantial bodies of theological ethical work on both war and capitalist systems but relatively little on their progeny, the Military-Industrial Complex (MIC) (xv). In order to begin filling this lacuna, *The Business of War* assembles twelve essays of both scholarly and popular Christian interest that offer ethical analysis of various aspects of the MIC, especially as it prevails in the United States.

Beginning the first part, Myles Werntz outlines the military-economic situation of Israel in the Old Testament and argues that both the New Testament and Christian political theology challenge any translation of Israel's arrangement to the contemporary nation state (18–20). Christina McRorie surveys various ethical approaches to economics and war, both theoretical and practical, taken throughout the Christian tradition.

Pamela Brubaker's essay begins the second part by helpfully sketching the development of the MIC in the US and treating the impact of that development on arms proliferation and the climate. David Swartz describes the fusion of capitalist economics, war, and evangelization within the Christian Evangelical imagination during the Cold War, noting that freedom became the central theme in a quasi-crusade against Marxism (83). Matthew Whelan discusses instances in which the US has supported corrupt regimes in Latin America to ward off the perceived threat of communism (96) and extols Latin American martyrs as witnesses to just resistance to MIC (107). In discussing the Republic of Korea's MIC, Won Chul Shin argues that the Democratic People's Republic of Korea's military superiority is a myth and that the true driver of the Republic of Korea's MIC is its inextricability from the US's MIC resulting from their military alliance (113).

In the third part, Bradley Burroughs addresses the ethical concerns associated with the US's use of private military contractors, which not only commodify war but also seek to cut costs by, for example, outsourcing security services (136–137). Kara Slade's essay offers a discussion of how engineering companies, the DOD, and the US educational system taps into the "techno-aesthetic" imagination of students in order to attract them to STEM disciplines, an intent that is ultimately grounded in the MIC's inexhaustible need for researchers (146–147).

In the final part, Bronson Barringer locates the mode of Christian resistance to MIC in the practices of simplicity, community, charity, and spirituality from the book of Acts, observing various prophetic American figures who embodied these practices (162). James McCarty's essay invokes King to argue that the triple evils of racism, materialism, and militarism are inseparable and therefore can only be rectified integrally. Tobias Winright and Nathaniel Hibner advocate for the incorporation of *jus ante bellum* and *jus post bellum* costs into just war theory as a means for ensuring its ordering toward a holistic understanding of peace (205). The volume concludes with an essay by Stan Goff, who argues that MIC can only be undone by subversion of money-dependency through intentional pursuit of local community interdependence, which will inevitably come either by immense government overhaul or by societal disintegration (226).

The volume is both challenging and engaging, prophetic and scholarly. All of its essays are certainly well-suited for undergraduates as well as scholars, though experts might desire book-length treatments of the topics, which can be found in other volumes. While the scope of the volume is impressive, certain topics could only receive brief or passing discussion that might have been worthy of dedicated essays, such as feminist theological or ecological theological accounts of the MIC. Finally, while this volume only aimed to begin the discussion on the ethics of the MIC, it seems the conversation would benefit from interaction with another burgeoning area of moral theology—Christian ethical engagement with critical realist sociology, such as that presented in Daniel Finn's *Moral Agency within Social Structures and Culture.* Critical realist tools of analysis would be of great use for deepening the investigation of systemic factors constituting the MIC and for assisting Christians in imagining paths of resistance. All of this is to say that the volume is sure to inspire further thought on the theological ethics of the MIC, which means that it admirably achieves its goal.

VINCENT BIRCH
Catholic University of America

Restoring Humanity: Essays on the Evangelization of Culture. By R. Jared Staudt. Belmont, NC: Divine Providence Press, 2020. 195 pages. $16.00.

In the midst of culture wars and similar conflicts, more conservative or traditionalist Catholics who disagree with many of the actions of the current pope have searched for the same themes and tone that were previously expressed by John Paul II. In his recent work, *Restoring Humanity*, Jared Staudt, Director of Formation for the Archdiocese of Denver and Visiting Associate Professor at the Augustine Institute, provides a work that will resonate with many of these same Catholics. The author of such works as *The Beer Option: Brewing A Catholic Culture, Yesterday & Today*, Staudt, in *Restoring Humanity*, provides a map for the restoration of Catholic culture as he understands it.

Drawing from the works of thinkers such as Benedict XVI, John Henry Newman, and St. Thomas Aquinas, Staudt argues that one of the Church's missions is the transformation of culture. Evangelization is not only for the conversion of individuals but of peoples and their cultures. The word "culture" itself is derived from the Roman philosopher and rhetorician Marcus Tullius Cicero who noted in his *Tusculan Disputations* that the process of education was similar to that of agriculture in as much as the soul, like the soil, is cultivated. With this historical reference, Staudt takes aim at the (post-)Enlightenment notion of culture as the accumulation of items or adornments. Culture, then, is an essential element of human formation. Christopher Dawson, Leo XIII, and Vatican II's *Gaudium et Spes* argue this is potentially a positive good for Catholics and something that, for John Paul II himself, is a positive good for human development.

Staudt argues that it is only the Gospel which can transform culture. Christians must further recognize and proclaim the Incarnation as the center of history, which ultimately gives meaning to human history. With the gifts of grace, the Church acts as "leaven" in society, transforming and healing it.

Like Gerard Manley Hopkins, Catholics are also tutored in the sacramentality of each thing, and like St. Thomas Aquinas, disciples of Christ can further recognize the beauty of each thing. This is the marked contrast to the nihilism and ugliness of postmillennial life. The Catholic artist especially should have the ability to recognize the beauty of being as well as ultimate beauty and meaning of such things as suffering and the seeming ugliness of everyday life. The land itself, according to Staudt, is a place for evangelization and is a gift from God. The loss of land is then, by default, a loss of connectedness to the sacramentality and beauty of being.

Catholic education must ultimately be directed to the Truth, which is Christ Himself, who provides the firm grounding for authentic culture as well as authentic freedom. Staudt writes that education, at its heart, should be a process of cultivation of the soul. Culture is further a gift from the past from which many in the West have been uprooted.

Ultimately, Staudt argues, the West is under assault, and it can be only revived by Christian faith. This belief does not reduce Christianity to a utilitarian role but rather emphasizes the fact that it is only by and through Christ that the West and, ultimately, the world has the potential to be saved.

JESSE RUSSELL
Georgia Southwestern State University

Morality and Situation Ethics. By Dietrich von Hildebrand. Steubenville, OH: Hildebrand Project, 2019; xxxvi +180, $16.99; *Graven Images: Substitutes for True Morality*. By Dietrich von Hildebrand. Steubenville, OH: Hildebrand Project, 2019; xxvi + 194 pages, $16.99.

Dietrich von Hildebrand was one of the early phenomenologists, studying under the tutelage of Edmund Husserl and sharing friendship early in his academic career with Max Scheler. Hildebrand influenced the Catholic sexual tradition by offering an early articulation of the two ends of marriage in the 1920s. He vehemently opposed the Nazi party before and during World War II, during which time he wrote *Transformation in Christ*.

Hildebrand originally published *Morality and Situation Ethics* and *Graven Images* with Alice Jourdain in the mid-1950s, during that critical period between the Second World War and the Second Vatican Council. The Hildebrand project, within its broader mission to make the ideas and writings of Hildebrand more widely known, edited these two works for consistency and style and now has re-published them as critical editions.

Morality and Situation Ethics, first published in 1955, follows Hildebrand's more comprehensive and systematic work on morality entitled *Ethics*. Accordingly, Hildebrand does not explain in detail his overall ethical theory. Readers of the two works under consideration would do well to know some central features of his broader value-response ethical theory. Hildebrand employs the word "value" in a distinct and technical sense. Value is something good in itself beyond the good or subjective satisfaction it might bring to the one acting. Moral goodness implies a capacity for self-transcendence—to recognize and respond appropriately to values (things that are good in themselves). He warns against the persistent danger of pride and concupiscence which can lead individuals to overlook or even respond maliciously toward values.

Perhaps Hildebrand's greatest contributions in *Morality and Situation Ethics* are his distinctions between different kinds of legalism and his insightful analysis of their relationship to pride. The work is filled with original insights, such as when he observes that the Pharisee attempts to borrow "the unique humiliating power inherent in the moral verdict, and to use it as a weapon for his pride" (18).

Hildebrand proposes that the cultural trend of situation ethics moves from legitimate criticism of legalism to a morally problematic justification or even praising of the tragic sinner. He sees this tendency evidenced in literature (e.g., Graham Greene and Francois Mauriac) and youth movements. A false dichotomy between legalism and the tragic sinner, according to Hildebrand, suggests that following moral norms is worse than not following moral norms. Hildebrand insists that if the tragic sinner possesses certain positive moral attributes "it is not because of his sinning, but in spite of it" (96).

For Hildebrand, situation ethics is a tendency to reduce moral insights to specific actions and to deny the validity and role of general moral norms. He proposes that while specific circumstances need to be considered to offer a valid value response, many moral insights have relevance beyond what should be done in a specific situation. Further, while one should avoid reductions of the moral life to moral rules, moral laws and norms serve a crucial function in guiding individuals towards moral insight and conversion, thereby helping to overcome false self-rationalizations rooted in pride and concupiscence. Rather than compare the tragic sinner to the Pharisaic or the self-righteous person, Hildebrand argues that one understands the error of the tragic sinner more accurately in relation to one who embraces the high calling in Christ living in charity, mercy, contrition, and humility.

In *Graven Images*, Hildebrand provides a profound analysis of the boundaries of moral analysis. He reflects on different ways in which individuals substitute concerns, moral or otherwise, for morality. The substitute "is identified with the general denominator of morality: moral goodness" (31). He offers many examples of moral substitutes: following tradition, following the laws of the state, progressiveness, honor, warmth of heart, duty, faithfulness, altruism, self-control, mediocre realism, the decent man, the gentleman (34–40). He notes that other common distortions of morality flow from giving too central a position to efficiency, duty, being genuine, fearlessness, nobleness, or ritualism (41–45). This tendency to replace morality with an individual moral value or extra-moral concerns, according to Hildebrand, results from making compromises with pride and concupiscence.

Hildebrand argues, for example, that while necessary for the cultivation of virtue, self-control is extra-moral because it does not assure moral goodness. The prideful person also finds the cultivation of self-control to be crucial (60–68). In his analysis of maintaining self-control, following tradition, cultivating honor, fulfilling duty, and acting with altruism, Hildebrand insightfully articulates how one can easily reduce the moral life to one limited concept. His rich descriptions provide a great resource for recognizing various common distortions of morality that are masked as authentic moral theories. His goal is to identify these distortions and substitutes to enable individuals to recognize and respond fully to moral values. Ultimately, Hildebrand calls his readers beyond moral prohibitions and reductions to the life of a saint committed to love of God—a life of holiness that frames all moral and extramoral concerns in relation to and in relationship with God.

These two works would be of interest to moral theologians for two different reasons. First, I recommend these works to those interested in Catholic ethics between the Second World War and the Second Vatican Council. Second, I recommend these works to those who are interested in specific topics. In *Morality and Situation Ethics*, Hildebrand offers rich phenomenological descriptions of different kinds of legalism, and he identifies concepts fundamental for discussion of situation ethics. In *Graven Images*, Hildebrand provides a masterful

analysis of how pride and concupiscence incline one to certain compromises in one's moral framework. His reflections provide moral theologians with language and distinctions for understanding the various
compromised frameworks that often remain hidden in ethical conversations and debates.

KEVIN SCHEMENAUER
St. Meinrad Seminary and School of Theology

Articles available to view
or download at:

https://jmt.scholasticahq.com/